Ohitika Woman

Mary Brave Bird

with

Richard Erdoes

HarperPerennial

A Division of HarperCollinsPublishers

HarperCollins books may be purchased for educational, business, or sales promotional use. For information please write: Special Markets Department, HarperCollins Publishers, Inc., 10 East 53rd Street, New York, NY 10022.

First HarperPerennial edition published 1994.

Designed by Laura Hough

Library of Congress Cataloging-in-Publication Data

Brave Bird, Mary.
   Ohitika woman / Mary Brave Bird, with Richard Erdoes. — 1st Harper-
Perennial ed.
     p. cm.
  ISBN 0-06-097583-0
  1. Brave Bird, Mary. 2. Brulé women—Biography. 3. Brulé Indians—Politics
and government. 4. American Indian Movement. I. Erdoes, Richard. II. Title.
[E99.B8B733   1994]
973′.04975—dc20
[B]   94-18040

94 95 96 97 98 RRD 10 9 8 7 6 5 4 3 2 1

To the brave women of

Wounded Knee

Contents

CONTENTS

Instead of a Foreword

This book is the result of a collaboration between two oddly paired human beings—an old white man and a young Native American woman. Our backgrounds could not be more different. I, Richard Erdoes, have been raised in Vienna, as a member of a family of actors and opera singers. I came to America at the age of twenty-eight, and even though I have lived in the United States for a lifetime, I am culturally still more European than American.

Mary Brave Bird, up to recently known as Mary Crow Dog, was born and raised in the tiny settlement of He Dog, on the Rosebud Sioux reservation, a member of the Brulé, or Sichangu, Tribe, one of seven tribes making up the larger Lakota Nation. While I was raised in the shadows of medieval cathedrals and ancient baroque buildings, Mary grew up on the prairie, where, as the old saying has it, "there is nothing between you and the North Pole but a barbed-wire fence." In spite of our different backgrounds, Mary and I have two things in common: We both grew up fatherless. Four weeks before I was born, my own father died of double pneumonia after an exhausting series of performances at the Budapest opera. Mary's father deserted his family while she was still a baby. And both of us had been youthful rebels fighting the powers that ruled over us. As a twenty-year-old art student I had been a member of the anti-Hitler movement in Austria and Germany, while as a teenager Mary had joined AIM, the American Indian Movement, fighting against racism and oppression. Mary and I finally met as the result of an accident.

During the first twenty years of my life in New York City I worked exclusively as an artist, particularly as a book and magazine illustrator. In 1964, two national magazines sent me west to do a painting portfolio and a photo essay on Indian reservations. This led to lasting friendships with several Native American families, many of them Sioux. One old medicine man, John Fire Lame Deer, insisted upon my "doing his book." In spite of my protests that I was an artist, not a writer, and that English was my second language, he kept saying: "My medicine tells me that you'll write my story." This went on for years until I finally gave in, and to our surprise, the book, *Lame Deer, Seeker of Visions,* became a classic in Native American literature. Lame Deer changed me from an artist into a writer, though I still paint whenever I have a chance.

The Indian civil rights movement started some ten years after the struggle for Black Power, but when it hit the Sioux reservations it did so with a vengeance. By 1970 many of the sons and daughters of my older Lakota friends had joined AIM. As a result my wife, Jean, and I became heavily involved ourselves. In November 1972, Jean, I, and our two sons took part in the Trail of Broken Treaties, which ended in the occupation of the Bureau of Indian Affairs Building in Washington, D.C. Mary was there too, sixteen and pregnant, but on that occasion we were not aware of each other.

At that time I was especially close to the Crow Dog family— Old Henry, his wife, Mary Gertrude, and their son, Leonard, who was the medicine man of the American Indian Movement. After having given birth to her first child, Pedro, during the siege of Wounded Knee in April 1973, Mary married Leonard, Indian style, and moved in with him at "Crow Dog's Paradise." It was there that I first met her face to face. She was small, feisty, very pretty, and standoffish. I heard her say once, during those days of confrontation: "There might be a good white man someplace, but I never met one yet." Observing the close bond existing between my family and the Crow Dogs, she tolerated my presence, ignoring me most of the time. I didn't mind, having learned something of her terrible experiences at a white-run boarding school and with redneck racists. When she couldn't avoid contact with us, she was politely cool.

In the aftermath of Wounded Knee and the big shoot-out at Oglala in May 1975, which resulted in the death of two FBI agents and one Native American, my wife and I became heads of a defense committee for Leonard Crow Dog and a few other Lakota friends who were indicted for strictly political offenses. Crow Dog was tried at Cedar Rapids, Iowa, and Rapid City and Pierre, South Dakota, and was convicted in every case. While he was released on probation by the judge at Cedar Rapids, the one at Pierre ordered him to be at once taken to prison. In handcuffs, waist chain, and leg-irons, he was dragged away so quickly that I did not even have a chance to tell him good-bye. At the time South Dakota was considered the most racist state in the Union as far as Native Americans were concerned; it was said that even Jesus Christ himself would have been found guilty of a heinous crime there had he been an activist Indian.

Crow Dog was sent to Lewisburg, Pennsylvania, to serve his time. The prison was some eighteen hundred miles distant from the Rosebud Reservation but could be reached by car from New York in a couple of hours. I therefore proposed to Mary that she move in with us, together with her baby, so that she could be near her husband. She stayed with us for almost a year and it was then, living together in the same apartment, that we finally became close friends. Even so it took her a long time before she hugged and kissed us as she did her Indian friends. She was as sassy, outspoken, and brutally honest as ever, but also bewildered, wide-eyed, and lost in what she called "the canyons" of the big city.

We had not realized how isolated and limited Mary's life had been before she came to live with us. After we introduced her to Lucy, an African American friend, she told us that this was the first black person she had ever met. She found out that many New Yorkers were unlike the racists who had made her life miserable in South Dakota and that there existed white people who would become her close friends. You could not pull the wool over her eyes, though. Coming home to us after a fund-raiser for minority causes held by some wealthy people in a luxury apartment, she told us: "Those people used me only as a prop, showing off 'their Indian,' trying to impress everybody with how liberal they were. They talked a lot about women's rights but left a mountain of dirty dishes for their black maid to clean up. I went into the kitchen to help her and we compared notes. Well, I'm breaking through the buckskin curtain."

She once caught me looking at her and at once confronted me, saying: "I know you are sexually attracted to me." I told her that, being an artist and photographer, I could not help studying people's faces, whether they were men or women, young or old, pretty or ugly.

She stared back at me for a moment, shrugged, and said: "Okay, I half believe you." We laughed and I was never again suspected of harboring designs against her virtue, but the remark was typical of her blunt way of confronting situations.

I also discovered that she had a beautiful voice, more like a child's than like that of a grown woman, and we all liked to listen to her Lakota songs and peyote chants—touching, sweet, and indescribably sad.

There were good days and bad, laughter and tears. I remember her bursting in on Jean and myself during breakfast, shouting: "Come quick, look, Pedro has a boner!" And indeed, two-year-old Pedro had a tiny erection, something to make a doting mother proud. But then there was the dark day when Mary and I were sitting in my studio, chatting. The phone rang. I handed her the receiver: "Mary, it's for you." I watched her listen, stiffening, her face distorted in grief. Somebody from the reservation was reporting that her best friend, Annie Mae Aquash, had been found brutally murdered in the snow, her eyes picked out by crows or magpies, her hands cut off and missing. And there were bad days whenever they were giving Crow Dog a hard time in the Lewisburg prison.

One of my publishers approached me: "Your Lame Deer book is doing very well. What else would you like to do in that vein?" I told him that books and magazine and newspaper articles were being written about Native American men, particularly AIM leaders, but that the Indian women, whose strength kept the movement going, were being ignored. I said: "We have just now a Sioux friend living with us, a young woman who gave birth at Wounded Knee during the siege. I would like to help her write an autobiography." We got a contract, and all during the time of Crow Dog's imprisonment we worked on the taping and transcribing of her story. We got Crow Dog out of prison with the help of the National Council of Churches, which raised funds for his defense, and Mary and Leonard returned to the res. I put the manuscript together like a jigsaw puzzle out of a huge mountain of tapes and delivered it a year or so later. The editor phoned, asking me to come and see him. He told me: "This book is much too radical. The political climate has changed. This radical shit is out. Mysticism is in. Make her into a female Don Juan! Make her into a witch. Make her fly through the air!"

I said: "Are you completely mad? Mary is not a spectral apparition but a flesh-and-blood Sioux woman. She's for real, not something out of my fantasies. If I faked her story she would come after us with her skinning knife, and rightly so." Whereupon he refused to accept the manuscript and, of course, we were not paid for a year's hard work. The manuscript lay around for over ten years. I forgot about it. Mary forgot about it. But our literary agent, Peter Basch, remembered. In 1989 he mentioned it to Fred Jordan, at that time a senior editor at Grove Press. He loved the book. *Lakota*

Woman became a best-seller. It is out in several foreign languages. We even got a movie contract for it. In a way, "our medicine was good." Had the book been published back in 1979 it would not have been as successful. Women, especially Indian women, weren't "in" at the time.

Our first book described Mary's life from her childhood until 1977. "What has happened to her since then?" the people at Grove asked. "Can you do a second book?" And so Mary, fifteen years later, moved in with us again, this time in Santa Fe, to do a second book, and here it is.

Richard Erdoes
Santa Fe, New Mexico
August 1992

Ohitika
Woman

CHAPTER ONE

Like a Candle
in a Storm

I was like a candle in a storm, a little candle in a big storm, barely flickering, almost snuffed out. On March 28, 1991, there was a power outage on the Rosebud Reservation in South Dakota. As the light bulbs went out in my mother's house she said: "I wonder if anything happened to Mary?" She still doesn't know what made her say this. Then she heard it on her scanner, with which you can listen to the tribal police band. She heard a policeman say: "Mary Crow Dog has been in a terrible wreck. She's dying. She's gone."

I had been drinking heavily, like most everybody else on the res. To drown my sorrows. To forget. To wash away despair in a flood of Jack Daniel's and "Buddy Wiser." I had no place to stay. Part of the summer I had lived in a dilapidated one-room cabin with an earth floor, a kerosene lamp, and a toppling outhouse, a veritable Tower of Pisa. Before that, for months at a time, I had lived with my children in a tipi at Grass Mountain. The advance money from the book was long gone. Every week I had to borrow money from Richard, my wasichu coauthor.

Because of some of the things I'd said in *Lakota Woman*, women on the res had liked my book. Some men had not and were giving me that "death look." One had sneered at me: "You are nothing and your book is nothing." Woman beating is part of everyday life on the reservation. The white man oppresses the half-blood, the half-blood oppresses the full-blood, and everybody takes out their anger, despair, and feeling of helplessness on the women. The men have a good and an evil side. Sober, they are angels. Drunk, their evil side comes out, and they are drunk a good part of the time.

Men and women drink because there is nothing else to do. There are no jobs. The poverty is unbelievable. Everybody is on public assistance, which is not enough to hold body and soul together. There is nothing to occupy one's time except partying and playing "quarter pitch." Partying means visiting back and forth in groups while getting drunk. Getting drunk means getting mean, and partying often ends in violence. Men fight men, women fight women, friends fight friends, big guys beat up on little women. They seldom beat kids. I will give them that. Sometimes a fight ends in death or serious injury. Most fatalities on the reservation are caused by DWI, driving while intoxicated. More people die because of this than heart disease and cancer combined. Some kill themselves by drinking "Montana gin," a deadly mixture of Lysol and water that is becoming popular on some reservations.

I have many faults, but dishonesty is not among them. I tell it like it is. I don't make myself better than I am. Being beaten up sometimes was my own fault. I don't have to go partying. I don't have to drink myself into insensibility, though given conditions on the res, insensibility can be bliss. When I am in that state my anger comes out. I get rowdy and foulmouthed. I talk back to the men and get hurt. Many a night I wind up in the drunk tank. I wrecked several cars while being "lila itomni."

On that night, March 28, I had been partying with some of my friends. We had already downed a few and went to the "club," where we had shots of Jack Daniel's and margaritas on top of that. Then I went to a girlfriend's house, where they were drinking beer. I joined in. Everything was covered with empty beer cans. When

I got up to leave, everybody said: "Don't go. You're in no condition to drive." But I went anyway. I wanted to pick up my cousin, Mike, who is part Navajo, and have some more Buddy Wisers with him. I never made it.

Somehow I got on the road leading to the trailer of my sister Barb and her old man, Jim. It was about one o'clock. I was on a gravel road, real loose gravel. I took the wrong turn and must have been going real fast, because I lost control of the car, and when I saw that utility pole coming at me, I said: "Oh, shit!" And that's all I remember.

When I came to I couldn't move. I yelled for help, but nobody heard me. Then I lost consciousness again. I had wrecked near a house. The man who lived there got up early in the morning and noticed my car from his window. He also saw the utility pole down and broken in half. Luckily he had a phone and called the police.

High-voltage wire was wrapped all around the car, and to get me out they had to call the electric company to turn off the power. I was pinned inside the car, drifting in and out of consciousness. I did not know where I was or what had happened. They thought I was dead, but one man noticed a pulse beating. When they moved me there was a terrible surge of pain that shot up all the way from my feet into the roots of my hair. Cuts from the glass of the splintered windshield had left tiny drops of blood all over my face. My mother said it looked like freckles. One of my ears was nearly severed. Six of my ribs were broken. One had punctured and collapsed my left lung. Another had ripped open my aorta, but this they didn't find out until later. At the tribal hospital they thought that my neck had been broken. They called my condition "code blue." They knew that my injuries were too severe for them to handle and that they would have to fly me to the big hospital at Sioux Falls, our largest city. They phoned my mom, and she came down from He Dog to be with me. My oldest son, Pedro, also came, together with my sister Barb. They all flew with me. I fantasized that I phoned my kids to tell them where I was, but of

5

course I was hallucinating. I was dehydrated and terribly thirsty, but they wouldn't give me any water on account of my injuries. In spite of the state I was in I got rowdy and kicked the nurse. Barb took this as a good sign that at least I was not paralyzed. Pedro, on the sly, gave me some fluid to drink from an IV bottle.

When we arrived at Sioux Falls, Mom had a priest give me the last rites before they wheeled me in for surgery. The doctors gave me only one chance in ten to survive the next twenty-four hours. They performed open-heart surgery to put a graft around my ripped aorta. They told me later that for some twenty seconds I had been clinically dead with my arteries disconnected. I could not breathe by myself, and they had to perform a tracheotomy. I was also put on a respirator. They put a tube in my left side to drain the lung and a catheter in my urethra, and pumped antibiotics and God knows what else intravenously into both my arms. They did not bother with my lesser injuries. Even now, ten months later, there are "no strings attached" between my left shoulder blade and upper arm bones, where most ligaments were torn and never repaired. To this day, it hurts and the arm is weak.

Before the accident I had been going through a lot, was depressed and did not want to go on with my life. That is why I got drunk and wrecked in the first place. So, during open-heart surgery, I had a vision. It was very real, like a down-to-earth experience. I went to see my grandma who had raised me. I was in a room with her in the house where I had spent my early childhood. I said: "Grandma, I came to stay with you." She said: "No, you can't." I told her: "I don't want to stay in the world anymore. I miss you." But Grandma insisted: "No, you can't. You have kids to take care of. Think of them. You have to go back. I'll be here for you, someday, when you're ready to come over. I'll always be here for you." So my grandmother was telling me to go back to the world and my responsibilities. After surgery I thought I was dying and I wouldn't let Mom let go of my hand. They took a CAT scan the next day, putting me into something like a giant tube to take X rays of my head. I thought I was dead and someone was putting me in the freezer.

They performed a series of operations on me, but every time they thought they were through with me, they found new injuries to fix. They discovered that my womb was injured and took out one of my ovaries. Before they did this they made me sign a paper: "I understand that after this operation I will never be able to have a baby," or something to that effect. At first I refused, saying: "Can't you avoid it?" They asked me: "Do you have any children?" I told them: "Yes, three boys, one girl, and a granddaughter." "Well, you've done enough," one of the doctors said. "Herewith we retire you from that messy childbearing business!" Ten months later I was pregnant again. That shows you how much you can rely upon what those big-shot doctors tell you. Here I was thinking that I didn't have to be careful anymore and then there was someone kicking again inside my belly. So it goes.

I stayed a month in the hospital. They put staples in my back and in other spots where I had surgery. They hurt whenever I moved. At first I couldn't move at all. I just lay there. If I wanted to change position I had to call the nurse. One night I got so tired of lying on my back that I somehow managed to turn over on my stomach. That was a mistake, because I got all tangled up in the sheets like a mummy. I couldn't reach the button to call for the nurse. I yelled for help, but nobody heard me. I finally managed to push the button with my foot. The nurse came and laughed seeing me in my mummified state. I didn't think it was all that funny. But the nurses were good to me. After a week or so they took out the catheter and the tube in my trachea. I could breathe again and go to the bathroom by myself. They took the IVs off because I could now eat solid food. They took me to the rehab place for physical therapy. I was still in great pain but considered myself blessed having all my body parts in the right place and functioning again. There were a lot of other skins in that hospital for the same reason as myself . . . DWI! Some were missing hands or legs, and others were blinded or brain damaged. They were much worse off than I. A lot of people were sending me get-well cards. I didn't realize how many people were praying for me. One guy, George, who partied a lot, even conducted a sweat for me. He later told me: "I thought of you every day. Even when I was drunk I prayed for you."

Once I was able to get around I even enjoyed myself, up to a point. I had hot and cold running water, a bathtub and flush toilet, all the conveniences of a middle-class wasichu home. I could order any food I wanted and raid the fridge whenever I felt like it. But I got restless and tired of being cooped up in a hospital. I missed my kids and friends. So, over the protests of some doctors, I checked myself out and had Barb and Jim drive me the three hundred miles home. I stayed at my mother's place, and she took good care of me. I still hurt, so the doctors gave me painkillers, Demerol and other highly addictive narcotics. The more you take, the more you want. I told them: "Take me off that stuff. I don't want to end up as a junkie." I drank to deaden the pain. When the pain stopped I quit drinking. Sometimes my heart muscle cramps, mostly when I am stressed out. So on certain days I still have trouble breathing. Singing with others at the drum during last summer's sun dance, I got short-winded and had to sit down. But that's my own fault, because I still smoke cigarettes. I smoke a little pej, too. I look upon it as a natural medicine that was put there for us. I never did drugs like crack, cocaine, or heroin. I never got into the hard stuff. It used to be that I couldn't get out of bed and through the day without a joint, but I put it away because it was no longer doing anything for me. I pray to Wakan Tanka, the Creator, and I'm honest with him and with myself.

Finally this episode in my life came to an end. I never was the same again after it. It changed my life-style for sure.

Three things stand out in my memory regarding my car wreck. Two are funny and one is very strange. I got a bill for fifteen hundred dollars—to pay for a new telephone pole. That struck me as tragicomical. After the wreck, when I got a trailer house for myself and the kids, the utility company wouldn't turn on the electricity until I signed an agreement to pay for the pole in monthly installments.

The second incident isn't quite as funny, come to think of it. Debbie, the person whose house I wrecked in front of, owns what calls itself a nightclub in Mission. Don't imagine that it's like a club in New York or Chicago. It's just a small, humble drinking joint for skins. Debbie is an old friend. I grew up with her, and we are really close. After the wreck, while I was recovering, I stopped in and saw her at the club. She said: "I'm so glad you survived! We were rooting for you! Drinks are on the house!"

The third thing that happened, the strange one, was this: As I was hallucinating on the operating table, I imagined that I phoned my children, telling them where I was and what had happened to me. At that time the children were staying with my sister Barb. When Barb came home from Sioux Falls, my son June Bug told her: "Mom called. She said that she was in a car wreck and is in surgery. She also said not to worry, that she'll be all right." The spirit works in strange ways.

That is all I can say about this accident that almost killed me. White readers will probably look upon it as something out of the ordinary. On the res it caused no ripple. DWI wrecks like mine happen all the time, to be dismissed with a shrug.

CHAPTER TWO

Ancestors

I am an iyeska, a half-breed, and there are some on the res who won't let me forget it. The full-bloods, the ikche wichasha, the "wild, natural beings," often look down upon the half-breeds as no longer living in the traditional Indian way, as being "apples," red on the outside and white inside. The half-breeds, in turn, look upon the full-bloods as backward. All this doesn't mean much. Ikche wichasha or iyeska, we are all no longer living like the old Indians—we all go to the same stores and supermarkets and have had to compromise, with one foot in the white and the other in the Indian world. Also, at Rosebud we are all related in some way, particularly as we recognize fourth, fifth, and sixth cousins as relatives. I am a half-breed. So what?

We are all descended from Chief Iron Shell, Pankeska Maza, a son of a warrior called Bull Tail. Iron Shell was a legendary fighter. In 1843 he killed eleven Pawnees during a single battle. He counted many coups* and received many war honors. In 1849 a

---

*Coup is a French word meaning "strike" or "hit." Counting coup meant performing a brave deed by which a young warrior could earn eagle feathers.

10

band of Lakotas went on the warpath and fell into a trap. Over eighty of their party were killed, and the survivors and their families were from that time on known as the Wablenicha, or Orphan Band. Eventually Iron Shell became the chief of the Wablenicha. In 1855, after a heroic defense, Iron Shell and his band were defeated at the battle of the Blue Water River. In the retreat, one baby was lost but was found by an officer and later returned to his father, Iron Shell. The baby, whose name was Hollow Horn Bear, grew up to become a great chief.

Iron Shell had seven sons—Bear Dog, the oldest, Hollow Horn Bear, Peter Iron Shell, Bird Necklace, He Frightens, Pretty Bird, and my great-grandfather, Stephen Brave Bird. At some time late in the nineteenth century, everybody got a permanent last name and a Christian first name. Brave Bird had only one son, and that is why there are so few Brave Birds left.

Each of Iron Shell's sons formed his own tiyospaye, the extended Lakota family that includes all people descended from a common father. Of all these sons of Iron Shell, Chief Hollow Horn Bear, Mato He Oglogeca, was the best known. He was a magnificent-looking man. His face appeared on an old fourteen-cent postage stamp and on a five-dollar bill. He was invited by President Teddy Roosevelt to come to his inauguration. As a young man he had been a great warrior. When only sixteen years old he counted his first coup on a Pawnee brave. As befitted a great chief he had a harem of seven wives. As a chief he had to be generous, feeding all visitors and giving away fine buffalo robes. One single wife could not have done all that cooking and hide tanning. One wife's name was Good Bed. He had his camp at Cut Meat, a small settlement so named because it was where the government-issued cattle were butchered.

In 1912, the chief had his first ride in a motorcar. Studying our ancestors' history, I am always struck by the fact that my great-grandfathers and great-grandmothers made the jump from the Stone Age to the industrial age in one single lifetime. Iron Shell and Hollow Horn Bear grew up making their fires with flint and steel and had gone to war with bows and stone-tipped arrows. They lived off the buffalo. In their old age they rode in cars, made telephone calls, posed for photographs, and had dinner with journalists and politicians in fancy East Coast restaurants. Hollow Horn Bear died in Washington of pneumonia during the inauguration of President Wilson. His body was shipped back to Rosebud, where he was buried in 1913.

Another well-known member of our clan was Fool Bull, Tatanka Witko, who fought Custer at the Little Big Horn. An old photograph shows him with a huge bear-claw necklace, each claw representing a grizzly or black bear he had killed. His son, Uncle Dick Fool Bull, took me to my first peyote meeting. He was the last maker of traditional Sioux flutes, which all ended in a bird's head, the sound coming out of the open beak. He himself could play the flute beautifully. These were instruments for courting, making the love music. Uncle Fool Bull died in 1975, almost one hundred years old. He still remembered the massacre of some three hundred Lakota men, women, and children at Wounded Knee, in the winter of 1890. Uncle Dick's son, Leslie, is a roadman of the Native American Church, the peyote church. Other Iron Shell relatives are also leaders, as well as members, of that pan-Indian religion.

My great-grandfather, Stephen Brave Bird, had five wives. One of them was named Zoe Gurue, also known as Zoe McKenzie, my great-grandmother. She was half French. Stephen was a cowboy. He went on long, epic cattle drives from Rosebud to Texas and to the Kansas hell towns . . . Dodge City, Ellsworth, and Newton. He became one of the early rodeo riders, bulldogging being his specialty. When he married Zoe he settled down on the reservation at a place called Hollow Horn Bear Flats. All the sons of old Iron Shell lived close together, each with his own tiyospaye. The Hollow Horn Bears at Cut Meat, the Iron Shells at Spring Creek, the Bear Dogs near St. Francis. They all lived up there on the flats, close together for mutual support. Stephen lived strictly on his own land, the original allotment. He had a little wagon, and he'd bring wood and groceries for my grandmother after her husband died in an accident. He was very affectionate and couldn't do enough for his grandkids.

My grandfather, Mom's dad, was Robert Brave Bird. He was a farmer, hunter, and trapper. All winter long he trapped beavers, mink, coons, and muskrats. Throughout the season my mother lived down by the creek in a tent. In the spring he'd sell all the furs he had. Mom said that this was her Christmastime. With the money from his pelts he bought all his kids new clothes and lots of candy. He'd buy new corn seed for his little farm and work his fields all summer long. After the harvest he'd move back to the river with his family. For food they'd eat turtle, beaver, whatever. It must have been a hard life, but Mom remembers it as a happy time. They had no electricity or plumbing or running water. They had oil lamps for light, and a stove with plenty of wood for heat. During the South Dakota winters, with temperatures often dropping to forty below, you had to be hardy to survive. Mom thought nothing of it. Mom also told me of some old customs that, in her words, "weren't very nice," like having multiple wives and "drumming" an unwanted wife out of camp so that she could never come back. She told me that wife beating was a way of life and that having head lice was considered part of normal living. When Mom was a young girl she could only speak Lakota. She still understands it perfectly, but nowadays she is slow in getting her sentences out. As a schoolteacher she comes in contact mostly with English-speaking people and has little chance to practice her Sioux language.

Grandpa Robert was a fine man, very kind, a good husband and father. He died during the early thirties. He had sold his corn and drove his wagon to the big general store to buy groceries. He had loaded his wagon with rations and was driving his team of horses when he had the accident. There was a storm. Lightning spooked the horses. They were dragging him along and he grabbed a fence to stop himself. The barbed wire cut his arm badly and he bled to death. A neighbor found the body the following morning. He found the horses, too, which I am told were exceptionally fine and beautiful animals. My great-grandmother killed them, shot them dead after the old custom. To make things worse, when Louise, his widow, had a giveaway in Robert Brave Bird's honor, people came from everywhere, descending upon the house like a swarm of locusts, stripping the place clean, down to the pots and pans. After that my grandmother's sister came and brought Louise's kids back to Rosebud, where Mom spent the rest of her childhood. Later, Louise did cleaning and washing for people, mostly whites from the Bureau of Indian Affairs. I am told that I look very much like this grandmother of mine. She was light-skinned but her features were totally Indian. She died only a few years ago at the age of eighty-five. Her maiden name was Flood.

The Floods left County Mayo, Ireland, sometime during the Great Potato Famine and came to America. My great-grandfather, Tom Flood, was born in 1863. He went west early and opened a trading post in Wyoming, close to what is now the South Dakota state line. Here he married one of the Yellow Hair girls, from Pine Ridge, whose father was a Roubideaux. There are still lots of Roubideauxs in Pine Ridge and Rosebud. Some are AIM activists and Wounded Knee veterans, others are conservatives, and one is a lawyer. They are all descendants of Joseph and Antoine Roubideaux—French trappers, mountain men, traders, and trailblazers. They came from a family clan that had settled along the Mississippi and Missouri long ago, when that whole large area was still French. These Roubideaux men first appeared in Indian country between 1820 and 1830. They were friends of such famous men as Kit Carson, Jim Bridger, and Broken Hand Fitzpatrick. They trapped beaver and put up little log cabin "forts" where they traded with the local Indians for furs, paying them with "rattlesnake whiskey" . . . one gallon water, one cup raw whiskey, a dash of strychnine for taste, a pinch of gunpowder "to give her a kick," and three rattlesnake heads for potency. The brothers bought whiskey at St. Louis for thirty cents a gallon and sold it for three dollars a pint to booze-crazed trappers in the Rockies. Antoine blazed an immigrant trail all the way from Missouri to California, and you can still see the deep ruts it made through our country. Both Antoine and Joseph married full-blooded Sioux women, because these were the only kind around. There's also a tiny bit of Spanish blood in there someplace, but it's hard to trace. The woman that Tom Flood married was a feisty lady, small of body but with a big heart. Legend has it that she once stabbed to death with her skinning knife a trader who had cheated her.

Great-grandpa Flood opened a saloon and tended bar. He also herded cattle, acted as an interpreter, and worked as an allotment agent. One day in 1906, when he was in the saloon, some cowboys came in there wanting a drink. Some dispute started, and Tom Flood was shot in the back. His wife found his body and carried it six miles on her back to his camp. He was a tall, dark-haired, good-looking man. We still have a photograph of him, in full Indian regalia, with a very large eagle-feather warbonnet on his head.

There was a man called Noble Moore, and he married my grandmother, Tom Flood's daughter, Louise, after my grandfather Robert Brave Bird died. They were wonderful, kind people who raised me during my preschool days in the traditional Indian way, as I described in my first book. Noble's son, Bill, married Mom. He was the no-good son of a fine father, but Mom didn't have much of a crop to pick from. The reservation, at the time, was a hellhole, the men totally demoralized, with no money and no jobs, drinking themselves to death out of sheer boredom.

My oldest living relative is Great-uncle Bernard Flood. He was born in 1900 and is ninety-two years old now. His mother died when he was only six months old. He never knew her, doesn't even have a picture of her. His father was already gone. So he was an orphan, living out at a camp near the Little White River in a tipi with his grandma, his brother, John, and his sister, Louise.

When Uncle Bernard was old enough, he went to school in St. Francis until he was about sixteen and the school burned down. Then he went to school in Haskell, in northern Kansas. At this time Indians going to high school went either to Haskell or to Carlysle, Pennsylvania, where my grandma went in 1911. Haskell was run like an army barracks. The boys had to wear uniforms and stiff collars that chafed their necks. The worst were the stiff, heavy, ankle-high shoes. He was not used to wearing them. Otherwise, the school was all right. In St. Francis, Uncle Bernard had played in the marching band for about three years. At Haskell he played the tuba in the Indian band. He was there for a couple of years, from 1916 to 1918. And then at age seventeen, he enlisted in the navy and was shipped to the Great Lakes Naval Station in Illinois. The U.S. was fighting in World War I, so nobody cared that he was only seventeen. He served two years there and during that time he was the only Indian on the base except for a Chippewa from Wisconsin. They had a big band there and, again, he played the tuba. He had it pretty easy being a musician, and it kept him out of combat.

In 1922 he went back to St. Francis, on the Rosebud Reservation, married a woman called Little Money, and worked on a farm. Life was rough on the reservation. People had to build their own houses, mostly cabins. They got rations of beef, a little flour, and wood. They didn't have commodities, government food handouts, in those days, although the government people gave you clothes for your kids to go to school in, shoes and stuff. They didn't have the regular school built until 1930. There were just two denominations, Catholics and Episcopalians. They got along pretty good, civilizing us, as they said.

Uncle Bernard had been all over in his younger days, from Canada to Window Rock, Arizona, on the Navajo reservation. Once, they wouldn't let him travel in a regular train compartment with the white folks, because he was an Indian. They made him ride in the baggage car. But that's a long time ago.

During World War II, he worked for the air force at their academy in Denver. Then he worked for the navy, as a production specialist, making forty-millimeter antiaircraft guns. Later, he was elected to the tribal council. Most of what they did was negotiate with the BIA, the bureau, for getting federal funds for the Rosebud Tribe. He went to Washington twice on tribal problems. But they never got enough money to work with, so they couldn't do much. He told me:

"Now my roaming days are over. I just look at the clouds, the birds, a young frisky pony running about. I'm ninety-two years old now. I'd like to live to see a new century starting. I would be a hundred years old if I make it."

Mom's oldest brother died when he was eighteen. Her last surviving brother, Richard Brave Bird, died a couple of years ago of cirrhosis of the liver. He was a rodeo man, and a great one with horses. He worked for a rancher and sometimes brought horses back with him for us kids to ride. He'd drink a lot and go off to do his bulldogging. He won many prizes but broke his back three times in the process. He always went back to his bronc busting though. He and my uncle Clifford Broken Leg were old-time cowboys. Their sons carried it on. June Leader Charge, Clifford's son and my cousin, is still a rodeo rider. He's got a whole remuda of horses and herds cattle. I loved to go to the all-Indian rodeos. The one on the Fourth of July is always the greatest. After the main events are over, they have a wild-horse race, in which they ride bareback, old style. That is really exciting. Some of those Indian cowboys become great riders at a very young age, and you can see which ones are going to be world champions. There's an old saying that we Sioux can ride before we can walk. The girls are great, too, doing their barrel races at a full gallop, with their whips clenched between their teeth. I wasn't too bad myself.

My mother, Emily, was raised the Indian way, way out on the river in a tent, isolated from the world beyond. But after her father, Brave Bird, died, she was taken to the St. Francis Mission School in Rosebud and she chose the white man's road as her way of life.

When I was six or seven, I was taken away from my grandparents and from then on was raised as a Catholic, in the white man's way. I was not taught my own language because "speaking Indian would not be good for me." As a teenager, I ran away to go back to the traditional Lakota ways. My mother has a shrine of Our Lady in her garden, surrounded by pretty flowers. She has an upright piano in her living room and plays the organ in church on Sundays. I go to peyote meetings, am a sun dancer, and pray to Wakan Tanka, the Great Spirit. So my mother and I are very different. We travel different roads. But we love and support each other even while we argue. As I once had harsh words to say about my mother's attitude, I think it only fair to make it clear that in my time of troubles and drinking my mother stood by me, nursed me back to health after my accident, and took care of my kids while I was recuperating. And I have to admit that I must have been a sore trial to her during the days I spent in an alcoholic daze. Our life philosophies are different, but we love each other. And whenever I am in a bad way, I turn to her for help.

After Grandpa Brave Bird's death, an aunt took his widow back to Rosebud, and they took my mother with them. Like everybody else, she wound up in the St. Francis Mission boarding school, run by Jesuit priests and Franciscan monks and nuns. This was a great shock to my mother, as it was to all other Indian children, being forcefully taken from their families to be raised by strangers who must have seemed like alien beings from another planet. The kids were forced to stay there for a whole year and could not leave the mission even for holidays. So it was no wonder that my mother always cried when the wagon taking her there got to the junction where she could see the church steeple. The priests and nuns were very strict and meted out harsh treatment. These were the bad old days when they tried to "whitemanize" the kids with a strap. My mother told me: "The kids used to run away, and when they were caught they put them in little cells and shaved their heads. Some students froze to death hiding in haystacks while running away."

While I rebelled against the unbearable conditions at St. Francis, my mother saw the key to a better life in what she learned at the school. She always said that while she was there the kids got a quality education. "They made sure you learned, even if they had to beat the knowledge into you. Kids were often mistreated in that school, but I got a good education from the teachers."

So, while my mother complained about the abuses, she still always says: "I'm grateful for what the nuns gave me." She was even taught some Latin and how to play the piano. So she put her Indianness aside and concentrated upon studying. It paid off for her, as she became, first, a registered nurse and later a schoolteacher.

Mom was baptized in the Catholic faith by Father Eugene Buechel, a German. At that time, all the priests and brothers at St. Francis were Germans. Buechel came to Rosebud as a young man, in 1902, and he spent the rest of his life on the reservation. He was a Jesuit and was quite a remarkable man. He founded a museum for Indian artifacts that he had collected. He gathered, cataloged, and described native healing herbs, photographed people on the res, and compiled a huge Sioux dictionary and grammar. My mother told me that through his books she not only learned English, but got a better understanding of her own Lakota language. Like other missionaries, he used to travel around in his horse and buggy, with a portable altar, to say mass in such tiny hamlets as He Dog, Upper Cut Meat, Soldier Creek, White River, Grass Mountain, or even isolated homesteads way out on the prairie. People liked him because he could speak Sioux flawlessly, ate whatever Indian food was put before him, and always had his pockets full of little gifts for the children.

The other priests were not so popular because they took the strap to the kids and always spoke German, so it was hard to understand them—men like Brother Hartman and Brother Joseph, who taught carpentry, and Father Shoemaker. That's what they called him, but his real name was Hinderhofer. He taught boot making to the students and slapped them down hard if they didn't obey. They tried to persuade Mom to become a nun, but, luckily, she didn't go for that, though she is a staunch Catholic. While Mom wrestled with math and Latin, Grandma supported her by doing cleaning and washing for people—that's how she made her living. She encouraged Mom in her studies, always telling her: "You'd better learn both ways, Indian and white man's ways; then you'll have a better life."

I have said harsh words about the mission school, because we were not allowed to talk Indian, or to pray the Indian way, or to go to native ceremonies. If we did, the nuns beat us, as I have described it in my first book. It is only fair to say that things have changed for the better at Rosebud and other reservations. St. Francis hasn't been a missionary school since the 1970s, and while it's still a boarding school, the staff is now Indian. It's grown, and they have a big library now. They're big on cultural education. For example, if there's a funeral, a priest will do the burial, but if it's a traditional family, they can also smoke the pipe, and sing with the drum, and sing for that person. The Christian and the traditional people get along pretty good. They come together for powwows and different activities. Now they have priests who take part in the sun dance and the sweat. My mother doesn't like it. She says that it goes against what she believes, that "you don't step into another church." Sometimes she looks kind of wistful and says: "Maybe it would have been better if we'd stayed out on the flats and lived the Indian life, and never went to mission school, because then, maybe, my children wouldn't have run away and joined AIM, and got into all that trouble." She means Barb and myself, and Joe and Sandra, too.

When the Depression came and everybody was poor, Mom didn't notice it, because poverty was all she knew. There was sharing on the reservation. People helped each other. Mom vividly remembers one summer when Texas had a drought and the ranchers donated to the reservation the surplus cattle they couldn't feed.

They had them all penned up at Rosebud, real skinny animals, but every family got a cow. All along the creek women were butchering. There was no refrigeration, so they were drying the meat, making jerky. You had to know how, and do it right, or the meat would rot. For the most part, the people lived on rations. They got coffee, sugar, beets, and dried fruit. Somehow the family survived.

Electricity came to Rosebud and Mission in the 1930s. The smaller hamlets had to wait until 1958. So, at that time, when the school at He Dog was being built, the people used kerosene lamps and coal stoves. Electricity was fine, but with it came TV, which was not so good. It made kids think and act the white man's way and forget their own language.

Mom says that when Myrl Smith, her present husband, married her, he made a good catch, and that is true. A damn good catch, in fact. But when she married her first husband, Bill Moore, she made a very bad catch. Bill was a handsome man with a good build on him. That's the only favorable thing I can say about him. He is part Indian but pretends to be white. He once brought some things made of silk home from the Orient. I later swapped them for books. My mother divorced him when I was one year old. We were living in Denver at the time. One day Bill sold all the furniture in the house, stripped it clean, and used the money to go on a big drunk. He wound up in a bar, where he picked himself up another woman who, he said, was not so goddam strict and moral as my mom. That was the last straw. I saw him only three times after that. Once he came to Rosebud to borrow money from his dad. The second time he came to Rosebud for his brother's funeral. He let everybody admire his brand-new, fancy cowboy boots and pretended not to notice me. I saw him for the third time only a few years ago. I was moving from city to city, and shelter to shelter, with all my kids and no money, desperately trying to find a place and some work. I had been in a shelter in Marshall, Minnesota, and from there took a bus to Sioux Falls, where things were even worse. In December, in the cold and snow, I struck out for Arizona, where I had friends and where it was warm. I had the kids with me—Pedro, Anwah, June Bug, and Jennifer, who was a little baby then. I still don't know how I was able to handle it. We made it to Omaha, Nebraska, and stayed in a shelter there. I remembered hearing that my father had remarried and settled in Omaha, working as a trucker. I looked up his address in the phone book and went to see him. He was unpleasantly surprised. He told me: "I'd ask you in, but I have a family. You see how it is." He did not even want to have a look at my kids, his grandchildren. He had washed his hands of us for good. I turned around and went to the homeless shelter. Next day I was on the road again.

After Bill Moore had disappeared into the wild blue yonder, Mom had to earn a living. She did not want to live in the usual reservation way, on insufficient government handouts . . . not quite enough to live on, but just enough to keep you from dying. She wanted to be independent. To become a nurse she had to go to a school that was almost a hundred miles away in Pierre, the state capital. So my grandparents had to raise us children. I was tiny then. Whenever Mom came back from school I'd jump on her lap and hug her. When she had to go back to school I cried and didn't want to let go of her. That was hard, very hard. Maybe that's why I am what I am. Maybe it had an influence on shaping our personalities. But what choice did she have? We had to survive somehow.

After becoming a nurse she worked three years at the hospital. Then Myrl came out from Minnesota to teach at the school in He Dog, where she lived. That's how she met him. Mom had five children, and he had been a bachelor all his life. When he married her, he got himself a good wife. Mom switched from nursing to teaching, and now Myrl and my mother teach at the same school. In another year, I think, she'll retire from the classroom, but not from working. She'll instruct at our little tribal college, the Sinte Gleska College, named after Chief Spotted Tail. English is her subject. She's an organist at two churches—St. Briget's and St. Agnes's—and plays whenever they have wakes. She never took lessons but taught herself. She does not accept money for this work.

The matter of religion kept us apart for a while, but now we understand each other's views about this. My sister Barb and I started seeking for our roots, for a faith, for a meaning of life. Mom now says that this was great; but she did not always think so. She does not go to ceremonies and is not interested in powwows. She does not know much about Indian religion. She must have known it as a child. Maybe she forgot, or wanted to forget, while I, and my sisters, went to Uncle Leslie Fool Bull to learn as much about our ancient beliefs as we could.

Mom says: "I believe there is a power there, a mysterious power, but I don't tamper with what I don't know. If you kids want to go that way, that's fine. If you live that way, and believe in it, that's good. If you come out of there and get drunk, it's not."

My mother now respects my beliefs, and I respect hers. I have matured, and become more tolerant. When you're very young, there's only one viewpoint—yours. Mom still uses an herb that grows wild where we live. She takes the root of this plant and boils it and uses it for sore eyes. And she makes tea out of the bark of chokecherry trees for chest colds. In spite of what Mom says, there's still a lot of Indian in her, and much of the old Lakota wisdom. Well, that's the story of my ancestors and relatives, living and dead, the story of my family, the Floods and the Brave Birds, a story that is not finished—yet.

CHAPTER THREE

A Little Backtracking

I have to backtrack a little bit. At the beginning of 1973 I was seventeen years old and pregnant, in my ninth month. The father was one of those young, good-looking radical warrior types. I was infatuated with him, but discovered soon that he was not the kind to have a solid relationship with. I considered myself part of AIM—the American Indian Movement—and so after the movement took over Wounded Knee in February, I joined my friends who had occupied the historic site, determined to have my baby there. Call it a statement, or a gesture of defiance. My sister, Barb, and my brother, Joe, welcomed me. My baby was born on April 11, during a firefight, with bullets whizzing through the air. It lifted up everybody's morale to have a new life born after Clearwater, an Indian from North Carolina, had been killed by the marshals. There was drumming and singing when my baby was shown to the people. I named my son Pedro, after a close friend, Pedro Bisonette, founder of the Oglala Sioux civil rights organization, who was later murdered by tribal police. He had been a great support and covered me with his body when we received fire from the feds.

My mother sat at home, watching the evening news, fretting.

Her kids were in the movement. She was not. She had two young daughters and a son inside Wounded Knee. My brother, who had been in Vietnam, had told Mom: "Those in the movement are going in there armed. It won't only be the goons and the marshals who'll have weapons. If they shoot at us, somebody might shoot back." With a ring of fire around the Knee, all of us surrounded by trip-wire flares and armored cars, no wonder she was worried sick, not only about her three kids but also the little baby inside me. She didn't even know if we were still alive.

I went to jail when I came out of Wounded Knee with my little baby. The marshals had promised me that I would not be arrested or prosecuted just for having been part of the occupation, but I was grabbed as soon as I was outside the perimeter. That was the same day Buddy Lamont was killed inside the Knee by a marshal's bullet. I came out of the Knee at the end of April, together with Kamook, Dennis Banks's lady, and Buddy Lamont's body. That was very sad. I kept thinking of those I had left behind inside, at the Knee.

So they took me to the Pine Ridge jail. There were feds standing around in bright blue jumpsuits. They all had M-16s with sniper scopes, ready to get it on with the red savages. One of them, a fat pig, came up to me and said: "Is that your baby? How cute." I told him: "I don't talk to guys like you." So he left me alone. They told me: "You can't take your baby in here. Jail ain't a nursery." I was upset, but Buddy Lamont's sister reassured me: "I'll take your baby, sister, until you come out. I'll treat him real nice."

They kept me in a cell, alone, for eight hours before they took me upstairs. There was an FBI agent there, sitting at a desk, shuffling papers. He looked at me with a nasty smile: "We got some heavy charges against you. You better cooperate if you know what's good for you." I answered: "What charges? It ain't no crime to have a baby. That's all I did, have a baby." He kept on grinning: "You're all guilty of rioting, armed uprising, criminal trespassing, and unlawful occupation, each and every one in that place. But if you behave, sign these papers, and give us some information, I'll see to it that they'll go easy on you."

I told him that we in the Indian movement had a policy of never giving information or signing anything, but he kept on badgering me: "Who's in there? We want names. What are those AIM guys up to? How many of them are there? How many guns?" That went on for quite a while. I just sat there like a deaf-mute, staring at him. He finally gave up: "Well then, lady, you're gonna spend some time in jail, until you decide to give us some info and sign some papers." "That will be a long time," I told him.

They handcuffed me and took me to the Pennington County jail in Rapid City. They threw me into a cell with another Indian lady, who had been in there already for three weeks without having been allowed to make a phone call or see a lawyer. I wasn't allowed to, either. They threw in a white girl with us. She was a sympathizer who had come to show her support. They let her make phone calls and get in touch with a lawyer right away, which showed us that, as far as the FBI was concerned, we were ranked even lower than a female left-wing radical hippie, the lowest on the totem pole. In the meantime my breasts swelled up and hurt because I didn't have my baby to nurse. I felt like a poor cow with a full udder and no one to milk her. Again they were running the same kind of shit on me: "Who's in there, at the Knee? We want names, we want to know about guns, we want you to sign papers waiving certain rights. It's up to you. Cooperate, or rot in your cell." I told them: "Okay, so I'll rot." They couldn't do anything with me. Somebody notified my mother and told her where I was. So Mom came out to see me. They told her that I couldn't get out because I wouldn't release any useful information to them. The feds almost locked Mom and Myrl up, too, saying: "You have come to protest and make trouble." The goons pointed their guns at my mother. She had disapproved of my joining the movement, but she's always there when I'm in trouble. They told her: "Lady, you've got five minutes to be with your daughter." She cried when she saw me in chains, but I told her: "Mom, don't let them see you cry. Don't let them see you that way." Mom told the feds: "My daughter is only seventeen. She's done nothing bad. Let me stay a little longer." They said: "It's not what she's done. The thing is, she's become a symbol." When Mom was forced to leave me, she reassured me: "Don't worry about the baby. I'll take him."

My mom went to Cheyenne, the sister of Buddy Lamont who had taken my baby. They had an all-night wake for Buddy at the morgue and my mother sat there all that time with my baby in her lap. Everybody was crying and singing the AIM song. Buddy's grave is at Wounded Knee, right on the hill where all the victims of the 1890 massacre, three hundred Sioux men, women, and children, are buried in a common ditch. The FBI came to the morgue and wanted to question my mother right there. She told them: "Have a heart. My daughter is only seventeen years old, and we are in mourning here for an ex-marine and veteran whom you guys killed."

The man took my mother out into the parking lot and said he would help her, but he also told Mom: "There's heavy charges against your daughter." My mother told him: "How can you be so afraid of a seventeen-year-old girl, and so small a girl, too?" But at least she had my baby.

Well, the FBI couldn't do better with me at Rapid City, where they moved me, than they had at Pine Ridge. They arraigned me, and took my fingerprints, but gave up on me in the end. They threw me out, saying: "We need your space for some real heavies." And there I stood outside the "iron house," which is what Indians call a jail, not knowing what to do, and with no place to go. I thumbed a ride to get back to the res, back to Rosebud, and with my bad luck was picked up by a goon. The goons were a private army organized by Dicky Wilson, the corrupt and murderous half-blood tribal chairman at Pine Ridge, who had declared an open season on all AIM members and everybody else who was opposed to his reign of terror. The goons were a bunch of thugs, some of whom were responsible for many, many murders that were never investigated. You can imagine how I felt when I discovered that I had been picked up by one of them. He wanted to take me to his home, "for a sandwich," as he said. I knew a sandwich was not what was on his mind. I told him I wanted to go home to Rosebud. He tried to force me to go with him. I managed to jump out of his pickup, ran like hell, and hid in a culvert, my heart pounding. I was only a teenager and scared stiff.

Leonard Crow Dog had been AIM's medicine man at Wounded Knee. He had made a tremendous impression upon me. All during the siege he had been the rock of fortitude and courage. I stood in awe of him. He was thirty-one years old in 1973. Shortly after I got back to the res he gave me a ride in his old, busted-up car. Suddenly he had his arm around my shoulders and kissed me. I moved in with him on the old original Crow Dog allotment at Grass Mountain. Old Henry Crow Dog, Leonard's father, had named this place Crow Dog's Paradise, and by that name it was known to every Native American in this country.

CHAPTER FOUR

Life in Paradise

Sometime after Wounded Knee I and little Pedro moved in with Leonard Crow Dog on his father's place. I married Leonard in the Indian way, with a blanket wrapped around us, holding on to the pipe, while being cedared and fanned off with an eagle feather.* This was not considered a legal marriage in a white priest's sense but it was good enough for us. The Crow Dogs still lived on their old place, some eighteen miles from the tribal administrative center at Rosebud. The land is quite beautiful—a large flat area, including the sacred sun dance ground, surrounded by pine-studded hills. A stream runs through the property and the Little White River is only a few hundred yards away. A steep path leads up to the hilltop where the Crow Dogs have their vision pit when going on a hanbleceya, a vision quest. Here also Leonard and

---

Cedaring and *fanning off* are terms you will encounter often in this book. *Cedaring* means burning as incense dry cedar, sage, or sweet grass. *Fanning off* means using an eagle wing to fan the cedar smoke toward a person who is being cured or purified.

his father had a ghost dance in 1974. In summer the air is filled with the songs of many birds. Overhead you can see flights of eagles and waterbirds, sacred in our beliefs. The air is also fragrant with the sweet scent of plants we use in our ceremonies—sage, sweet grass, cedar, and washtemna—Indian perfume. Willows grow along the stream to serve as material to build sweat lodges. Here also grows mint for native tea, and chokecherries to make wojapi, a kind of berry pudding. Also, unfortunately, there's a lot of poison ivy.

The place was very picturesque. The entrance was formed by two long crossed poles. Fastened at the top was a buffalo skull and an oil painting by Old Henry, depicting the peyote Christ, with the feather fan and gourd rattle in one hand and the tufted staff in the other. Visible from afar stood a huge monster-sized truck tire, almost as tall as a man. Painted white, it had written upon it in large letters: CROW DOG'S PARADISE. For me it was sometimes hell.

When I first lived in this earthly Eden, there were still standing a number of different structures. First there was the main house, which Henry had built with his own hands around 1930. It was a funky but picturesque dwelling made of whatever Henry had been able to rustle up—parts of an old railroad car, car windows, ancient discarded lumber, and God knows what else. The whole outside was painted bright blue with red window trim. Inside, upright tree trunks held up the ceiling. The walls were covered with stiff, heavy, brown crating paper. As you came in, you first entered the kitchen. It had an old-fashioned iron cooking range. Next to it was a rough bench with a pail of cold water from the brook and a good-sized dipper. This served for cooking, drinking, and washing as the house had neither running water nor indoor plumbing. Beyond the kitchen was the large main room, or living room, with a number of beds and a big wood-burning stove. Here was also Grandma Crow Dog's out-of-date foot-pedal sewing machine. On the wall were old family photographs, a number of Henry's paintings, a large poster advertising a movie, *Stagecoach*, in which Henry had had a bit part, and a large poster of a smiling Henry, which he had got for himself for two bucks in New York's Greenwich Village during the mid-sixties. Hanging from the ceiling were bundles of dried medicine herbs, warbonnets, dance bustles, and other paraphernalia. In this room peyote and yuwipi meetings were held. There were two smaller side chambers, one of which served as sleeping quarters for Henry and his wife, Mary Gertrude.

Across from the old blue dwelling was Leonard's house, into which little Pedro and I moved. This was a so-called transitional house, jerry-built, flimsy, and resting on cinder blocks without a basement. It looked nice from the outside, painted red with white trim, but it started falling apart even before it was finished. The government put up these transitionals all over the res. People referred to them as "poverty houses." It had some modern conveniences. Henry's blue and red palace had recently gotten electricity and we ran the juice from the old place to the transitional with a wire. The place had a gas range fed from a propane tank and, off and on, running water and a sink. It had a bathroom and a toilet, but somehow these never got connected. When I moved in I found a hippie sleeping in the tub. As for the toilet, Old Henry sometimes dragged it into the living room to use as an easy chair, with the water tank serving as his backrest. The kitchen was combined with the living room, whose walls were covered with Leonard's sacred things—pipe bags, peyote gourds, beadwork of all kinds, some quillwork, photographs, and many other things.

Leonard already had three children from his first wife, Francine—one son, Richard, and two girls, Ina and Bernadette. By and by, I added four more. The place became too small for all of us. There were always hangers-on at the Paradise, coming from nowhere and, sometimes, staying for a long time—months, or even years. One of these guests was Roque Duanes, who made himself useful by adding a wooden addition and second floor to the transitional. This part was painted white and decorated with Crow Dog's wotawe, what you might call a totem or family crest—two round balls representing bullets, and two arrowheads. This crest was designed by Henry himself, symbolizing that his grandfather, the first Chief Crow Dog, had been a great warrior who had been hit by two bullets from white soldiers' guns and by two Pawnee arrows. The stairs up to the second floor were not built for the timid. A huge oil drum on cinder blocks served as a wood stove. I gave birth to my third son, June Bug, in Roque Duanes's add-on.

Once we had a plague of wood ticks on the second floor and, downstairs, an invasion of bedbugs brought to us by one of our less desirable guests. We had a hell of a time getting rid of them. Further, there was the cookshack, to the right and back of the entrance; a brush shelter for summer outdoor cooking, the so-called "squaw cooler"; a never-quite-finished Navajo-style hogan; the sweat lodge; and far back by the stream a few tipis; and three outhouses, badly in need of repair. For a while there was also the bare shell of a red VW camper left there by a New York friend when it broke down. Without wheels and totally cannibalized, it served as a temporary home for a family of four. There were several horses on the place. Leonard's favorite, Big Red, sometimes came into our kitchen, through the back door, looking for hand-outs. The Paradise was swarming with dogs. The puppies regularly wound up in the cooking pot whenever we had a yuwipi ceremony, which is also a solemn ritual dog feast. Once a week I did all the washing, in a tub with the help of an old washboard.

Today, nothing is left of all these quaint structures that for a while had formed a veritable little village. The first to go was Henry's old homestead. I was there when it burned down. Leonard was at that time in jail, at Lewisburg, Pennsylvania, on trumped-up political charges stemming from Wounded Knee. He always was convinced that the goons, who hated the movement, had put the torch to the place. I think that the fire was caused by something else. Henry was also away when it happened, gone for a few days on some business or other. I was left alone with Grandma and the kids. I was staying over at the transitional house. I went over that morning and Grandma was doing patchwork pillow covers and she gave me a pillow. I went back to do housework, and I was reading a catalog when I heard a noise from the electric cord connecting our houses, like it had shorted out. I got up and ran to the other house, and I saw smoke coming out. Grandma was standing there all freaked out. The inside walls, which were made of paper, were in flames. She wanted to stay but I grabbed her and got her out of the house. There was that little side room, and she said: "My trunks!" So I busted that window and went in and got one trunk and heaved it out the window. I tried to get the other one, but by then the walls were ready to go up. Grandma started screaming and crying, telling me to come out, so I did. I jumped out the window, and then the house went down. It all happened really fast. By the time the fire department came it was too late. Leonard's sister Berta was still alive then, and she came over, and everyone felt really bad. The kids came home to find that they didn't have a home anymore, and they were in tears. Ina, who had just gotten a medal for basketball, just stood there and cried. I felt so bad for her. For all of them.

So then they all stayed in the house I was in, Leonard's house. Grandma Crow Dog was a chain-smoker. The greatest gift one could give her was a carton of Pall Malls. She used to flick the used matches away from her with a snap of her fingers, and sometimes there were still-smoking cigarette butts on the floor. Maybe that had something to do with the fire. Eventually Henry and Grandma had to move into the primitive cookshack, which was really a step down for them.

The next item to go was Leonard's red transitional house. Leonard, I, and the kids had been away for a couple of weeks gathering sacred medicine at the Mexican border in what Leonard calls the "peyote gardens." When we came home, the transitional was gone. Someone had stolen it. White people might wonder: "How can a house be stolen?" They wouldn't ask this question if they ever had seen, or been inside, one of our transitionals. The way they are built you can just pick them up and walk away with them. The VW camper also disappeared mysteriously. The hogan disintegrated by itself. In the end only two tipis and the sweat lodge remained.

When I first came to the Paradise I had a hard time. I was an outsider, I was a half-breed, I spoke only a little Sioux, and I arrived with a baby that wasn't Leonard's. My greatest crime in the view of some members of the Crow Dog tiyospaye was that I had replaced Francine, Leonard's first wife, a Lakota-speaking full-blood. Certain relatives of Leonard's were really mean to me. They accused me, again and again, of having broken up Leonard's family. They called me a homewrecker. This was ridiculous, because Leonard and Francine had split up long before I appeared on the scene. Leonard's parents also looked upon me as an intruder. Old Henry was the more tolerant of the two. As a traditional man he still lived in conformity to the old tribal customs, like never talking to one's daughter-in-law. There's this taboo that a father-in-law never speaks to his daughter-in-law, and a mother-in-law never speaks to her son-in-law. There is a tremendous fear of incest, that a father-in-law might be attracted to his son's wife, or a son-in-law to his wife's mother, no matter how unlikely it is for such a scenario to become reality. There was a way around this. The old man might mutter to himself: "I'd sure like it if someone would fry me up some spuds and bacon." And I'd be daydreaming aloud: "It sure would be nice if somebody would chop some wood for me." Henry made some concessions to modern times. He would speak to me briefly when it was absolutely necessary and when I was in despair he would grudgingly say a few kind words to me. But most of the time he was a deaf-mute as far as I was concerned. After I left Crow Dog, my new husband, Rudi, introduced me to his father, saying: "This is my woman." It was really quiet. I didn't talk at all. Then Rudi told me: "This is my family and my reservation. You can talk."

I have to admit that I liked Henry. He had a fantastic full-blood face, and a lean young body though he was almost eighty. He was still riding his horse dragging a load of firewood behind it. He was always busy with his hands, making a dance bustle, a horned headdress, or some other artifact. He was a fine dancer, even in old age. When he did the eagle dance you forgot that he was human. He became an eagle, flapping his wings, moving and turning his head like a bird. He had a wicked sense of humor and it was great fun to listen to him. He spoke English after his own fashion, a Henry-Crow-Dog-English of his own invention, full of quaint, strange, poetic half-Indian and half-white word creations. He was insanely proud of being all Indian and of his family history, often speaking of the "royal Crow Dog blood." I was hurt that the two old people always called me takoja, grandchild, and never wiwoka, daughter-in-law.

Henry's wife, Mary Gertrude, was a kind, very brave, broad-faced woman. She was a fine beader and moccasin maker, but so nearsighted that her nose almost touched the stuff she was working on. At first, she just wouldn't accept me.

In the end we came to love each other. A lot of women would always come to Grandma Crow Dog for advice. After all, she was an elder and she always knew what to say, even if it was just common sense. She was really down on drinking but had no luck in keeping other people from the stuff. Before the old folks' home burned down, early in the morning I'd get up and cook—I'd usually make fresh bread or pancakes or muffins—and I'd bring them over something while it was still hot. Then we'd all sit down and they'd talk about relatives, and just gossip. It was always lively, especially at breakfast time, drinking coffee and talking. Grandma often took to talking Sioux, oblivious to the fact that I could only understand half of what she said. It didn't matter. I got the drift. I never saw her idle. She was always busy with her moccasins, which every so often she took to town to sell.

My mother and Grandma Crow Dog went together to the Catholic boarding school at St. Francis. Mom told me: "Mary Gertrude was a strong, traditional woman, even when we were just kids. Her English was not too good. She went to the old ways, and I to the new."

Of Leonard's sisters, Christine was always friendly to me. She is a fine peyote singer with a mellow, deep, resonant voice. Leonard stood up for me most of the time but I sometimes wondered whether he had been attracted to me because of my looks and personality, or because I had at Wounded Knee given birth to Pedro, upon whom he looked as a symbol of renewal, as a rebirth of the Lakota Nation, and whom he groomed to be his successor.

Life at the Paradise was like a twenty-four-hour three-ring circus. There was never a quiet moment. We were never alone. Privacy was a strange white man's notion that was never taken into account. People would come asking for money all the time, thinking that because Leonard was a chief and medicine man he should be their sugar daddy. The remarkable thing was that Leonard thought so too. No, I am wrong because from his point of view it was unremarkable. In his traditional way it was the custom to expect a chief to be generous, to make gifts to all and let himself be stripped of all possessions. And so he gave money away that should have been used to buy food for the family. Sometimes he would give away the food itself, leaving us hungry and dinnerless. I admired him for that, but I was eventually the mother and stepmother of seven children, and never having any money sometimes drove me to the edge of a nervous breakdown. Leonard was in many ways a truly great man but he does not know what money means. I can't handle money either, but I was a little better than he in managing it. Some people would come and bring him a few dollars to perform a ceremony and he would immediately give it all away.

People came to Leonard with all their troubles. I kidded him, saying that he was the tribal psychiatrist. Like certain specialist doctors, he was always on call. People dropped in night and day to discuss tribal politics, religion, reservation economics, family tragedies, treaty rights, and a hundred other subjects. Because most of the visitors are full-bloods, short on reading and writing skills but brought up in the great oral tradition of our people, such talks tend to be long, wonderfully flowery, and poetic. But when they go on and on into the wee hours of the morning, speechifying can tire you out.

There is Indian time and white man's time. Indian time means never looking at the clock. It means doing what you want when you want it. In the case of some people it means having dinner at midnight or going to sleep at noon. In the old days we had no clocks or wristwatches. Nature was our clock. If we wanted to get up early, we drank a little more water the night before—then our bladders would wake us up in the morning. The sun, the moon, and the seasons were our timekeepers and that way of looking at time is still in our subconscious. There is not even a word for time in our language. Even the sophisticated, city-bred AIM leaders, great speechmakers who can twist the media around their little fingers, sometimes still move on Indian time. I remember, during the Wounded Knee crisis, some of our top men wanted desperately to get on TV to tell our side of the story. One network invited them to speak for an hour on prime time, on a Tuesday evening, I think. They never showed up. They arrived the next evening, on Wednesday. The TV people were livid with rage. "Never, ever, try to get on a show with us!" they told our leaders. "You put us in a horrible situation. We had to take whoever was willing to take your place at a moment's notice. It was a real bummer. You embarrassed us." Our men couldn't understand. What was all the fuss about? Tuesday or Wednesday, what did it matter? Who could understand white folks making such a stink about dates? White man's time and Indian time are just two entirely different concepts.

What with taking care of the children as well as visitors, I got little rest, or even sleep. Even when Leonard was away people came, expecting me to take his place handing out money or providing a meal and a place to sleep. Whenever Leonard stayed for any time at the Paradise there would be ceremonies—sweats, yuwipis, and the regular meetings of the Native American Church. Yuwipi rituals usually lasted throughout the night, and peyote meetings went from sunset to sunrise or even longer. That always

meant one to three dozen people coming to the Paradise to participate. After a night ritual most people did not want to drive home,
so they stayed to sleep it off and get fed. On such occasions the
floor was covered with bodies, the scene resembling a seal island.
I sometimes did not dare to go to the privy for fear of stepping on
someone. There was simply no space left to put my feet. Some
visitors were old friends, some were total strangers. They came
from all walks of life—Indians, whites, blacks, Asians. They came
from Mexico, Europe, and Japan. Many were curiosity seekers
wanting to meet the "great shaman" and to learn about Indian
spirituality. Many were groupies, hippies, and most of all New Age
people. Some stay for a few hours, some for months, some a few
years, becoming part of the household. We even had Buddhist
monks settling in, with one of them, Junji, becoming a friend and
sun dancer.

I became totally worn out and freaked out by constantly being
overwhelmed by crowds of visitors. It got to the point where I
yearned to go for a ride just to escape for an hour and get some
peace and quiet. When Leonard was in jail at Lewisburg, I grabbed
little Pedro and went to New York to live with my coauthor,
Richard Erdoes and his wife. I went there not only to be closer to
Leonard, but also to get away from the wear and tear at the
Paradise. What a relief it was to be able to take a hot bath, to get
a good night's sleep, and to eat something other than frybread,
fried potatoes, and greasy hamburgers.

When I got back the misery started again. I got pneumonia from
sheer exhaustion. Henry was away, which meant that I was "the
man of the house." In other words, chopping firewood was up to
me. I got a chain saw, cut wood for the night, and then stacked it
up. One night I was so tired I could hardly move. I lay down and
covered myself with a blanket but it was icy cold and I couldn't get
warm. My teeth were chattering. One moment I was hot and
sweating, the next I was freezing and shivering. I hitchhiked into
town the next day and went to the hospital. They said I had

pneumonia. As usual when I am in deep trouble I went to my mom's place. For a week I didn't go back to the Paradise. I couldn't handle going back down there. Mom nursed me back to health. So this was a ten-day "vacation."

Back at the Paradise we didn't have a house to live in. There was just the old cookshack that leaked, with a dirt floor. Eventually we rented a trailer house in Antelope, and it was nice at first. It was hard finding a place that would rent to us with as many kids as we had. So we rented a trailer at the edge of the community from this Indian lady. It was all right—I got along with the neighbors. We had cable TV and a phone, but we didn't have hot water there because the place was in need of new plumbing. In the spring and summer people would come by bringing tobacco, wanting advice, wanting to visit and talk. People would come to hock things, too. In fact there were these young boys that hocked us a microwave oven for thirty dollars. I thought it was great, until the police came about a week later and said that it was stolen and that if we didn't give it back we'd be charged with receiving stolen property. We gave it back, and about a month later we got our money back from the boys. After that we were more careful. The trailer had three bedrooms, a bathroom, a kitchen, and a living room. The trailer rested on cinder blocks, about two feet from the ground. The floor was rotten and I fell through. I could have broken my hip. Eventually, we went back to the Paradise and camped out in two tipis like in the days of long ago.

Leonard is a medicine man. Performing ceremonies is all he can do. He cannot read or write because Henry kept him out of school, fending off the truant officers at the point of a double-barreled shotgun. The old man claimed that school would "spoil his sacredness and bury his Indian mind under the white man's learning." They knew that he was destined to be a medicine man because of certain dreams and visions he'd had in his childhood. So he makes his living, if you can call it that, by performing Indian rituals all over the country. As he does not charge for his healing and cedar-

ing, he has to hustle and scrounge around, trying to find a founda-
tion or some sympathetic individuals to support his work.

His being a medicine man meant that we were traveling all the
time, like a caravan of gypsies, with the whole kit and caboodle, the
kids and, nearly always, an entourage of relatives or hangers-on.
Leonard is a chief, and chiefs do not travel alone. He also felt that
it was easier to raise money for a big group than for two or three
people. We always traveled in two or three cars that just loved to
break down. He's always surrounded himself with people. He's
always been that way. It was not enough that we took off in a bunch
of six or eight people, but he would also pick up hitchhikers, often
rather suspicious-looking characters, some of whom I suspected of
being federal agents checking up on us. We traveled all winter
long. With the kids. They did not get much schooling that way,
but, like his father, Leonard doesn't believe in book learning or the
three Rs. I will admit that he took the boys along in order to teach
them the rituals and raise them in the traditional way, but it
seemed to me that we were spending our lives in moving cars.

We would go someplace to perform a ceremony, like Texas or
California. They'd send him maybe a hundred dollars for gas,
which did not get us very far, so we made stops wherever we had
a friend or acquaintance and hit them up for gas money to get us
a little bit farther. We always had to hustle all the way and it
was a drag because often I didn't know whether we would eat.
Always the cars were overcrowded, like that little VW beetle in
the circus that stops in the center of the ring and thirty guys come
out. We should have performed that trick for money. One day we
would have to sleep in the cars, or spread our bedrolls by the side
of the road; the next day we might live it up in the mansion of
some wealthy admirer, to be treated to a huge gourmet dinner in
a fancy restaurant. We met more people than I can remember—
Indian and white, good and bad, rich and poor, some conventional
and some oddball types. Many of them were really very nice,
sympathetic, with an understanding of what we were doing. Some

went to extremes, and a lot of inconvenience, to put us up and feed the whole gang. I learned much and gained a lot of insights, but still the raggle-taggle gypsy life got me down. As a runaway teenager I had roamed from city to city with gangs of radical AIM kids, but it is different when you are ten or fifteen years older with kids on your hands.

Some people looked upon Leonard as a sort of magician who could fix just about anything. Some years ago they had a drought in Ohio. It seemed it had hardly rained a drop there for twenty-four months and the farmers were desperate. They contacted Leonard to do a rain ceremony for them. They flew him out and escorted him in a limousine, and they had a Hopi elder come, too, to help, two medicine men being better than one. But Leonard had the lead part. He did the ceremony and it rained, and rained, and rained. The whole area was flooded out. It was shown on nationwide TV. That Ohio town is even putting up a fountain in Leonard's honor with his statue on top. They paid him some two thousand dollars to come, but he had five or six people with him, besides our son Anwah, who was nine at the time. So it cost him more than he made, as usual.

At some time or other we had met Oliver Stone and he said that he could use us in the movie he was doing then—*The Doors.* So the whole caravan traveled to San Francisco. We were in a background scene of hippies clapping hands and music blasting away at the same time, so loud that I thought my ears would fall off. Leonard, Pedro, and I were all dressed up Indian style. They wanted one Indian to dance and then fly up in the air. At the same time we were supposed to be dancing around him and singing. Oliver was busy directing the crew and the cast, and he came over to us, and he said: "Don't just stand there like Ma and Pa Kettle, move around—do anything you want to do." In the background there were nude women dancing. And there was the actor playing Jim Morrison, and then Leonard, and an Indian woman, all dancing around a fire, a big fire. The concert was going on full blast.

When Oliver came onstage, I could see he was under pressure and kind of stressed out, but he kind of yelled at us. He has his nice side, but he has his business side too. I got mad and said: "I don't have to stand here and take this."

That scene was the last part of the movie to be filmed in San Francisco, and when it was over they had a party for the cast and the crew at the Holiday Inn. It was pretty good. There was a big buffet laid out, all kinds of food. The bar was open and people were milling around. Then this guy walked in with a stereo, with the Doors on full blast. Then he set it on our table. Pedro, who was seventeen at the time, was sitting up there with Val Kilmer, the actor who played Jim Morrison. So Pedro gets up and goes to the tape player, and he takes the Doors music off and puts on Indian powwow songs and an Omaha round dance, blasting it.

I was going up to the bar, and Leonard and Oliver were talking, and Leonard was telling him off, saying that he was just another white man and that he had a John Wayne attitude for the way he treated us on the stage area. Then I got two triple shots of Jack. Some guys from the crew were talking about a party, and they said: "Follow us." I did, and went into one of the rooms, and partied some more, and I fell asleep in a bathtub. This was on Fisherman's Wharf. So one of the guys took me back to the Sheraton, and somebody took me to my room. I took a bath and fell asleep in the tub, full of warm water.

Not all our travels ended in such a spectacular way. Frequently we traveled south across the Mexican border, to gather our sacred medicine, peyote. It doesn't grow in Sioux country. It never comes farther than some ten miles north of the border. It is legal for us to get it, provided we have a license and can prove that we are tribally enrolled Indians and members of the Native American Church. The people owning ranches along the border have made a commercial crop out of our wild-growing sacred medicine. We have to pay big bucks in order to be allowed to harvest it. On the way down we usually stopped and found shelter with other peyote roadmen, particularly a Navajo friend at Lukachukai, in Arizona.

Our longest treks were the so-called "walks" and "runs": the Trail of Broken Treaties, the Walk for Survival, the Longest Walk, the many runs for Native American rights, for Red Power, and what have you. These walks went all over the country, from the Pacific to the Atlantic Ocean, winding up usually in New York or Washington. We traveled in large caravans of cars, but people took turns running. Once we traveled to New York State on a Walk for Leonard Peltier, who was doing two lifetimes for allegedly killing two FBI agents during the great shoot-out at Oglala in 1975. I say "allegedly" because we all know that he was railroaded on a phony charge. We caravanned first to the Mohawks, to Rooseveltown, where they put out *Akwesasne Notes,* probably the best Native American newspaper in the country. Then we went on to Onondaga County, also in upstate New York. Both Mohawks and Onondagas are part of the Iroquois League of the Six Nations. We were treated very well, housed and fed. They took us into their longhouses, the men sitting on one side, the women on the other. That was the first time I met the clan mothers, who looked upon Leonard as a spiritual man and vied with each other to massage him, or knead his feet.

One time we went to Attica, after the big riot there, during which many inmates were killed. In the end only one man was still imprisoned for this uprising—a Native American, of course. His name was Decajawiah Hill. His relatives wanted our support. They thought it was unjust that he was being made the scapegoat for the Attica riot. We were not allowed inside the prison to hold a ceremony there. The warden would not permit Leonard to enter even though he was a medicine man. They did not even let us send a pipe in. The best we could do was to hold a big rally outside the prison walls. We had an overnight vigil and kept a fire going. People were drumming and singing, and we smoked a pipe for Decajawiah Hill. We hoped that maybe he could hear the drum, and through it find strength.

On the Long Walk for Survival, we had more white "walkers" than Indians. One white girl insisted that she was a witch. She chanted and danced in the moonlight all night through, covered with veils, keeping everybody awake. She made so much trouble that I got into a fight with her, giving the witch a bloody nose.

Often we ran out of money and had to camp by the roadside. We did not know from one day to the next at what place we would wind up for the evening, or where the gas money was coming from to get there. But something always turned up. Maybe it was the spirit working for us. Occasionally we stayed in luxurious homes along the way and I have to admit that, at times, I found myself envying the people who owned them. I am not materialistic, and I am used to being poor, but I started thinking about having a nonleaking roof over my head, and a little security. We roamed around the country so much, helping other people, that we never paid attention to ourselves. Leonard and I never settled down. As long as the old folks lived we had a home base, but after they died, it didn't seem the same anymore—it seemed empty. I was weary of the everlasting gypsy life, with no real home to return to.

While I lived at the Paradise, so many people came and went that I remember only a blur of many faces. Some, however, stayed for long periods, became friends, and had an influence on our lives. One of them was Cy Griffin. We met him at Richard Erdoes's place in New York. He dropped in to borrow a T square, had one wide-eyed look at the assembled Crow Dog tribe, left his family, and joined the wandering Sioux. That was over twenty years ago. At that time, Cy had a magnificent, shoulder-length bright orange-red jungle of hair and a huge beard of the same color. It made him look like St. John the Baptist. He had been in advertising, a Madison Avenue type, but when he saw Crow Dog he was born again. He became a faithful friend, stayed for long periods at the Paradise, and made himself useful, chopping wood, doing errands, helping Grandma Gertrude. He later became involved in almost all the AIM confrontations and was inside Wounded Knee for most of the siege.

Cy showed up last summer for the sun dance and we talked about the old days and the Knee. Cy's daughter, Janet, and her boyfriend, Bob Young, had stayed for more than a year at the Paradise, together with Cy's youngest daughter, ten-year-old Tracy. In time, Grandma Crow Dog looked upon Janet as her granddaughter. Bob joined the Native American Church, ate huge amounts of "medicine" during the meetings, and became a good singer of peyote songs. One time Bob and Janet wanted to go from New York to the Paradise. They had no car so they went to the George Washington Bridge to thumb a ride. A guy stopped and said: "Hop in." He asked them where they were going. When they told him they were going to the home of a Sioux medicine man, he got so excited that he took them all sixteen hundred miles to Rosebud and stayed there with them for a while. That was a hitchhiking record for sure.

Another longtime visitor at the Paradise, and sometime travel companion, was Roque Duanes. He was mostly Chicano and originally from Central America, but before he showed up at our place he had lived in the Northwest. Roque stayed with us for a few years. Leonard accepted everybody who came, no matter for how long, and somehow provided a tent, bedroll, and food for them. Roque made himself useful. He helped putting up the addition to the transitional house before it was stolen. He always helped prepare peyote meetings, helped with the wood, and became a real good peyote singer. He picked up the songs real quick. I still have him on some of our peyote tapes. He joined our caravan and went along to the peyote gardens, picking sacred medicine. Roque was unusual because he didn't drink. Never touched a drop. He didn't smoke grass either, but he did not condemn people who did. He said that was between them and the Great Spirit. He was always at the Paradise during sun dance time. He worked real hard during the vigil we had in D.C. for Leonard Peltier. If anyone ever deserved another trial because of a growing mountain of new evidence, it is Peltier. But he's still in jail, slowly going blind.

Well, Roque worked real hard during the vigil. He was always running around, doing paperwork, hustling food, finding places to stay. He became heavily involved in Peltier's case. When Peltier broke out of Lompoc Prison, in California, Roque was outside in his car waiting for him. He left Peltier at a place where a white woman was supposed to pick him up with a van and get him to Canada. But before the woman could get Peltier, an Indian showed up and told her: "No. You are white. I'm Indian. It's my job." He took the van and the eight hundred dollars she had on her for the trip, took off, and was never seen again. When the van did not come, Peltier wandered around for a day or two until he was picked up by the police. Curiously enough, Roque never did time for the part he played in Peltier's escape. As far as I can remember he was not even indicted. On another occasion, when people needed guns he supplied the stuff. But when some brothers got suspicious and went through his billfold and found a list of the serial numbers of the guns, word went out that Roque was working for the Man, that he was an informer. We had a hard time with him, because many people said that he was a rat. Some thought that he might have had something to do with Leonard going to jail. He left Rosebud and the Paradise to set himself up as a fisherman on the Northwest Coast. One day he set out in his boat and did not come back. He vanished without a trace. His body was never found. Some said that he drowned in a storm. Others thought that the government had killed him. Maybe it was his own people. We will never know. Before he disappeared he sent some tobacco and a sack of medicine to the Navajo elders at Big Mountain to hold a meeting for Leonard Peltier. They heard what had happened to Roque, but held the meeting anyway, to honor Grandfather Peyote and the smoke he had given them.

Another outsider who came to the Paradise to stay was Brad Zais. His chief achievement was getting my sister Sandra pregnant and cooperating in the making of a pretty baby girl. Brad lived at the Paradise off and on for a few years. He became a veritable slave for Leonard, a real gofer. He brought and fetched, made phone calls, wrote letters for us, drove to town for groceries, and traveled with us. He took good care of Grandpa and Grandma Crow Dog. Brad chopped wood and helped put up the arbor for the sun dance. He always said that Henry and Gertrude were the best people he ever met. Grandma Crow Dog soon started to call him "son." He would spend hours sitting by her side, sipping "black medicine," listening to her stories of the olden days. Often she would speak for a long time in Indian, and then suddenly stop herself, saying: "Oh, I forgot, you can't understand." Then she would go on with her story in English, but soon slip into Lakota again. She taught Brad how to make frybread for her.

And then there was Junji, half Japanese and half Ainu, the indigenous, bear-worshiping people from Hokkaido, Japan's northernmost island. We had met him at the Longest Walk, and then again at Big Mountain. Junji came to America in 1980. At first he was a kind of Japanese hippie, but once he joined a group of Buddhist monks on the Longest Walk he became one of them. He showed up at Big Mountain in a saffron-colored robe with his head shaved. He is now celibate and can no longer fool around with women. He is very saintly now. He pierced and sun danced at the Paradise for four years running. At sun dance time he is always up before everyone else, when it is still dark. He then wakes the camp by beating his monk's drum.

Many people came to the Paradise from Latin America, particularly Mexico. One came with a bunch of large condor feathers. Another man, half Huichol and half Nahuatl, came to participate in the ghost dance at the Paradise in 1974. He said his Indian name was Warm Southwind, so we dubbed him "Mild Disturbance." One Yaqui, whose name was Nacho, was some sort of a revolutionary who called himself general-in-chief of Aztlan. Another sun dancer from Mexico named himself Tlacael after a famous fifteenth-century Aztec leader. One Indian from Central America walked for three months on foot to participate in last summer's sun dance.

A young law student, Eric Biggs, stayed at the Paradise for over a year doing Leonard's law work and letter writing. Later he worked for the Navajo Tribe. He is now a big-shot lawyer in Santa Fe and no longer interested in Crow Dog or the movement, but that takes away nothing from the help he gave us years ago.

We even had some devil worshipers coming to the place who boasted of having sacrificed cats and chickens to the Prince of Darkness. We got rid of them fast. And, of course, there were the Germans—Hanz, Fritz, and Stephan. It is impossible to remember all the people who made their pilgrimages to the Paradise and lingered on for weeks, months, or years.

There was also the problem of always being spied on. Our greatest shock came about five years ago. Richard Erdoes had flown to Custer, South Dakota, to testify for Dennis Banks. Dennis was being sentenced there in connection with the great riot at Custer, in February of 1973, when many Sioux people protested in front of the Court House, because the white man who had killed Wesley Bad Heart Bull went unpunished. The morning after the trial, Richard was having breakfast at the Alex Johnson Hotel in Rapid City. He was sitting at a table together with Bill Kunstler and Bruce Ellison, Dennis's defense lawyers. Crow Dog and a few of his friends came in. He, too, had wanted to testify for Dennis, but, as so often happened, his car had broken down and he had arrived during the night, after the trial was over. Kunstler called out to him: "Leonard, come over here. Do you know that your brother-in-law is an FBI informer?" As Richard told me, Crow Dog stood there openmouthed, in shock. All he could say was: "NO!" "It's true," Kunstler went on. "Before I came here for Dennis, I was up in Fargo, North Dakota, for a rehearing of the Peltier case. When the prosecution ran out of believable witnesses, they blew his cover and he testified for them, saying he had worked for the FBI for years. He ratted on you, sending out a whole stream of lying reports. Your own brother-in-law, your sister's husband." Crow Dog did not know what to say. He kept standing there openmouthed, shaking his head, his appetite for breakfast gone. So we had to deal with such things at the Paradise. We found out that after the Pine Ridge incident he had told his bosses that Peltier was staying at our place and they had believed it. That's why we were raided by 185 marshals and agents with helicopters in September 1975, and why Leonard was arrested on a trumped-up charge and went to jail.

As a matter of fact, Peltier *had* been staying at the Paradise, but that was *before* the shoot-out. He was a big flirt with the girls on our place but they didn't care for him too much until later on. Such was life at the Paradise.

Grandpa Henry always used to get up early in the morning. Grandma had arthritis and could hardly move around. She was also in pain all the time because of a broken hip. When they were living, they'd hold hands when they walked, and he'd cook for her and feed her. He was spry for his age, and real loving to her. And they'd talk, like after peyote meetings. She had been really sick, and gotten well from using the peyote, so she continued to use it.

One winter we went to Kilgore to get some beer, and were drinking and partying, and he got a little high. We all did. Leonard went to bed and fell asleep. When I went to check on the old man, I didn't see him anywhere. I thought maybe he'd gone to the other house. About an hour later, Bern, Richard, Ina, and some of the grandchildren came up and asked where he was. I said: "I thought he was down there." But he wasn't. The snow was high and it was cold. We looked all over for him. He never came in.

Apparently he had fallen into a ditch full of snow somewhere. Early the next morning Wilson White Hawk came knocking at the door: "Leonard! Your dad's at Diane's doorstep!" Diane, his daughter, lived next door and he was always going over there, but it happened that this week Diane had gone and locked up her house. We rushed over and he was lying there. We got him in the house but we knew he was already gone. We called an ambulance and they tried for three hours to revive him but he had frozen to death. He was eighty-six, I think. No one was really sure of his age.

They decided to bury him up at Ironwood Cemetery by his

mother. It was a big funeral—people came from all over the country, and there was big media coverage. They had Christian and traditional Indian services.

Henry was always making something—a tomahawk or a shield—always doing crafts. In the morning they'd always have cornmeal and coffee. Sometimes we'd eat over there and sometimes they'd eat at our house. With Old Henry passed a piece of history and a way of life. He was the last of his kind. There isn't anybody like him left now. We were in Phoenix when Leonard's mother died soon after. Leonard didn't want to go back because he knew she was dying. I guess he just couldn't handle seeing her die. My mother went to her wake, and they had Henry and Gertrude's marriage certificate there for all to see. They had been married in church, in the Christian way. That surprised some people. They held a mass for her and buried her next to Henry.

Year after year, things at the Paradise went from bad to worse. All the troubles of the world landed at our doorstep. There was a total lack of privacy. The house was always full and the grounds resembled a permanent camp. People came to borrow money and never paid it back, not even once. They took from the house whatever they needed, even the pots and pans. Leonard would give his last dollar away to help someone. We never got on our feet. We never had a home. For years he told me he was going to build me a home, but there was always something more important—a ceremony here, a sun dance there, a political meeting, tribal affairs. We ended up with nothing. We never knew what the next day would bring. And Leonard will live that way all his life, because that's all he knows. I am not materialistic at all. I have the sharing spirit of our people, but the life at the Paradise simply wore me out. It got to Leonard, too, even though he had grown up this way. We got short-tempered with each other. We exploded emotionally. Simply because of the maddening condition of our existence. He strayed. I strayed. In the end we no longer shared the same bed. Finally, two years ago, things became unbearable, and

I left him. The life we led took its physical and emotional toll on me. I had become scrawny and you could see the bones under my skin. I couldn't sleep. I had nightmares. I was so tired that I stumbled around like an old woman. We were both stressed out.

The last time I lived with Leonard, we didn't even have a house. We just camped out. We had a propane gas stove outside. That's how I aged so much, from cooking out in the sun. The elements got to me. It was okay, except when it rained. Then everything got wet, no matter how much I tried to tie down the tent. I always ended up having to do laundry, washing everything. You get a lot of fresh air but it's hard. You get up in the morning and try to beat the flies to the toilet. I don't like camping out, especially with a lot of kids, because they're hungry, and then when you do cook, they're not around to eat. They'd rather munch cereal, anyway. Sometimes we'd cook over a big fire, like if we needed a lot of coffee, or soup or something. That was my home for the whole summer. I wanted a house. And I told Leonard: "I'm not camping out here forever." Water was from a pump pretty far away from camp. You would have to bribe somebody to carry it for you. All there was were those big five-gallon buckets. You'd have to keep the cleaning water separate from the drinking water. And after cooking, you'd have to clean everything in the whole camp, and then after everybody left spray and clean it again for the bugs, because there's literally millions of flies. You could be twenty yards from the outhouse and hear them already. It was pretty bad. Then there was poison ivy. And last year they tested the water table and found arsenic in it. I guess they were treating it, but I don't know if our well was being treated, because Leonard would never let the public health people come in and test the water. Anwah and Jenny got sick from the water, and June Bug, too.

For some time I slept in a little U-Haul trailer. The boys slept with Leonard in the tipi. I've had enough of that. When you're young, you're gung ho, and it's all right. But not when you get older. I want a push-button washing machine now, and running water. Leonard would tell me: "This is my grandfather's ways. I live in a tipi. But you've lost the spiritual side of it."

One day our friend Rod Skenandore brought us a buffalo pipe for Pedro because he was born at the Knee. It had a bowl in the shape of a buffalo. The stem had beautiful quillwork on it. He also gave me a beautifully beaded pipe bag. One day pipe, stem, and bag disappeared. Another time my medicine bundle given to me at the Knee was gone. Up to this day I don't know what happened to these things. When I told Leonard that these sacred things had been stolen, he said: "Yeah, the spirit told me that you were drunk in a bar and maybe you dropped them in a ditch somewhere."

I said: "No, they were just plain ripped off like all our other things. I don't go drinking when I have a medicine bundle on. I don't dishonor sacred things that way." We were rubbing against each other. We rubbed ourselves raw. It wasn't his fault and it wasn't my fault. The conditions were at fault. I left.

Leonard and I still care for each other. He taught me so much about ceremonies and how to prepare for them. He took me on walks and taught me how to recognize the different healing herbs. He had a good influence on me. He opened the door to me, a door that led me back into being Indian and not merely a half-breed. He was always there for the people. He brought me back to the pipe, and shared with me his dreams of spirituality. And to suffer at the sun dance was good for me. And now, even though I am no longer with him, I have it in me to go to the sweat lodge, or a peyote meeting, or a sun dance, or to be around when people are praying in the good old Lakota way, to share dreams and goals for the future and our children. And I feel sorry for him that I'm not there anymore to help him, because it will be hard for him without me. He told me how hard it would be to teach someone else all those things that I learned over the years, and that brought tears to my eyes.

There's not much left of Crow Dog's Paradise as I found it when I joined Leonard there in 1973. The houses are gone and so are many of the people who had once spent their lives there. Now there's only last year's sun dance pole left, and the ruins of the tar-papered cookshack, and the skeleton of a sweat lodge. But, come August at sun dance time, there returns that old feeling, the excitement, the elation, the trance, the ecstasy, when the drums are pounding, and the songs reverberate, and the sound of eagle-bone whistles fills the air, and the sun dancers circle around the sacred tree with their red kilts and circles of sage around their heads. It is during these short days that I wish I'd never left.

CHAPTER FIVE

Womb Power

I had one child, Pedro, before I came to Crow Dog's Paradise. I had three more children during the years I stayed there. Recently, I had my fifth, a girl, with my new husband. I have already described Pedro's birth at Wounded Knee in my first book. I had gone to the Knee for the purpose of giving birth to my first child there. He came into this world during the siege, with bullets going through the wall and the drums beating before the window greeting the arrival of a new life. Pedro's birth was looked upon as a symbol of renewal, a tiny symbol, a tiny victory in our people's struggle for survival. But my other birth-givings were likewise symbolic, or at least different from most women having a child in a hospital.

My second child was also a boy—Anwah. He was born in 1979, during a month's vigil for Leonard Peltier in Washington, D.C. We were holding candlelight demonstrations in front of the FBI Building, and John Trudell, a friend and AIM leader, ceremonially burned an American flag on its steps. That very same night John's house burned down and his family, including his pregnant wife, perished in the flames. John Trudell wanted to bury his family in the traditional way and so he, Leonard, and Roger Eagle Elk left the vigil for a few days to fly to Nevada to perform the funeral ritual while I stayed with the vigil in Washington. During our demonstration for Leonard Peltier a howling blizzard struck the town, the first such blizzard they'd had in twenty-three years or so. Nine months pregnant, I slipped and fell on some ice. During the vigil Steve Robideau's wife at that time, Tico, who was a Clallam (a people from a Northwest tribe), said: "Mary, you'd better go on to the hospital." I said: "I don't want to go to the hospital." She said: "You'd better go, because nobody here knows how to deliver a baby." Tico took me to D.C. General, located right in the ghetto, and all the patients there were black people. I was in and out of labor. Finally they tried to induce labor but that didn't work. John Trudell called me at the hospital and said: "Mary, you go ahead and have a nice baby—I really care for you and what you're doing for Leonard Peltier." And he said what happened to his family had been done by the government and it was a setup. After they buried John's family Leonard and Roger Eagle Elk flew back into Richmond and took a bus to D.C. When they got to the hospital the doctors were ready to do a cesarean because the baby seemed stuck inside me. Roger Eagle Elk was a member of the Native American Church, so Leonard asked Roger to pray for me. Roger made me four peyote medicine balls that he gave to me. He then prayed for me and fanned me off with his eagle-tail fan. Within an hour I had Anwah. There was an intern there who didn't think the baby was coming because my blood pressure and everything was normal, so he sat down to eat. I asked if Leonard could be in the room because I knew the baby was coming. Sure enough the baby came. He didn't have a name then, he was just "Baby," or "Baby Crow Dog." I had him on a Thursday night.

It was the first time I had been among black people and they treated me really good, like a family member. When Anwah was born I felt really sad. They said: "Aren't you happy?" I said: "No, I feel sad," because I was thinking about what had happened to

John Trudell's family. Then that Saturday Leonard's sister, Berta, was killed in a car accident. So from the hospital we had to fly home for the funeral. Before we left we went to the place where the Japanese monks stayed. They had a big feast and an honoring ceremony. It was really nice. Leonard did a ceremony and Roger was right there being his helper. The monks had never seen a newborn baby. They greeted us with drumming and chanting.

The monks were going to make a plate of food for my newborn baby who was only two days old, and I had to explain to them that I was nursing, and that the baby was too young to eat solid food, because they didn't know anything about children. After that we flew back for the funeral. At that time Leonard's mother and father were still alive. Henry gave Anwah his name. His full name is Anwah Tokakte, something like Warrior Killing Enemy. So that was how Anwah was born.

My third child, also a boy, was born at the Paradise in 1981. He is a sun dance baby because he came into the world during the sun dance, on July 30, the first day of purification. I had him in the red transitional house's upper floor, which Roque Duanes had helped us build. I knew already the night before that I would give birth the next day. I was supposed to lie down and breathe rhythmically, but I felt like walking around outside in the fresh air, and when my labor pains would start I'd just stand still until they passed. Some guys were making coffee, and I said: "Let me have some!" But they told me: "Get back in the house, you have a job to do." Roque and some young men were pacing back and forth in front of the house and they were also heating up fifty gallons of water—for me. Men always think that when a woman is in labor they have to heat up bathtubs full of water. Why, I don't know. I guess they have seen it in the movies. I didn't want the big crowd at the dance to know that I was going to have a baby, but Leonard was running through the whole camp yelling: "Anybody got a pair of scissors? We need them to cut the umbilical cord. Mary's in labor!" So there was a big excitement when word got around that there would be a birth at the sun dance.

I had the baby early in the morning. Leonard's sister Christine was supposed to act as midwife, with his daughter Bernadette to help her. At the last moment, Christine lost her nerve. So Bern did the whole job alone, cutting the navel cord, helping with the delivery. She was only fifteen at the time and had never done it before, but she handled the whole matter like a professional. The tiny human being's first cry was high-pitched and piercing, like an eagle-bone whistle. He had long black hair with three little "whirl-wind" curls in it. All the time it had been raining, raining, raining. The house was leaking very badly and the whole floor was wet, so I put him in a laundry basket together with the clean clothes. Francis Primeaux, a peyote man and World War II veteran, who died in 1991, named the newborn Warrior Boy.

That year the prison wardens had let out a number of Indian prisoners so that they could sun dance, so they were having all kinds of ceremonies outside my leaking room, for these inmates as well as for my baby. I couldn't join them, however, since they had the pipe there and all the sacred things, and for four days after giving birth you are like a woman on her moon, you can't be in a ceremony. Instead I watched from the house.

The baby's English names were Leonard and Eldon, after a relative, Eldon Low Moccasin, but I got to calling him Junior, and then June, and finally June Bug. So everyone now calls him that. It just stuck.

June Bug's birth caused almost as much joy and excitement as Pedro's had at Wounded Knee. The sun dance is a ceremony of life renewal, the lives of our people and the buffalo who gave themselves so that the tribe could survive. So a new life at this, our most sacred ritual, was received as a good omen.

Next came Jennifer. Hers was the most "normal" of my births so far. I was watching a soap opera when I felt the first pains of labor. I could feel the pains starting and I knew it was time to go to the hospital, but I had to finish *The Young and the Restless*. When it was over at noon, I told Leonard it was time to go. He took me to the emergency room, where they examined me and rushed me into the delivery room because I was already fully dilated. Leonard left me there in the delivery room. The nurse asked me: "What do you want it to be?" I told her: "I know it's going to be a boy, because I already have three boys." She said: "But what would you like?" I said: "I'd like a girl." The baby was born, and she said: "Guess what? You have a little daughter." I felt really happy, and I was looking at her, and I couldn't believe I had a baby girl. I didn't even have a name for her, because I had been expecting a boy. My mother named her Jennifer Louise. She'd had a grandma named Jennifer, and her own mom was named Louise.

I married my new husband, Rudi, on August 24, 1991, in Santa Fe, and immediately got pregnant, though I didn't know it. After I had my big car wreck, the doctors at the hospital told me that I would never be able to conceive again. "Relax," they said, "let others do the work." From Santa Fe we went to Arizona for three months and then went back to the res. I went to the tribal hospital for a checkup, to see how my recovery from the big accident was going, and found out that I was three months pregnant. Rudi said that when I came out of the examination room, I seemed to be in shock. I had trusted the doctors who had told me that I could never have a baby again. It shows you what they know. I did not think I could handle another pregnancy. I had four kids already. I had not yet fully recovered from my injuries from the car wreck. My one arm, separated from the shoulder blade, was acting up. I was in pain. I felt old and worn out. I thought: Oh, no, not again! But already there was a new life forming in my belly.

I consider myself a feminist. So you might ask why, under the circumstances, I didn't terminate my pregnancy. Well, there is a difference between white and Indian feminists—we think that abortion is all right for everybody else, but not for us. There are only one and a half million tribally affiliated Native Americans left. For centuries, we have been the victims of physical and cultural genocide. Whole tribes have been wiped out by bullets or by smallpox, introduced by Europeans. We have been dying of "benign neglect." So there is within us the subconscious urge to reproduce, to make sure that we are not a "vanishing race." I would carry my baby to term.

The first time we got to hear the baby was through ultrasound, when I was four months pregnant. They put this little contraption on my stomach and we were able to see the baby taking shape. We could hear the heartbeat. That was pretty exciting. We didn't know whether what we were seeing on the screen was a boy or a girl, and we didn't care. We were concerned about complications. After all, I had my thirty-sixth birthday behind me. Years of a hard life, drinking, and injuries had taken their toll. Then on New Year's Day I started spotting and was rushed to the hospital. The doctor thought that I might lose the baby and they kept me there for two days, but I came out of it all right. They told me: "Stay off your feet and relax." Easier said than done. I got bigger and bigger. I looked at myself in the mirror and thought: Could this be me? I was a grotesque sight. I no longer walked—I waddled like a doped-up, drunken duck.

Throughout my pregnancy, Rudi was a total wreck. It seemed that he was the one who was pregnant. He suffered from morning sickness. My ankles swelled up, his swelled up even more. My back hurt, he said: "My backache is killing me." I threw up, he threw up twice. I got mad. Here I was, big as an elephant, and he was having worse symptoms than I had. I said: "Who is going to have the baby, you or me?" We got on each other's nerves sometimes.

It was late May and I was a week overdue. I was worried. On Saturday the thirtieth we were all at my mom's place—Rudi and I, my sister Barb, and her Jim—having a barbecue, when my water broke. Everybody was excited—"Here comes the baby!" They rushed me to the Rosebud hospital, but the pediatrician wasn't there. He had quit. He'd had his license revoked in the city but was good enough for the res; not fit to treat white people, but good enough for us redskins. Then he got his license back and lost no time in getting back to civilization and better-paying patients. It pissed me off. To guys like him we are just guinea pigs to practice on. Here I was on the verge of giving birth and in that whole goddam hospital there was no physician competent to deliver my baby. They told us I would have to be flown almost two hundred miles to Yankton, which has a good hospital. We had to wait the whole night for the plane. It was a little medical plane, a two-seater, really. I still don't know how they crammed us all in there—the pilot, myself, a nurse, and Rudi. The one-and-a-half-hour flight was awful. We were jammed against each other. The nurse was practically sitting on my belly. I could hardly breathe. There was a storm and the winds whipped our tiny plane around so that it was bouncing up and down. Sometimes I had a feeling like falling from a two-story window. An ambulance picked us up at the Yankton airport and rushed us to the hospital. They put me on a gurney and wheeled me into a cubicle next to the delivery room. The doctor told me: "I have to give you something to induce labor. You're not dilating." He also reassured me: "Sit tight. You'll have a baby by dinnertime." They hooked me into an IV to make me dilate. Rudi was biting his fingernails. He hadn't slept a wink, so I told him to go outside to the lounge and find himself a sofa to stretch out on. Soon after he left the pains started and I sent a nurse to call him back. I was hyperventilating. I told Rudi: "I can't handle this. Tell the doctor to give me something to knock me out!" He tried to calm me down, telling me to breathe deeper. He talked to me. He had a washcloth and was sponging me off. For the first time I had a husband at my side when giving birth.

The doctor came back, had a look at me, and told the nurses to wheel me into the delivery room. Rudi asked: "Could I go in there, too?" They said: "Sure," and made him put on a set of greens and a mask and told him to scrub up. I was in the stirrups with my legs in the air, and the doctor said: "Okay, go ahead and push!" So I pushed. He said: "Stop, stop, I can see the head. Okay, push again!" And that was it. We had been in the delivery room less than five minutes. The baby just came sliding out, like toothpaste out of a

tube. I saw right away that it was a girl. Mom had already told me
a few days before: "You're going to have a girl." She was right, as
usual. My newborn had a lot of hair already. The doctor grabbed
the baby from me and handed her to Rudi. She still had the
umbilical cord on her and Rudi was in an absolute panic, not
knowing what to do, holding this screaming and squirming baby.
She was twenty-one and a half inches long and weighed eight
pounds, seven ounces.

The doctors hooked up a suction apparatus and started sucking
fluids out of my baby's nose and mouth. They said that she had
fluid in her lungs and that they were concerned because she might
develop pneumonia. The nurses cleaned her up and took her into
intensive care. Rudi, a sentimental and overprotective worrybird,
started crying when he saw this poor little thing hooked up to all
those IVs in her arms, and all those little monitors on her chest. He
said: "It's so sad seeing her lying there like that, with her breath
real wheezy," and he cried some more. I tried not to let him see
that I also was concerned. We prayed the Indian way and just hung
in there.

We had still another problem. When we had first gone to the
Rosebud hospital we had expected the baby to be born there. Rudi
came in just a pair of old Levi's and a T-shirt. We had brought no
money, not expecting to need any. Now here we were in Yankton,
with no money for Rudi to go to a hotel, or even for a bite to eat.
The doctor was nice. He had a cot put into my room and let Rudi
sleep there, and even eat the hospital meals. This doctor became
a real friend. He later drove all the way to Rosebud, during his
vacation time, to see how my baby was doing.

Well, they came to me with the birth certificate and said: "We
need a name for the baby." We didn't have a name for her yet, so
they hung a card on her: "Baby Girl Olguin–Brave Bird." My sister
Barb was sterilized and can't have a child, and so, to honor her, I
thought she should have the privilege to name her. I was thinking
that Summer Dawn would be a nice name. We called Barb, who

said: "Call her Summer Rose." We had been on the same wave-
length. Summer Rose it was.

Barb made a beautifully beaded umbilical turtle fetish from the
baby's navel cord. She said: "This will give Summer Rose a good,
long life. I will keep her on a good path, and she won't stray, and
she'll always come back to her roots and be a true Sioux." Actually,
there is more to this than just what Barb said. In the old days, until
recently, when a child was born someone made two identical
beaded or quilled turtle fetishes for the newborn. One of them
contained the umbilical cord, and that one was hidden inside the
baby's cradleboard. The other one was hung up in a tree or some
other place where the evil spirits could see it. It was believed that
these spirits always tried to get possession of the navel cord and
thereby gain power over the child. Not knowing that this fetish did
not contain the navel cord, they vented their fury and evil magic
on it to no effect. The little amulet is made in the form of a turtle,
because this animal represents longevity. For days after you kill a
turtle, its heart keeps on beating and beating.

Summer Rose did not stay long in intensive care. She turned out
to be a healthy and fat baby. She was only a few days old when,
lying on her stomach, she raised herself up on her tiny arms as if
she were trying to do push-ups. The doctor said: "See how strong
she is." Summer Rose looks very Indian, much more than I do. She
looks like a genuine little full-blood. I like that. She almost makes
me feel like having more kids, but I keep my fingers crossed that
she is the last. If somebody had told me a year ago that I'd be
married and pregnant again, I would have laughed. I felt strange
bringing new life into the kind of world we have but the spirit
moves in strange ways. Maybe there's a reason for babies to be
born. Maybe this generation is not vanishing or dying. Maybe the
earth will still renew itself as the ghost dancers of old had hoped
for.

The kids are growing up developing their own personalities.
Pedro, my oldest, is twenty now. In 1972, my mother was in

summer school at the college in Vermillion, South Dakota. During a visit there I was introduced to Pat Spears, a half-blood and a sort of Indian hippie—he had long hair, smoked grass, and had big college parties in his trailer house by the Missouri River. He was unlike anybody I had met before, different from the reservation kids I knew. He fascinated me and turned me on. I was not yet seventeen, innocent, and very naive. I didn't know anything about sex at all. I ended up staying with Pat for a while, out there by the river.

When Mom found out I was pregnant she was horrified. Myrl, my stepfather, was mad. He said: "That's the last thing I expected from you, getting pregnant." Grandma Flood was embarrassed and read me the riot act: "How could you do such a thing?" I could have told her that getting pregnant was the easiest thing in the world, but said nothing. I was the ornery, radical black sheep of the family and had disgraced them. In Parmelee and He Dog people gossiped about me. At that time having a child out of wedlock was still looked upon as being very shameful among the so-called respectable, churchgoing half-bloods. I was ostracized and felt unwanted at home and so I turned to the movement. The AIM became my family where I found my brothers and sisters. I went to Wounded Knee and Pedro was born.

From the beginning, Crow Dog accepted him as his own. He groomed him to be his successor, to become a medicine man.

Pedro grew up in the movement and was raised in the traditional Sioux way. Almost from the day of his birth he was included in the rituals of the old Lakota religion. As a baby he sat in my lap during peyote meetings. He pierced for the first time at the sun dance when he was only six years old. When he could not break free, I told him: "We'll pull you off." He was crying, but told us: "Don't touch me. I'll do it myself." I was so proud. He's been going to ceremonies all his life—pipe ceremonies, Native American Church ceremonies, vision quests.

I think that for Pedro, growing up in the movement has given him a special wisdom and philosophy that he will hold on to for the rest of his life. He has run Native American Church meetings ever since he conducted one in Phoenix when we all lived in Arizona. I was not present when Pedro ran his first yuwipi ritual. He was traveling with Leonard at that time while I stayed home with the three younger children. He has pierced at the sun dance, and hung from the tree, and pulled buffalo skulls. Of course my mom doesn't like this. It's not her way. But she accepts it now. We have both mellowed and respect each other's beliefs. So she comes to the sun dance whenever Pedro or I pierce and sits under the arbor, probably confessing this sin next time she goes to church. That's one advantage of being a Catholic. You get absolution. No such luck for the poor heathens who have to forgive each other.

Pedro did very badly in school and ended up dropping out, telling me that he wanted to walk the traditional road. He has followed in the footsteps of Leonard, who has little use for the white man's schooling. Pedro does not want to go back to high school and would rather get a GED—that's a general education diploma. He is strong willed and I could not persuade him to change his mind about this. He was going to school for a while in Rosebud, after we came back from Arizona, but he just couldn't get along.

Pedro is a big guy, six feet one and 190 pounds, but slender. He is very good-looking in the Brave Bird way. He is a good kid, respectful to his elders. He doesn't scare easily and although he never looks for trouble, he will defend himself if he has to. He is not stingy. If he's got something and he sees you're admiring it, he'll give it to you. He always has a little gift for Grandma Emily whenever he comes to her house. Mentally, he's still a kid. He likes to go out with the boys and party, cruising the streets and looking at the girls. I am grateful that he is not into drugs or alcohol. He'll drink a little beer now and then, but that's all.

I want Pedro to go back to school, learn a trade or have a profession. He's a good singer with a strong voice. Right now he has a drum group called the Eagle Lake Singers. His group gets paid at powwows. They travel all over Indian country, on the so-called powwow circuit, but it isn't a whole lot of money. Every time they hear of a powwow, they jump in the car and go. They've gone to Minnesota for the Wild Rice Festival of the Ojibways. They traveled to Kansas for the Kickapoo Dance. During powwow season they get jobs about twice a month.

Pedro made me a grandmother at the age of thirty-six. It is a bittersweet story. Pedro always traveled with us from coast to coast, especially to Big Mountain, in Arizona, where he had a Navajo girlfriend, Evangeline. I loved Evangie and hoped she'd be my daughter-in-law. She and Pedro were childhood sweethearts. They used to play together when they were little and, when they grew older, planned to get married. Evangie is very pretty. She comes from a large traditional family. Both kids belonged to the peyote church, and they were both sun dancers. Whenever Pedro was in Rosebud they would write long love letters to each other. Evangie is a fancy-shawl dancer and she always makes her own beautiful outfits. One year she was elected a powwow beauty princess.

But there was a little problem named Percetta Little Bear. Percetta is cute and lively and she was *here*, in Rosebud, while Evangie was a thousand miles away in Navajo country. And Percetta got pregnant, courtesy of Pedro. At sun dance time Evangie came with her whole family to visit us. And so now here in Rosebud were Evangie and her whole family looking upon Pedro as one of theirs already. It was quite a situation for an eighteen-year-old to handle. Anyway, Percetta and Evangie ended up being friends. Evangie proved to be very understanding. I would have liked Evangie to be my grandchild's mother, but I have learned to appreciate Percetta. She's a good woman, a good cook, a good housekeeper. She and Pedro help each other. In time, Percetta gave birth to a girl whom they named Vanessa.

I went to a peyote meeting at Fort McDowell and the roadman

called me Grandma all night: "Thank you for coming, Grandma," and "We really enjoy your presence, Grandma." He did it to show his respect, but I really don't want to be called Grandmother—yet. I guess I'll have to get used to it. Because of the powwows, Pedro and Percetta are frequently away from each other on the weekends, and then she stays with her mom. I think they are happy having a break from each other now and then. Percetta is good for Pedro because she keeps him away from drinking and partying.

Of course, the fifty bucks here and there Pedro gets for a weekend couldn't feed a sick sparrow, so he went and applied for a regular job, which is a requirement if you want to get any type of welfare. It's just a formality, because there are no jobs on the res. So they got GA. They get four hundred dollars for food, rent, and utilities. Their rent for a tiny rotten trailer is two hundred a month. That doesn't leave much for food, clothing, heating, and electricity. They got food stamps and still can't make it. In other words, they lead a normal reservation life. That is the story of Pedro, so far.

My second son, Anwah, is pure Crow Dog. He has Leonard's broad full-blood features and hefty build. He follows in his father's footsteps. He has already run sweats and peyote meetings. At age twelve, at a sun dance, he pulled buffalo skulls for Leonard Peltier, suffering to make the Spirit let Peltier go free.* When the skulls wouldn't come loose, my youngest children, June Bug and Jennifer, were made to sit on the skulls to make them heavier. When Anwah finally broke free, John Trudell, who was watching, said: "This is the boy, this is the future!"

Anwah is torn between Leonard and myself. Sometimes he runs

---

*"Pulling buffalo skulls" is one form of self-torture men undergo during a sun dance. Skewers are pushed through the flesh, high on the back. Thongs are attached to the skewers and connected to the skulls. The dancer then pulls them around the circle until the skewers break through. It is a very severe form of piercing.

away from me and joins his father at Crow Dog's Paradise, and then comes back to me again. It's hard for Anwah. He has a lot of anger in him. I try to convince him that even though Leonard and I are no longer together, he has parents who love him.

Anwah is a good, smart kid. He's a whiz at reading and math and because of this it makes me sad to see him out of school much of the time. It's the old Crow Dog attitude that the white man's learning prevents a boy from becoming a traditional Sioux. Anwah is rebellious. I can relate to him because I was pretty much the same. If he doesn't want to do something you can't make him. He is at an age where he thinks he is a young man, but he's only thirteen. He is full of self-importance, a real little chief. He argues a lot with the other boys, and especially with me. He wants to be the tough guy. Well, as I said before, I acted in exactly the same way when I was his age.

At an all-night peyote meeting, June Bug and Jennifer will sometimes lie down and go to sleep, but not Anwah. At one meeting, whenever it was my turn to sing he drummed for me, from sundown to sunup, and all the elders were watching him. He was only twelve and his arm got tired, but he went on drumming to the end. That night Anwah really made me proud of him.

June Bug is the mellowest of the kids, and he's lovable. He's small for his age. He's real quiet. When you're alone with him he'll talk. He's not violent, he's respectful. He's a good artist—he has an eye for detail and draws from his mind. He's into the Indian ways. Anwah will draw a gangster with a machine gun wearing a red headband with low-rider sunglasses, but June Bug will draw the buffaloes on the prairie, or tipis along a river, or eagles. He loves eagles. He'll draw peyote rattles, and prayer fans. That's what he's into. He's into his culture, and he's eager to learn. He sun danced for the first time this year, and pierced on his arm.

I'm sure June Bug will be an artist. He made himself his own little studio in his room. Rudi has been trying to teach him neatness in his work. He'll sit there all by himself while the other kids are playing, and draw. There's no doubt that he's gifted. He has trouble with math, but otherwise he's pretty smart. His hobbies are karate, martial arts, and, you guessed it, Ninja Turtles.

Jennifer, my fourth child, is great. She likes to be dainty and dress up, but then she'll go outside with the boys and play in the mud. She is mature for her age and very smart. She loves to read. She is a straight A student and her teachers love her. She is very outgoing and affectionate. She gets along with other kids. She and June Bug are real close, but she and Anwah are always hollering at each other. Jennifer is very pretty and, I am sure, will at some time be a powwow princess or American Indian beauty queen. Like all my other children, she goes to meetings of the peyote church and will carry the morning water. She likes to have a part in the ceremonies. It makes her feel important. She takes medicine at the meetings and knows the songs. She's been taught that way.

Like Anwah and June Bug, Jennifer shows a talent for art. She likes to draw. Anwah draws Batman; June Bug draws eagles; Jennifer draws flowers, birds, and clowns. When she was five, I started Jennifer doing beadwork, and she was beading Barbie dolls. I'd buy doll outfits and she'd bead the clothes. I hope she keeps up her beading. Jennifer wanted her ears pierced and talked about it for a year. I did not want to have her ears pierced in a jewelry store. Among us, for a girl to have her ears pierced is a religious ceremony, just like the ball-throwing ritual, later, at the beginning of puberty. So I had this done in the traditional way, during a sun dance. Leonard's sister Christine did the actual piercing, and she gave Jennifer little earrings of Black Hills gold. There is usually a giveaway on that occasion. I wanted to give a horse but didn't have the money. My mom usually does not come to the sun dance. It's not her way, being a staunch Catholic. But for Jennifer she came, together with her last surviving uncle, Grandpa Bernard Flood. We brought him out into the circle, presented him with a star quilt, and did an honor song for him. And he contributed money for the giveaway. I was happy to have Jennifer's ears pierced in the sun dance way. It was one more thing to make sure that she wouldn't walk the white man's road and throughout her life would listen to our elders and have the stability that comes from being a part of our traditional life. For me it was good to have my little girl's ears pierced in front of Grandpa Bernard, my mother, and all the sun dancers. It was the last ceremony of the four-day-long Wiwanyank Wacipi, and Jennifer will always remember it.

My kids are as tough as they have to be. They are survivors. If they have to live in a tipi, with a rock for a pillow, they will. And I am proud of that. Last year they donated a lot of their toys to poorer kids because they know that being a Lakota means being generous. I don't know what the future holds for them. They are facing heavy odds, but I know they'll come through. If ever, God forbid, I should have another child, I hope it will be a normal birth, not one under fire, or during a ceremony with somebody frantically searching for a pair of scissors to cut the umbilical cord, or needing an emergency flight in a storm-tossed two-seater.

CHAPTER SIX

Song of the Waterbird

I am a member of the Native American Church, the peyote church, whose symbol is the waterbird. This is at the very center of my life. Taking the sacred medicine, singing the ancient songs to the beat of the water drum, sitting in a circle with my elders, with people I trust, makes me feel my Indianness, makes me feel as one with the people of all tribes. I was baptized in the peyote religion and I will die in it.

The use of peyote in Indian ceremonies goes back to the beginnings of history. The medicine's name comes from the Aztec word *peyotl,* meaning "caterpillar," because this cactus plant has fuzz at its top like the hairs of a caterpillar. The Spaniards first encountered people who used peyote sacramentally when they conquered the Aztec Empire almost five hundred years ago. They called peyote the "devil's weed" and the "diabolical root." They proclaimed those who prayed with it "devil worshipers" and "witch doctors" who performed ungodly pagan rituals dancing in a double circle around a flickering fire. Today, we still talk of someone "having a fireplace," meaning a place where members of the Native American Church hold their meetings.

The Spaniards tried to suppress the peyote faith because it kept Indians from becoming good Catholics and submissive slaves. When they introduced the Inquisition into the New World peyotists and other adherents to the old native beliefs were whipped, hanged, and burned at the stake, from Yucatán in the south to Santa Fe, in New Mexico. While they no longer burn us at the stake, attempts to criminalize the use of peyote continue to this day.

According to one ancient legend it was a grandmother and her granddaughter who brought peyote to the people. The two of them had been lost in the desert for days and close to death from thirst and exhaustion. The young girl heard a voice saying: "Eat me!" She looked around and saw this little plant, picked it up, and swallowed it. And immediately she became enlightened, grew strong, knew not hunger or thirst, and clearly saw the way that would lead her out of the desert. The grandmother then ate one of these strange plants and also grew strong and saw the way back to their home. And again one of these plants spoke: "Take me!" and the two women, one very old and one so young, gathered up peyote in a basket and brought it back to their tribe. And the spirit of peyote instructed the grandmother how to pray with it, and how to put on a ceremony with this sacred medicine. And so the ritual was born. There are variations of this legend of how peyote came to the human beings, but I like this one best. The important role women play in the Native American Church is symbolized by the woman who brings in the water of life as a new day dawns, representing the All-mother of the Universe and the Great Life-giver. There is a parallel to her in the legend of Ptesan Win, the White Buffalo Calf Woman, who brought the sacred pipe to the Sioux Nation. It pleases me, and strengthens me in some strange way, to see women playing such a central role in Indian religion.

Peyote does not grow north of the Rio Grande and until about some hundred years ago the sacred medicine was unknown among the North American tribes. The man who founded the Native

American Church was Quanah Parker, son of a Comanche chief and a captive white woman, Cynthia Ann Parker. Already a warrior chief himself, Quanah became curious about his dead mother's white relatives. He traveled to Chihuahua, where John Parker, his maternal uncle, was living. After getting there he was attacked and gored by a maddened bull. The wound was terrible and blood poisoning set in. He was consumed by a raging fever and on the point of death. When some local Indians heard he was dying, they brought him a medicine woman, a so-called curandera, or bruja, who gave him a potion to drink of something she called woqui. It was peyote tea, and it cured him. He wanted to know more about this medicine and questioned many people who used it among the Huicholes, Tarahumaras, and southern Apaches. He learned to respect this peyote and to pray with it. He brought this medicine to his people. He taught his people to worship with it in the "half-moon way," which he had learned in Mexico. He made up a song to go with it—"Ya-na-ah-oway," meaning "The eagle flies to the sun." This was the kind of song after which all our North American peyote songs are patterned. He adopted Christianity, though he told the missionaries: "I accept your faith as long as I do not have to give up peyote or any of my wives." He founded a new religion on the Great Plains—the peyote church. It combined both Christian and ancient Indian beliefs, because, as he said, it was a religion for all people. When partaking of the sacred medicine and "in the power," his eyes shone with a bright, strange light. Then nobody could resist his preachings. Quanah was a great chief and his influence reached far. He introduced his new religion to the Caddo, Ponca, Kiowa, Cheyenne, Osage, and many other tribes in the area that is now western Oklahoma. From there the new faith was passed on to the more northern tribes and, eventually, to us Lakotas. Old Henry Crow Dog was among the first to put on peyote ceremonies among our people. I should emphasize that peyote is a natural plant, not a drug or chemical. It is not habit forming. You take the medicine only once a week, during a cere-

monial meeting. When I first started in the Native American
Church I was uncomfortable because it had so much Christianity
in it and so many songs had to do with Jesus. Why did they always
have a Bible in their meetings? Wasn't this an Indian, not a white
man's, religion? It took me years to open my mind to religion in
its various forms, to realize that we are praying to one great
Creator. When I told my Grandma: "I'm getting myself baptized
in the Native American Church," she felt so bad that she cried, and
she clung to her rosary. "Go ahead," she said, "fall away from the
church." And I replied, "Grandma, I'm not falling away from God,
it's just a different way to worship, it's the way I choose. I'd rather
worship with the elders, with the sweat lodge, with the medicine.
My uncles are road chiefs in the Native American Church—I want
to pray the Indian way." Now that I'm older, I have respect for all
religions. Praying with the pipe has opened up my mind. You're
supposed to have good feelings. You're not supposed to pray
against someone else, or use bad medicine on another person. I
have my own pipe, waterbird fan, and black ebony drumstick that
I use in peyote meetings. I've made a lot of prayers with those
three things. And I hold on to my sacred things, but now I can just
pray without a gourd or a staff, and it's good to be humble in front
of Grandfather Peyote, and tell him: "This is just me, this is all I
have, I don't have any fancy feathers, I come to you just to pray."

The Native American Church has always had to fight for its
right to exist. The use of our holy sacrament has always been
suppressed by whites, by the priests, and by federal and state
governments throughout the United States. The missionaries
preached against it because it kept Indians from joining their
particular churches. This oppression persists despite the fact that
James Mooney, a sympathetic anthropologist, had helped Quanah
Parker make the peyote religion widely acceptable, and the Native
American Church was legally incorporated at Rosebud as early as
1924.

In the 1920s, the great apostle of Prohibition, William Pussyfoot

Johnson, ranted and raved not only against "demon rum." He also wanted peyote included in the Prohibition legislation because it "induced Indians to become drunkards." This in spite of the Native American Church forbidding the use of alcohol. Though the use of our medicine has been legalized everywhere when taken by Native Americans in a religious setting, efforts to suppress and outlaw it continue. As recently as 1991, the Supreme Court upheld a Washington State ruling outlawing peyote. Freedom of religion, as I said before, seems to apply only to whites.

For years Leonard Crow Dog has traveled across the country testifying in cases involving the Native American Church, and quite recently he testified before Congress. In 1978, our whole family, including Leonard's usual entourage, drove halfway across the country to the Colville Reservation in Washington State. This state still outlaws peyote, even in religious ceremonies, and two of our friends and relatives, Roger Eagle Elk and Ken Little Brave, were arrested for possession of sacred medicine on a visit to the Colville Tribe. They were held under the outdated Drug Abuse Control Act of 1965. On that occasion Leonard testified for the defendants and helped run a Sioux-style meeting, appointing Ed Eagle Elk, Roger's father, to be the road chief. Roger and Ken were eventually released, but the antipeyote laws in that state are still on the books. I can't even remember all the places we went to testify on behalf of the Native American Church—Washington, D.C., St. Louis, Texas, Arizona—just about everywhere.

The Native American Church has a state charter. There is a chairman and a vice-chairman, a secretary and a treasurer, a sergeant-at-arms and a custodian, who takes care of the medicine. In the past different people have misused and abused the peyote. Now it's well taken care of by the custodian and the church members. You can have medicine in your house as long as you abide by the rules. Uncle Leslie is the custodian. He goes down to the peyote gardens about twice a year to collect medicine for meetings.

Done in the right way, a peyote meeting is beautiful. It is very precisely structured, spiritually and symbolically, just like a Catholic mass. It is a solemn ritual. The three main things needed for a meeting are the peyote, the fire, and the tipi. And of course the food. Then you have like a ten o'clock brunch in the morning. Also they usually have a big dinner. So it can run five hundred or six hundred dollars to put on a meeting. People have meetings for different reasons—birthdays, memorials, Thanksgiving, different things.

Years ago, when I first went to meetings, the Christian element was very strong. Now you have some meetings with little or no reference to Christianity, the result of the Indian civil rights struggle, the return of ancient beliefs, and the rejection of European ideas of spirituality. The nature of the meeting depends on where it takes place and who runs it. To the end of his days, Old Henry Crow Dog had a Bible in his meetings and chanted songs like: "Jesus, light of the world," or "Jesus, unsimalayelo, nita canku wanyanka makiye lo"—"Jesus, pity me. Lead me on your road." When I was seventeen and eighteen, in my early white-hating days, that would have made me squirm. But now I know better. I have become aware that real "Indianness" means being tolerant of my brothers' and sisters' beliefs. Now it doesn't matter to me whether it is a cross-fire or a moon-fire meeting, whether there is a Bible or not, whether the meeting is run southwestern style, with cornhusk cigarettes and Bull Durham, or with the red-bowled pipe and kinnikinnick. It does not matter whether the meeting is held in a house or a tipi. It is the feeling of being Indian, of being in the power, of being as one with all other tribes that matters. And it is not important if you call the Great Spirit Wakan Tanka or Maheo, Masaau or Manitou, or whether you conceive him as a woman, or both male and female. You still pray to the same Creator or creative spirit. You are born in this religion. You are married in it. You die in it.

Let me describe a typical peyote ceremony as I experienced it a hundred times. The person who runs the meeting is called the roadman or road chief, who leads us on the road of life. He is assisted by the firekeeper, the doorkeeper, the cedar man, the drummer, and the woman who brings in the morning water—the water of life. A meeting always begins at sundown and ends at daybreak, when the morning star comes out. The ceremony lasts all night. Whoever runs the meeting always has a chief peyote, a large button, sometimes kept for generations as a sacred talisman, handed on from father to son. The chief peyote is placed on a bed of sage in the center of the altar. Though some altars are different, the half-moon altar is the traditional one. In a half-moon, the altar is crescent-shaped and formed out of hard-packed sand. At the very heart of the ceremony is the fireplace, the sacred fire, peta owihankesni—the fire without end, the flame passed from generation to generation. Four times during the night its red-hot, glowing embers are formed into different shapes—a half-moon, a morning star, a four-directions cross, and, at one part of the meeting, into a heart, a glowing heart pulsating to the beat of your own heart and those of all others who have come to pray with the sacred medicine.

The paraphernalia used in the Native American Church are beautiful, full of symbolic meaning. They are the same among all tribes, the same in a cross-fire or moon-fire ceremony. There is the tufted staff, denoting authority, a link between humans and God, or as Leonard used to say: "A hot line to Tunkashila, the Grandfather Spirit." When you hold the staff you communicate with the supernaturals, communicate in a sacred universal language. Then there is the water drum, the heartbeat of the Indian Nation. It is the voice of thunder, the spirit of rain, the murmur of the spirits. It comes with its hardwood drumstick and is formed from a three-legged iron or copper pot covered with buckskin or moosehide. Depending on how wet the buckskin is, the drum can have a deep, rumbling voice or a high, clear one. The beat is very fast. The drum has seven round, marble-sized stones. These are tied into the hide, forming knobs by which the hide can be fastened to the pot with rawhide thongs. When they are putting up the fireplace before the meeting, whoever brings the drum will go into the tipi by himself and tie the drum. He says a prayer for each stone as he ties it into the hide. When this is done, the rope forms a star design at the drum's bottom.

Then there is the fan made of macaw, magpie, scissortail, hawk, or pheasant feathers. You hold on to it while you are singing. It is said that you can catch songs out of the air with the feather fan. We also have the gourd rattle, which we shake to the beat of the drum. Its handle is finely beaded, Kiowa style, and fringed at the end. The gourd itself is crowned with a tuft of horsehair. The gourd represents the Indian's head and thoughts. The rattlings of little stones inside it are the voices of the spirits. When shaking the gourd you are communicating in a universal language. The little talking rocks inside are small crystals picked up from anthills. In this way the ants, too, are connected to our religion—tiny relatives of us humans.

Then there is the bag of cedar for incense. They say that by burning cedar in the fireplace you are making a garden, planting seeds, cultivating a soul. When you put cedar on the fire, it pleases the spirits. The cedar is evergreen. It represents life everlasting. We also have the eagle-bone whistle, the eagle's voice sent to the four directions, and, with us Lakotas, the sacred pipe. We smoke canshasha, Indian tobacco. We pray with it. It will take you on. It will always be there to help you.

The meeting is divided into four parts—four being our sacred number. Four times the medicine goes around, either in the form of buttons or chopped up like relish. Some people throw up after eating medicine, it has that kind of effect on them. That is no reason to be embarrassed. There will be somebody handing you an empty tin can for that purpose. Nobody minds.

The roadman always sits at the back of the altar. He opens the meeting with a prayer. On his right sits the drummer, on his left the cedar man with his rawhide bag of incense. On the opposite side of the circle, at the tipi's door, the fire man has his place. Near him sits the woman who acts as the water carrier. The other participants sit wherever they please. The meeting could also take place in a house, in a room, but the arrangements would be the same.

The singing starts as the paraphernalia are handed around clockwise. The singer holds the staff and the fan in his or her left hand and shakes the gourd rattle with the right. Both men and women sing. You don't have to sing. If you don't know how you just pass on the paraphernalia to your neighbor on the left. If you want to sing, the drummer will come over and drum for you. The beat is very fast. It races your heart. It makes you feel that your heart beats in rhythm with the drum, but the drum is faster. The drum, the gourd, and the song unite in the same rhythm. When I was pregnant I felt the child inside of me moving to the beat of the drum. Every time it's your turn, you sing four songs. These are the songs that unite us, that we learn from each other—Lakota, Cheyenne, Kiowa, Navajo, Ponca, Arapaho songs—and above all, the songs that have no words, just the sound of a universal Indian language that makes us one. I learned peyote songs just by listening. I learned some from friends and some from the peyote spirit when I was in the power—precious gifts to be treasured.

Years ago I was at a meeting down near the Mexican border where we ate fresh green medicine. When the staff came I started to shake the gourd. Leonard gave me an eagle fan, with the black-tipped tail. And when I started to shake the gourd, the medicine started to work on me. I could hear wind blowing, and through the wind I heard a tune. I started singing the tune that I heard through the wind, and when I did, the eagle feathers started to move around, and each feather had a different tune. They were almost harmonizing. They were dancing. It was as though the feathers had come alive. Another time, in Minneapolis, we were having a peyote meeting with the Winnebagos. They blessed the staff, and when they passed the drum, I put my hands on it to bless myself, and it was almost like I was inside the drum. And my heart beat very fast in rhythm to the drum. I could hear people's thoughts. In the morning, when a lady brought in the water and the food, I could hear the music. Sometimes I'll hear or see things like that through the medicine. My voice has changed from the high, child-like voice of my earlier years to a deeper, more mature voice, but the songs are the same, though new ones are added all the time.

The fire man brings in the water at midnight. This is where nighttime ends and you start toward another day, toward another time in life. So the fire man prays for whatever the meeting is about. He usually says a word of thanks, to greet the relatives there in a good way, and then they'll pray with the water. The road chief blesses the water again with cedar, or he uses tobacco. They'll fan off the water. When the water is going around, someone will talk, usually an elder, and if it's a birthday meeting for a child, they'll have somebody talk about how it's good to have your culture and your religion, but to have the best of both worlds you should learn the white man's ways so you can survive. Then the meeting goes on, and the medicine is sent around again. The roadman will always say a few words. No one ever goes in front of the medicine, or in front of someone who is singing. If you have to leave the tent you do it without walking in front of the roadman. And the cedar man has his purpose there, too. If somebody is enlightened to the spirit, or somebody wants to pray, or rejoice, or worship, the cedar man will burn cedar for them. The meeting goes on throughout the night. Then there is the morning water call, which usually happens when the morning star comes out before the dawn. It's a belief that when you pray at that moment, your prayers will come true. Praying to the morning star is an old tradition. The roadman's wife will bring in the water, and she'll pray. Before she prays she always has the privilege to address the congregation, and thank the sponsors, and thank the roadman, the drummer, the cedar man, the fire man, the door man—basically everyone who worked for the way that night. She's the one who carries the generation. She's the water woman, she brings life and she's honored for that. If she's not the roadman's wife, she's usually his daughter. The Lakotas are real strict about this. Different tribes will borrow water women; if there's an extra woman around, they'll let her bring in the water. But not the Lakotas. You have to be family in order to do that. You can't just pick any woman from the circle. The woman prays with the water, and then she burns the cedar, or sometimes the men will burn the cedar for her, and she'll use the fan to bless the water and fan toward the four directions.

The water always starts from the doorway and travels in a circle. In a cross-fire ritual, the roadman will wait until the water completes the circle and he gets it last. He blesses the water with his eagle-bone whistle. While the water goes around the sponsor can address the meeting, talk about its purpose, and give thanks to all present. When he's finished speaking, the roadman allows those in the circle who want to speak to do so, encourages them to say a good word about the meeting.

In a Christian cross-fire ritual the roadman is looked upon as a reverend who can perform baptisms and marriages. The fireplace is laid out in the shape of a horseshoe, representing the hoofprints of Crazy Horse. In such a ceremony the cross stands not only for the four directions, but also for the four angels mentioned in Revelation in the Bible. The cross-fire people are real strict. Members are supposed to be legally married and have one set of children with one spouse only.

The half-moon fireplace is the traditional, non-Christian one, where they smoke cornhusk cigarettes during the meeting. Their altar represents the moon, the generations. In Lakota it is called peta wichoichage, the generation fireplace. They use the pipe in there, too, depending on how the sponsors want the meeting run. They offer the roadman cornhusk tobacco or the pipe. It's usually four smokes. That comes from Quanah Parker's fireplace, the Comanche-Oto fireplace. Philip Eagle Deer was a half-moon man.

When his wife, Julie, would bring in water, he'd say: "We're trying to pray here. Don't be crying around this fireplace," because she'd start weeping, asking for forgiveness for her sins.

In the cross fire they form the embers into a moon until midnight. When the fire chief is going to bring in the water, right before the staff gets back to the roadman, they shape the glowing coals into a heart. That represents Jesus Christ, and love. Toward the third round, when the morning star is coming out, they'll form up a star. That's when they have the main prayer. Whatever the purpose of the meeting, the roadman will say the main prayer. After midnight, the roadman goes outside and prays to the four directions around the tipi. Most roadmen will let the staff and the medicine and the prayers continue on while he does this. Some will stop the staff. The last fire will be shaped into a four-pointed cross that represents the four directions, or they'll make a chief with a bonnet out of the embers.

After sunrise, when the meeting is over, they bring in the sacred food. First, the woman brings in the water of life. Then we have corn and papa, which is jerked meat, and sweet wasna, which is pemmican: dried meat pounded together with kidney fat and lots of dried berries. Also we have wojapi, a sort of pudding made from chokecherries, and we drink chokecherry juice. Later we sit outside in the open, talk and gossip, and finally end up with something the white man brought us—pejuta sapa, black medicine, our word for coffee.

The church is strict about drinking, but everybody has weaknesses, and I had mine. They'll tell you right in the church, "You have to live a good life. You have to be upstanding. You have to stay away from alcohol and drugs. Raise your children in a good way and don't be led into temptation." The reason for this is all the death, the tragedy, the domestic violence that is caused by alcohol. The church is set against people that do drink. Sometimes people who have a drinking problem will say so in the meeting. The roadman will listen to their problems, and he'll take some time to pray for this person. He'll have the cedar man burn some cedar and he'll bless the person. He'll fan him off. If a person has any problems with drinking, the roadman will talk to them and encourage them.

When I left Leonard I had the awful feeling that I was also leaving the peyote church, because I had been his water carrier and he had been my teacher in the use of the sacred medicine. I did not know how people would take it if I went all by myself to a different fireplace, to meetings run by another road chief. When I went to Santa Fe to work with Richard on this book I went to a meeting arranged by old friends of ours, a couple who live in Abiquiu, some fifty miles north of Santa Fe. They are wonderful people and great singers. He is a fine painter who came to pierce at the last sun dance. His wife makes truly remarkable sculptures out of painted clay. They raise huge parrots, macaws and cockatoos, and we always get a few large red, blue, or green tail feathers for peyote fans. They have a fireplace, or rather two fireplaces. In summer he has meetings in his tipi, next to his sweat lodge right by the Rio Chama. In wintertime he has meetings inside an ancient round watchtower, probably built by early Hispanic settlers as a refuge from Apache raiders. Leonard acted as the roadman there a few times. After I had my car wreck in March of 1991, these friends arranged a meeting for me run by Charlie, a Navajo medicine man.

Charlie really gave me a talking to about drinking and everybody prayed for me. I cried, and sang, and took a lot of medicine. I loved the way he doctored me. In one way the meeting was terrible. It happened at a time when I was drinking myself to death. I had walked away from my kids and needed help badly and for that reason went to this ceremony. That was good, but I had few illusions that I could redeem myself instantly. It was up to me which way to choose—the bottle, meaning death, or life. I felt like a wild horse being stampeded. There was one moment in that meeting when I really wanted to head straight out the door, but I knew there was nothing out there for me. The roadman gave me a lot of medicine, and it got a little better. All that day his family stayed and talked to me, to see if I felt better. If I didn't, they were going to have another meeting for me the next night. Charlie told me that if I'd quit drinking he would run a thanksgiving meeting for me, four meetings in a row, similar to what we Sioux call a wopila. I liked the soft chanting of the Navajos, so different from the loud, piercing singing of Leonard and the other Lakota peyote people. It was heavy. It was a powerful meeting. It shook me to my roots.

David went all over me with his eagle tail–feather fan and bone whistle, and he followed it up with a doctoring on the next day, also. When I closed my eyes I saw an eagle flying. I looked down into the glowing embers and saw the eagle there, too. It was beautiful. At one point I looked across that round stone chamber and I could see Leonard sitting there, just the way he does in his meetings. I could not read his face, whether he was frowning or encouraging me. This meeting made me realize that I had been living in the fast lane. It forced me to have a good look at myself. I will be forever thankful for what these friends have done for me.

Back at Rosebud, before I started to go to meetings again, I talked to different people to see how they felt about it. I told Uncle Leslie, who is a road chief, that I felt I could not go back to Grandfather Peyote because I wasn't with Leonard anymore. He said: "This is your church, you are baptized in it, and so are your children. Come!" After I married Rudi, I was encouraged to bring him, too. Even Leonard visited me and reassured me:

"You can still go to meetings. You can still run sweat lodges. You can still be in this way." And the kids found feathers in the house, and he made peyote fans out of them, and we had our medicine things around the house, and he said: "I'm not here, but the sacred things are here. Go on, continue." He even called Rudi "nephew." And he and Pedro ended up singing a peyote song together.

CHAPTER SEVEN

Peyote Memories

Certain Native American Church meetings have remained vividly in my mind. I remember the first meeting I went to after my car wreck. It was at my uncle Barney's. I ate a lot of medicine, and it was mush, chopped up like relish. I ate four spoons and passed it on. Every time I tried to relax the medicine would work on me—my mind wouldn't be on anything. I ended up sitting on my knees all night, paying attention to everything, because if I wasn't paying attention, the medicine would start working against me—I'd start wanting to get sick, or I couldn't breathe. If I sat up and listened, everything would be okay. But if I tried to relax, it would work against me. Uncle Barney said: "When I first saw you years ago I understood that you were a nice lady, and that you had a lot of patience, and I understood that you had a heart, and you always liked these ways." He was glad that I was there, and he said: "It doesn't matter what anybody says, keep on coming to the meetings." When I go into meetings I always have dreams and the medicine will show me things. It always gives me more understanding. Peyote can make you gag or vomit when it is dry or chopped up. I like peyote when it is fresh and green.

Then it does not have that gagging taste, a taste that makes you feel as if you were eating earth.

In the old days a special ceremony was given for a girl who was on her first moon. A feast was held for her. Horses were given away in her honor, and she got a new, shining deerskin outfit together with many other gifts. Something of this old custom has influenced the Native American Church. I remember a meeting held way out in the boondocks, somewhere on the res, at old Hairshirt's place. There was a young girl, maybe twelve years old, though she looked younger. The drum went to her before it went to anybody else, and in the morning, when the sacred food was put out, she was served first, and she was also the first to get the morning water. It was obvious to all that she was honored for having her first period—to all, that is, except to her. She was dumbfounded at being served before the elders and never caught on. The morning after, she was laughing and playing the tomboy with some little kids as if nothing unusual had happened.

I remember one birthday meeting for Crow Dog's oldest son. The roadman was Emerson Spider, and he ran this ceremony in the open, right out on the grass, with nothing above us but the sky. This happened on the day of purification during a sun dance. So many people wanted to take part in this meeting that there was not a tipi big enough to hold them. Emerson and his helpers put up his sacred things right around the sun dance altar amid the sweat lodges, near the main fire that burns from purification to the end of the sun dance. Crow Dog put a star quilt around his shoulders, and he started his singing with that quilt on. The singing, on that occasion, was particularly haunting and beautiful. It was a wonderful meeting. Everybody was sitting around the fireplace, and you could see the stars. One girl was acting strangely, waving her fan frantically this way and that way. She called out to one of the singers: "Here, use my fan!" and threw it at him across the circle. The medicine was acting on her in a strange way. Then someone said: "Excuse me, can I go outside?" and we all laughed, because we were already "outside." This was the only time I had been at a peyote meeting out in the open, without walls and canvas, with the stars looking at us.

I remember the people who came over the years to Crow Dog's Paradise, who went to the meetings, and how the medicine affected them. In May 1975, many of the AIM people who had been at Wounded Knee knew that they would be facing arrest and trials on political charges, particularly Leonard Crow Dog and his closest friends. They asked Richard Erdoes to fly out, saying that we had something to tell him. He came. Leonard told him: "We'll all be arrested and tried. We know nothing about the law. We don't even understand the language they use in court." Richard said: "I'm an artist. I don't know anything about the law either." Leonard did some arm-twisting: "You're white. You live in New York. You'll handle it for us, get us a good lawyer. Raise some money." Richard answered: "I don't know any lawyers. I never tried to raise money." Leonard said: "I know you can do it." So Richard gave in: "Okay, I'll try."

Richard, at that time, was a magazine illustrator and he had to hand in a certain double-page drawing for *Life* magazine the following week and he had to fly home on Saturday in order to make the deadline. Now, all our peyote meetings are held from Saturday night to Sunday morning, but Leonard said: "We must have a meeting for him on Friday night. He must take medicine and be blessed so that he'll do a good job for us." So we had this meeting on a Friday night. All day Friday Richard drove around in his rented car, together with Alex One Star, who was supposed to teach him four peyote songs. Then we had a good sweat to purify ourselves, and then, at nightfall, the meeting started.

Richard had been in a number of meetings before and had taken medicine, but it had never really worked on him. He had always been sitting there, a little dreamy like, and contemplative, but peyote had never really taken hold of him, but this time, suddenly, the drumming and singing stopped, and everybody was staring at Richard, and Leonard proclaimed: "At last, Richard's in the power!" And he sure enough was. When the drum came around to him and it was his turn to sing, he sang only the one song he knows. . . . "Heciya ya ya, wichoni ye yelo . . ." and then stopped. He'd forgotten all the songs Alex had taught him. And he was clearly hallucinating. He told us later that Leonard had appeared to him in the shape of a red horse, and that people were gunning for it, laying out traps for this horse. The strange thing was that we had such a horse at the Paradise and Richard had ridden it. Its name was Big Red, and a few months later, when the marshals and COINTELPRO men raided Crow Dog's place, they shot and killed Big Red, out of sheer spite and meanness. After morning water, Richard said: "Well, I've got to make tracks. My plane leaves this afternoon and it's ninety miles to the airport at Pierre. I don't know how I'll manage it. My legs don't obey me. I see everything in glow-colors. My hearing is off, and that red horse won't leave me."

Leonard just said: "You'll be all right."

So Richard took off. He told us later that the red horse was always in front of the car. Finally he just opened the door and let this imaginary horse climb into the backseat. He had to drive real slow. When he got to the airport the plane was just taxiing on the runway. He ran like crazy and caught it. The horse climbed with him into the plane. As soon as he was in the air, all the forgotten peyote songs came back to him with a vengeance, together with an irresistible urge to sing. He was chanting loudly and all the wasichu passengers looked at him as if he had gone crazy, except one old Sioux who said: "Hau, kola," and sat down in the seat next to him and joined in with the songs. Richard had to change planes in Minneapolis and was still singing. A Sioux lady, Velma One Feather, happened to be in the lounge, and she sat down beside him and helped him sing. The horse was there too. He phoned his wife Jean and told her: "Maybe I've gone mad, but there's a red horse with me in the booth, and he won't go away. Maybe I'm just dreaming this, but maybe you should get hold of a bale of hay. If this critter is for real, we'll have to stable him in the bathroom." When he finally got to La Guardia and stepped out of the plane onto New York soil, the horse vanished instantly along with the power and the songs. New York will do this to you.

Native American Church people are always visiting each other across the country, men and women from many tribes holding meetings together, teaching each other new songs, talking about things concerning their religion. We frequently stayed with our Navajo friend and road chief, Leo Harvey, who lives at Luka-chukai, Arizona, right out in spectacularly colorful desert country. He got acquainted with Crow Dog at a peyote church convention in South Dakota. I first met Leo in 1977 while traveling through the vast Navajo reservation with the Red Nations caravan. There were quite a few carloads of us. We arrived at night and camped near Leo's home. The next morning our friends made a big feast for us—mutton stew and frybread, Navajo style, with a lot of hot, red chili sauce, which I love. That evening we had a ceremony and prayer meeting. There were so many of us that they made one huge tipi out of two smaller ones and set up a half-moon fireplace. This happened to be a little girl's birthday and special prayers were said for her. The Navajo ladies had all come in their tradi-tional crimson and olive green velveteen blouses with silver but-tons. Squash blossom necklaces dangled from their necks and turquoise bracelets encircled their wrists. Many had silver concho belts around their waists. They were beautiful to look at. The whole scene remains vivid in my mind, as if it were on a large canvas. The soft singing of the women mingled with the coyotes howling at the moon. Then during a terrific thunderstorm, with rain pelting down into the tipi through the smoke hole, my son Pedro was baptized in the Native American Church. The Harveys acted as godparents. The roadman running the meeting put the chalice at the altar next to the Grandfather Peyote and used an eagle feather to fan Pedro off. He also blessed the tipi with the morning water. We also held meetings at Big Mountain for our Navajo friends, particularly women, who wanted our prayers whenever they were in trouble, such as being threatened with relocation.

We had one peyote meeting where the wind was so strong that it lifted the whole tipi up, and lightning was hitting the ground everywhere around us. It was like an earthquake. A lightning bolt struck the tipi of our friend Rod Skenandore while he was inside. A fireball was rolling around on the floor and he was quite shaken up. Our meeting went on all the same though a few people camping out got scared and made a run for the house. The next day we set out in the caravan for California. We went through Denver and, while there, joined the Crusade for Justice, led by Corky Gonzales. In Oakland we stayed at the survival house, performing ceremonies, making speeches for the cause. Next we set out for Santa Barbara in a big truck followed by ten or twelve cars. Fifty miles out of Oakland I noticed that little four-year-old Pedro was missing. We thought he had been sleeping in the truck. It was so full of people, jammed together like sardines in a can, that nobody noticed he was missing. I counted noses, as I always do when traveling, and he wasn't there. So we turned around and went back to Oakland, where we found him with some people sitting on a park bench. He had not missed us, either. In Santa Barbara we had a big meeting on top of a mountain for a girl named Alice. She was living with her kids in a tipi, and the welfare people were giving her a hard time because, as they said, living in a tent was "unsanitary." They wanted to take her children away to a foster home but we managed to prevent that with the help of one of our movement lawyers. Unfortunately she was killed a year later when a drunken driver plowed into her car.

While we were living in Phoenix, we took part in the life of the peyote people there. I used to go to peyote meetings on the Salt River Reservation, or to rituals at Fort McDowell, along the river. I went to a meeting run by a Chicano named Mendoza, half Pima and half Hispanic, where some of the songs were chanted in Spanish.

For a while Brad, my sister Sandra, and their baby daughter lived in New Mexico. Brad was employed to do construction work, such as building fences, for a man named Ray who had a big place some fifteen miles southwest of Santa Fe. Ray is a dealer in gemstones who had lived for years among the Huichol Indians in Mexico. He has a fireplace and Leonard ran a meeting there, partly in the Huichol style. Ray had all kinds of Huichol and Tarahumara paraphernalia, beautiful woven sashes and bags in which peyote is carried. The Huicholes' name for the sacred medicine is *hikuri*. Every year they make a solemn and arduous two-hundred-mile pilgrimage north from their home country in Jalisco to San Luis Potosí and Chihuahua to harvest the peyote. The pilgrimage lasts fifteen days and during this time the men and women taking part in it fast and abstain from sex and salt. Upon coming back, a great feast is given that includes dancing, singing, and eating deer meat. Tobacco plays a great role in these ceremonies. The Huicholes also pray to the God of Fire and use the peyote medicine for curing all kinds of diseases, for snakebite, and for healing broken bones. Occasionally they use it to ward off witchcraft. Their singing is very different from ours. Instead of the water drum, they have a bowstring, which they play by pressing it against their stomach and holding a gourd against it, playing it real fast with a stick. They move the gourd around so that it makes different sounds. Traveling with Leonard, I learned a lot of the peyote ways of other tribes.

We have to go all the way south to the Rio Grande to get medicine, to what Leonard calls his peyote gardens. Sometimes we harvest south, and sometimes north of the border, usually near a town called Miranda. You can also order medicine if you can produce papers and show that you have a charter from the Native American Church and that you are enrolled in a tribe. You can show your papers to a dealer and order however much you want. Then he sends somebody to harvest medicine for you.

The first time I went to pick medicine, to harvest it, I did it the hard way. I found my first peyote under a big, spiny cactus and I got its needles all over me. Leonard told me to say a prayer first. I did, and then saw that the whole landscape was covered with peyote plants. I couldn't see it before. After I prayed it was easy pickings.

I have been to the peyote gardens twice. We went to a lady I'll call Amanda Cardenas. She is half Indian and half Chicano. She donated her land, which is full of peyote, to the peyote church. She calls it the holy land because of the medicine growing there. Besides peyote, her land is dotted with cedar, juniper, sage, and large saguaro cacti which, silhouetted against the sky, look like giants with outstretched arms. Some have big holes in them in which tiny owls and other birds are nesting. Amanda lets us pick peyote on her land for free. She told me that she has been using medicine since she was young and that it brought her health and good luck. She has opened her home to many tribes and holds meetings there. Amanda has a real nice place with a beautiful mural of a peyote meeting painted on one wall of her living room. She has a peyote altar and people come to pray, to touch the medicine, and to make offerings to it. The last time we were down there an untimely frost killed a lot of medicine on her land. So we had to go to a dealer to get peyote. There are a number of dealers down there. They own land and they treat the harvesting as a business. You might have to shell out as much as two hundred dollars or more for a thousand buttons. The price goes up every year. There is also a black market in medicine coming up from south of the border. You can buy the peyote fresh or sun-dried. When we harvest medicine we cut off and use only the top so that the root can grow new buttons. We never use the whole plant.

One time, back in the 1970s, we went down there to harvest medicine, a whole bunch of us in a big caravan. We had Arapaho, Cheyenne, Mandan, and Sioux guys with us, and some Arikara women. I had Pedro along, who was two years old at the time. That's where I met a young woman called Joanie Sue Young Bull.

We had kids of about the same age. The men were gone for a couple of days and Joanie Sue and I got restless at the motel. It was a nice day, so I said: "Joanie Sue, let's cross the border and check out Mexico." So we got our sons and we went down to Nuevo Laredo. And we bought the boys some little trinkets there. In the late afternoon, we decided to go back to the motel. As we were coming to Customs, I realized I didn't have a driver's license. The only ID we had were some Native American Church membership cards. As we sat in a long line, looking around the car for these, I all of a sudden started finding peyote, fresh buttons of all different sizes. I didn't know if it was legal for us to bring peyote into Texas and was afraid they'd arrest us and seize the medicine. We had no choice but to eat the peyote. We sure ate a lot of medicine. I looked over at the Customs and prayed that everything would be all right. When we finally got to the station, the agent asked what we'd bought, which we showed him. Then he asked where we were from. I said: "We're from South Dakota, see our license plate?" He said: "Okay, you can go." He didn't even ask for any kind of identification. By that time the medicine had started working on us. When we got back to the motel, we opened up the car trunk, and there were about a thousand buttons of peyote in there that we hadn't known about. That was a close call. We were both peyoted up. We took the kids to the carnival. It was a cloudy day, but the clouds had taken on pastel colors. As I looked at them I saw tropical birds flying in the trees, but it was the medicine that was working on me. Later we went for an evening swim, and that sobered us up.

Looking back, I have to say that Leonard Crow Dog, in his own strange way, is a great man. He has somehow created a pan-Indian belief. You could call it a religion in which it no longer matters whether you run a meeting the moon-fire or cross-fire way, whether you believe in the White Buffalo Calf Woman or the Corn Maiden, whether you perform the Pueblo cloud dance or the Sioux sun dance. Of course, he is always the traditional Lakota medicine man, doing the ancient Sioux ceremonies exactly how they should be done, but he has been a uniting force for all Native Americans and you can't take that away from him. He has influenced legislation on both the federal and state levels and has made the acceptance of Indian religion a simple fact. That goes not only for the peyote church, but for all Native American beliefs. He helped get Indian prisoners in penitentiaries the right to receive the support and consolation of a tribal medicine man just as white prisoners can have their priest, minister, or rabbi. It is thanks to him that you can have a sweat or a pipe ceremony inside prison walls. And he has achieved this not with a gun, but with his spiritual power. So when I say he is a great man, you'd better believe it.

Many months after I left Crow Dog I met Rudi, the man to whom I am married now. He proudly calls himself a Chicano. He is descended from Mexican Indians, from Zapotecs, possibly also from some Plains Indians. He is gentle, and he is good to me. I wanted to go back to the church, but I didn't know how to go about it. I used to be a water woman, but I wasn't sure how people would feel about me being at meetings now that I was no longer a part of Crow Dog's life. But I got an invitation from Joanne, a real good friend of mine who always had something nice to say about me in the meetings. She'd come to the house and visit, but she died not long ago. There was a memorial meeting for her son who got trampled by some horses, and that's when I rejoined the church. I wanted to take Rudi along and introduce him to the Native American Church. So I took him to the meeting and I introduced him to Auntie Dee, Uncle Barney, and the Reverend Burnette Iron Shell. I told them that we were getting married soon, and I called Barney "Uncle." He said: "That makes me feel good. I've known you for a long time, and when you were young I always understood that you had a lot of patience and understanding, and a good heart." By the time we went into the meeting the prayers had already begun. The medicine was going around, and then the singing started. It was late, too—I think it was after midnight. They had already changed the fire. Later, after Rudi had taken a lot of medicine, he reached over and pinched me in the butt. He didn't mean anything by it but I got real mad. He felt bad about it. He didn't mean any disrespect and later apologized.

Barney had said that it was a special meeting, and a very serious one. Uncle Barney said: "It's a memorial meeting, so don't go outside when you take this medicine." But then Rudi had to go to the bathroom. He'd drunk a lot of peyote tea, and he had to go. I said: "Oh, man, can't you hold it in?" So he was a good boy and sat there all night. Because he'd already had medicine he didn't know it was peyote tea and thought it was water, so he was drinking full cups. Then toward the early morning, the fire started burning his chin, and he could see the smoke coming toward him. Even with his eyes shut he could see the smoke. I thought for a minute he was going to get sick, but he turned on his side and got a couple of breaths of air, and that's when I poked him and said: "Sit up." As soon as he sat up and started praying again he was all right.

That was the first time Rudi had experienced the medicine. He had been to meetings before but never took medicine, because at that time he was messing with drugs and didn't think he was purified enough to partake of the sacrament. But I had been drinking a lot and decided that we had to go back to the church in order to make it. We need the medicine in our lives.

It was a good meeting. Cleveland Never Misses a Shot was drumming. And he plays and sings beautifully. It was an honor for Rudi to go to that meeting, and the people really welcomed him. Uncle Barney was talking to him, and he said: "I've always been a good judge of character, and I can see that you've got a good heart. I'm glad you're with Mary. Take care of her, and stay close to the medicine, and you'll have a long marriage and a happy one." I told him that Rudi had been in prison, but Barney was very understanding. He said that we were back on the right road, and that it was good to come to the medicine. After the meeting ended,

I was really proud of Rudi and told him that he had handled the medicine well. He did not realize how much it had affected him until the meeting was over. We went outside and saw the sun rise in a great red ball above the grass-covered hills. Everything was all right. I was at peace with myself and the world.

CHAPTER EIGHT

Wrapped in a Hot, White Cloud

Our oldest ceremony was taught to us by Ptesan Win, the White Buffalo Calf Woman. I am talking about inikagapi, or inipi, about taking a sweatbath, or "sweat" for short. The sweatbath is a prayer, a song, a healing, a purification, a communing with the spirits. There can be no Lakota ritual—be it a sun dance, a vision quest, or a yuwipi ceremony—without the participant having a sweat first. But a sweatbath is also a solemn rite all by itself. Having lived for so many years with one of our tribe's foremost medicine men, and having assisted in so many of our old rituals, I finally came to the point in my life when I was allowed to run women's sweats.

I ran my first sweat at Big Mountain, in Navajo and Hopi country. Nobody wanted to run the sweat for white women. The women went around trying to find somebody who'd run the sweat for them, and I guess I was the last resort. It was really confusing for me, because they were running it different from me, doing things differently. They just dropped their towels and crawled in naked. There were all these men around. And I got after them, saying: "This is sacred ground. Have a little modesty. Respect yourself. It's an embarrassment for us, to show your body like that." That happened more than once, and they'd roll around, and come out dirtier than when they went in. Some of them cried to get out, but some of them were really strong.

Men and women sweat separately. In the old days they sometimes sweated together, but no more. There was a heavy influx of white outsiders who did not know our customs. There were some incidents where some of these visitors, in the total darkness inside the lodge, copped a feel of the women next to them, saying: "It was a spirit." So we have become very strict in the way we run our sweats, not mixing the sexes and making visitors behave, reminding them that this is not a white man's sauna, but a meaningful, religious purification. But, when there are no outsiders, there are still some mixed sweats.

When I run a sweat, white women sometimes treat me like a medicine woman with knowledge of all things. They flatter me and shower me with gifts. That does not go over well with me. It makes me feel out of place. I tell them: "I'm just a woman like you." When I take them into sweats, I start talking to the person next to the door, and I go around and welcome everybody in the sweat lodge. Before they come in I warn them that once they come in they aren't allowed to leave, and if it gets too hot for them, to think of people in this world who are suffering, and need help, and to put other people's pain or problems in prayer. I tell them that we're all equal in the circle, and if one is weak, to try to give her strength and try to help each other. I always want to make the point with the women who come around that I am no better than they are. And that they aren't any better than I, even though they might drive a fancy car. They might be better off than I am, but in the traditional sense we're all the same. In the sweats we pray for the men to understand us better, too. When they enter the lodge on all fours, I tell them it should remind them to be humble, that we are no better than our four-legged relatives. When we huddle close together, our bodies touching, the darkness uniting us, I remind them that in the dark we cannot see our faces, or the color of our skins, that in the sweat lodge we are all the same and we cannot see whether we are Indian, white, or black. I tell them that our little lodge has become our universe, our galaxy. I remind them to turn inward into the vastness of their own minds. I sing to Kate Wiohpeyata, to the Spirit of the West. I sing so that the supernaturals will come in and take part in our purification and bless us. I ask for a sign. When they can't stand the scorching heat, I teach them to say: "Mitakuye oyasin"—"all my relations"—the signal for the doorkeeper outside to open the flap and let the cool air in, to give them some relief.

I love to sweat at night, under the stars, when you can see the steam rising from the lodge like a ghostly, magic mist. Whenever we had a sun dance at the Paradise, I'd pick a night to run a sweat. I'd always warn the women: "You don't have to come, because it's going to be hot, and I don't want to hear you scream, 'Let me out, I can't handle it!'" And I'd tell them: "I'm just running the sweat. I'm not a leader. I'm just part of the circle. There are no leaders here, just women supporting each other."

I've sweated with women of all colors—with Asian women, with people who have been facing down tanks in Tiananmen Square. I've sweated with South African women from the antiapartheid movement, with women from San Salvador and Guatemala who are Indians like myself. I tell them all: "I can relate to you, because I've been where you are. Whether at Wounded Knee or Soweto, or at Tiananmen Square, it's the same. This sweat is for freedom." And I also sweat for our men to be strong, for the children to be strong against the things that destroy our people.

I usually use fifty rocks in my sweats. That's pretty hot. I like to sweat with women because we support each other and exchange our spiritual thoughts. Some women cry during a sweat, because some family members are in prison, or doing drugs, or live on the street, or drink too much. Some women are real hardship cases, and they come to pray for a better life. But there is laughter too.

It is good to keep your sense of humor, to laugh through your tears. That's what a heyoka is for, a sacred fool, a clown. People who suffer as much as we do need laughter. These sweats get very emotional. We'll talk about the purification process. Women purify themselves every month, so they don't really have to sweat, but it is good to talk together, to exchange our troubles, swap our tragedies. We need that. One woman came to the inipi because she had lost her mother. She felt so bad when she went in, but she prayed hard, and after some cedaring she felt better. She was happy after the Fourth Door. She was sitting way back and I kept on pouring the water and she seemed to float in that white cloud. The spiritual part is just being able to understand yourself. That's something that is strong in Indian beliefs. It does not even have to be a ceremony. You can get up at dawn and pray to the morning star. Or you can burn some cedar or sage. I use the medicine or go to a ceremony or sweat whenever I start going off track. I want to keep up with it because this way I pray for my children, pray for them to have a future. I've sweated with Navajos, Apaches, Utes, and Arapahos, all over the West. That was another good thing for me. I met a lot of elders. I watched their different ways, heard different tongues.

Sometimes you have women in a sweat who have never done it before, particularly white women who have come for the wrong reason, maybe out of curiosity, so they can brag later: "I've been in a ceremony with real Indians." You've got to keep a tight rein on them. You've got to run it to them, make them behave. I ran a sweat, and we were praying, but one white woman paid no attention to it and got caught up in her own ego trip, getting macho, talking about "kicking some ass." I told her: "Watch your language when you come in here. You don't sweat in order to make speeches. You're here to learn something, and get some understanding, to have a good look at yourself. So keep your mouth shut and try some silent praying. Just be quiet and observe."

When I was in Phoenix, there was a guy from White River

named Bob who had a white girlfriend. We all ended up taking a trip to Bakersfield. Well, in a sweat one of our Rosebud men, Art, was sitting next to that white woman. In the darkness she grabbed Art's thing, his manhood, whispering: "Oh, Bob, oh, Bob!" He told her: "No, damn it, this is Art. You've got the wrong address." She had the surprise of her life. Art was mad as hell. There he was praying, trying to cleanse and purify himself, while this white woman acted like a bitch in heat. You are supposed to have only spiritual thoughts inside a sweat lodge. That woman ruined the whole inipi for us.

In the old days, after a winter sweat, men and women would take a plunge into the icy waters, sometimes even breaking the ice in order to do it. I wish we could have done that after the Phoenix sweat. It would have cooled that woman down. During a sweat you must have only pure thoughts, sing with the spirits, experience the beauty of being united with all living things on this earth. You must think of the White Buffalo Calf Woman who came to us singing: "With visible breath I come walking." Visible breath, to me that means the white hot cloud rising from the sweatlodge. For me Lakota ceremonies are my way of living in balance, of recognizing myself as an Indian. They are the drumbeats of my heart. They open a magical door for me. I walk through it and, on the other side, see a different reality, the true image if the universe. This power dwells in the secret valley of my heart.

CHAPTER NINE

Ceremonies

I want to talk further of the meaning our ancient beliefs have in our daily life, not as a medicine person, which I am not, but simply as a tribal woman. I do not want to "teach Indian religion." I don't want to give away any secrets because I do not have secrets of the sort that whites expect to get from Native Americans, secrets to "give them power," or to "enable them to have an extrasensory experience." I have no medicine to sell. I am talking of basic concepts, of everyday living. Indian religion—I use the English word *religion* for want of a better one—is an all-the-time thing. Whether you eat breakfast, or sweep the floor, or get the kids to school, it is always with you. We are not like the many white people who go to church on a Sunday for two hours and that is the sum total of their weekly religious experience. And we are not like Catholics who, once in a while, go to confession and come out of it bathed in innocence like newborn babies. The concept of what the white man calls sin, particularly "original sin," is utterly alien to us. As for the devil, as one of our old medicine men put it: "You whites invented him, you can keep him." I also agree with our elders that there are some things one should never talk about with outsiders.

People who believe in the religion will burn cedar in the morning, and drink water with a prayer, and bless the house and the surroundings. They'll pray for their family and their loved ones. If a relative has passed away, you'll remember them in your prayers that day. That's a daily thing. It affects your whole life. You start out with a prayer in the morning, and in the night before you go to bed, you end with a prayer. Even during the day, you think of the great Creator. You more or less fill your whole life with prayer. I pray whenever I see a waterbird, or an eagle circling above me. I pray when I am making tobacco offerings. Sometimes you put a spirit plate out during a meal. Some people do this every day. They say that then there'll always be food on the table. Even my sister Poco did it on Easter. She said: "I wanted to put a spirit plate out for Grandma." I've seen it done a lot of times after ceremonies and even after a peyote meeting. In the same way, some people, if they're going to drink a bottle of liquor, will spill a capful. Or they'll break a cigarette in half. I knew an aged alcoholic who always spilled a few drops of Jack Daniel's on the ground, saying, "Here, old departed wino brother, is something for you. Wichosani. Enjoy it," after which he said a short prayer.

It is easy to relate to Indian religion. You don't need a church or Sunday clothes to communicate with Grandfather. A certain rock or tree could be your church, a buffalo skull your altar, your pipe a bridge to the powers above. You can come into the sweat lodge and purify yourself, pray, and find comfort from the rocks, the water, and the sage. You can go up on a hill and be a church all by yourself. You don't need a priest between yourself and the Grandfather Spirit. Most of our older full-bloods trust a medicine man more than a missionary or white medical doctor.

We believe in herbs rather than pills. My mom still uses an herb that grows near where we live. You take the root of this plant, boil it, and use it for your eyes. And for chest and lung troubles Grandma made a tea out of the bark of a chokecherry tree. When your stomach's upset you can use sage tea. I never studied herbs until I was with Leonard. Then he'd show me their uses—not just for me, but for other people, too. Like if somebody came for doctoring, we'd go into the sweat lodge, and there he'd understand what kind of medicine they'd need. So we'd go up in the hills, just him and me sometimes, and we'd go and he'd say: "This medicine here is for kidneys." And he'd show me how it looked. One time he used this one plant for somebody—I can't remember what the illness was—but it was just a little plant with a certain kind of flower on it, but when you dug it up the root was huge. He told me: "Learn to recognize these plants. Someday I won't be here. Somebody might need your help." And Old Henry was the same way.

There are certain phenomena we take for granted, that we are comfortable with, though the white man is not. I went to the wopila, the memorial service, for Delphine, Crow Dog's sister, who had been killed by a drunken tribal policeman. That's when Leonard smoked the pipe with her killer, and forgave him. Her killer admitted that he had done it. That was pretty intense. But the night before, the family—Leonard, his mom and dad, his sisters, and I—took spiritual food up to the graveyard, and then talked to Delphine. I was standing there when they started talking to her and I could hear things, and I looked around and I saw all the spirits standing by their graves. Nearby was the grave of Estes Stewart's wife, Eunice, and her spirit was standing there making a high-pitched cry. The spirits were everywhere. I wasn't afraid. I never thought in my wildest dreams that I would be able to contact spirits through the spiritual food, with medicine, water, corn, meat, and fruit and I think a little bit of the ashes. And we offered that like at a meeting.

At the ghost dance, there were eagles flying overhead in formation. And when we were resting in the circle and Leonard's father was praying, and the spirit really moved everybody and they were almost like in a trance, Jerry Roy said: "Look, there's eagles." And we all looked up and there was a flock of eagles. I never knew they traveled like that, but they were in a formation that was almost like an AIM symbol. We took that as a good sign, that we were doing something good. Also at the ghost dance, I wanted to see my ancestors, talk to them—like my grandpa. When you hear the wind blowing through the pines, you can hear people, you can hear spirits during the dance. The spirits are in harmony with the dance, and they'll sing and talk with us. That's the closest I came to experiencing anything like that.

One time, at Crow Dog's Paradise we had a tame bald eagle. It just walked in one day as if it had always been a member of the family. It had a broken wing, which was drooping a little. It was always walking all over the place—slowly, like an old man, with a faraway look on him. Now Leonard's daughter, Ina, had a bad ear infection and, during a ceremony, was crying with pain. The eagle waddled over to her and scratched her ear, and immediately she got well. The eagle stayed with us for months, eating meat from our table, and then suddenly he was gone. I guess his broken wing had mended itself.

For whites, the most awesome of our ceremonies is the yuwipi. It is a finding-out ritual—finding a missing person, or object, or the cause of a sickness. It is also a dog feast and a celebration of Inyan, the rock, who is unchanging and forever. A yuwipi ceremony is put on at the request of a sponsor who wants the spirits to give him the answer for what he wants to know. At the core of the ritual is the yuwipi man, the interpreter, who will translate to the sponsor and the other participants what the spirits have told him.

For the yuwipi you need chanli—tobacco ties, tiny tobacco bundles tied into a long string that represent offerings and prayers. There are 405 tobacco ties, and they are laid out in a square. There is an altar with its red and white staff to which an eagle feather and a deer tail are tied. There are the staff with the eagle head, and the four direction flags at the corners of the square. And there is the sacred food.

Whoever has sponsored the ceremony will sit behind the altar, right next to the medicine man's wife, who will sit with the pipe. The altar is made, and there's a bed of sage. When the medicine man is filling the pipe, he sings the pipe song. There's also a drummer that sings and fills the pipe. During this time a helper brings forward the sweet grass and the medicine man will fan the pipe down with sweet grass. When that's finished he'll pray with it in each direction and he'll give the pipe to the lady who is going to hold it. That's when the prayers start and the ceremony begins. Then the medicine man, or interpreter, will go back inside the square of tobacco ties. His hands are tied behind his back, and his thumbs and fingers are tied together. He's wrapped in a blanket, which is then bound with leather ties. He is made into a mummy, into a large, living medicine bundle. He is wrapped into a star quilt. The medicine man is then placed facedown on the sage-strewn floor. He's lying facedown with his head by the altar. They'll put sage on each of the seven knots he's tied with. Then they smoke everything with sweet grass. After this the helpers go out, leaving the medicine man inside. They close the altar with the ties. The ties are never walked on or stepped over. If there's light bulbs, they'll put sage by them. If there's a mirror, they'll cover it. Before the ceremony starts they make sure that not a speck of light can enter. Yuwipi has to be performed in complete darkness. The helper will have a bundle of sage, and the first person will put some sage behind her ear and hand the bundle to the next person, so that each person will have some sage behind their ear. This will make the spirits talk to them. Everybody takes their place and the lights are shut off. Gourds are placed in the four directions around the medicine man. The singing and drumming starts. During the singing the medicine man prays. Four songs are sung. When the fourth song is sung the spirits enter the square. They'll make a loud noise. The rattles will start shaking. Sometimes you can hear an eagle in there. Sometimes you hear little voices from the gourds, and there are lights coming from the gourds, sparks that travel around the altar real fast, at lightning speed, and it's all in rhythm with the drum. Whatever happens, and whatever you see, comes through the power of the ceremony. There are always the spirit lights flickering through the air, rushing back and forth across the ceiling like tiny shooting stars. And spirit voices are whispering in your ear in a spirit language that only the yuwipi man can understand. The gourd rattles are flying through the air, sometimes touching you, speaking to you through the power of Inyan, the rock, talking to you through the gourd's tiny little crystal rocks picked up from the ant heaps. And I'd see things during these ceremonies. One time we were smoking the pipe at the end of the ritual, and when it got back to the oldest man there, and he started smoking it, the smoke rising from the bowl was bright red. I had beautiful visions, such as you only have during meetings of the Native American Church. Once I saw a campground as it was hundreds of years ago, as if painted by an artist-magician. It was so beautiful it brought tears to my eyes. I have often had visions during yuwipi rituals that are much like the ones I've had at peyote meetings after taking a lot of medicine. But you do not take medicine during a yuwipi. While they are singing, the gourds are still shaking, rattling, talking. There are special yuwipi songs for the ceremony, and when these are sung, it's really breathtaking because everybody's in the spirit, in one mind. Everybody feels united in prayer. The feelings are real strong, real intense, and while the singing is going on the gourds are flying through the air, and they'll come up to certain people, and the lights go all over. There's been times when the spirits have taken the drum from the circle and lifted it up in the air.

When the last four songs are finished, the gourds are still rattling and talking. Then the spirits themselves will leave—they'll go back where they came from. Then the interpreter prays, and after he is finished, he'll explain what the spirits have told him, he'll give the people their answers. Then the lights come on and that part of the ceremony is over. When the lights come on, you discover the tobacco ties are all wrapped up in a ball tightly, and so are the

leather ties that were used to tie up the medicine man—the work of the spirits before they left. Then the pipe is smoked. The pipe is passed all the way around the circle and everybody takes four puffs. Then it goes back to the medicine man, who still sits in the altar, and he smokes the pipe. When he's finished, he'll hand the pipe back to his wife, and she'll empty it, take the pipe apart, and clean the bowl. She'll put the ashes at one of the direction flags. Then the water will be given to her. She'll drink some of it, and bless herself with it, and she'll say: "Mitakuye oyasin." Then the water goes around and everybody will drink some.

The medicine man, the interpreter, will talk to the people. The spirits talk through him, and through him they will answer the question the sponsor, and other participants, have asked. After that comes the sacred food, which includes the dog soup. There are also dishes set out with wasna—wagmiza wasna, papa wasna, and chanpa wasna. Wasna is pemmican: kidney fat pounded together with corn, jerked meat, and chokecherries. There'll also be wojapi (a kind of chokecherry pudding), frybread, and chayaka—Indian tea. This is the traditional yuwipi food.

The dog soup is always waiting inside the altar, that is, inside the square formed by the tobacco ties. The dog is a ritual sacrifice. It is usually painted with a red stripe from the tip of its nose down to its tail. They face the dog toward the west and choke it with a rope, which kills it almost instantly. It is usually a well-kept puppy, not just a mongrel off the street. The dog brings the spirit that comes into the ceremony. At the feast, everybody is served in the circle. There is one helper who will bring the soup, and another one who will bring the frybread or the wasna. It will all be passed around clockwise. The head of the dog is given to the medicine man. Later, it will be placed outside where nobody walks, where nobody will bother it. During the feast, people talk and visit. They're still in the circle, and people are happy and they have good feelings. Then after everybody has eaten, a helper will light his sweet grass again and fan everybody off in the circle. Then the

ceremony's complete. The medicine man starts putting away his wope, his sacred things, his medicine bundle. The flags will be taken up. The flags and the ties are taken to another place and, like the head, put somewhere where nobody will bother them. From there everybody is excused. Sometimes these yuwipis will go until four in the morning. It depends on how many people are there and how long the prayers take. Some run real late because they start late at night. There's usually a sweat before the ceremony.

I learned a little about the yuwipi from Leonard's mother. She was always making tobacco ties. The same with her sister Nellie. Nellie was Moses Big Crow's wife. She's still alive. Laura Black Tomahawk, who passed away this past winter, was an elder, and these three were the main older women who were real strong in the yuwipi. They'd have their dog feasts. Laura always had a dog ceremony right in St. Francis. She lived in a traditional log house. I liked her dog feasts the best, because she always singed the dog real good, and she was real clean, and the meat was always tender.

I've seen yuwipi doctoring ceremonies where the person who's going to be doctored will stand with the pipe by the altar, and by a flag that's chosen—the spirit will say: "Stand at the north." They'll stand there with the pipe while the songs are being sung, and during that time the spirits and the gourds will go over the area where that person is sick. If the person is sick in his stomach, the gourds will touch his stomach. After the songs are sung, the medicine man will ask: "Where did the spirits touch you? Is that where the sickness was?" And they'll say: "Yes." So that's how the spirit works. Then the medicine man, who knows about herbs, will tell him what plants to use, like a prescription. The medicine they're given is always kept in a certain place, and they are told that while taking this Indian medicine, they have to stay away from any woman on her menstrual cycle. And a woman with her period can't go anywhere near the medicine, or even in the room where it is kept. That would interfere with the power of the medicine.

There can also be a yuwipi for a wopila, a thanksgiving for

mething good that happened, for a person getting a good job and
anting to have a ceremony to thank Grandfather in the hope that
ings will continue to go well. I've also seen people get married
a yuwipi, making their vows and being blessed. It can also be a
ming ceremony, hunkapi. Many ceremonies have been con-
ucted through this yuwipi.

Crow Dog once ran a yuwipi for a man who was trying to find
missing relative. Through Crow Dog acting as interpreter, the
spirit indicated that the missing man had been murdered and
described the spot where the body had been buried. The body was
found through the power of the yuwipi. During a yuwipi among
Oneida Indians the spirit dumped a whole bucket of water on a
man who had made fun of the ritual.

We also have medicine women in many tribes, usually older
ones. There is one Lakota woman who runs sweats in Phoenix, and
there's a middle-aged lady running women-only sun dances for an
organization called Women of the Red Nations. I know a Navajo
woman who runs peyote meetings where she doctors the sick by
pulling and sucking the sickness out of them. I met a Shasta
medicine woman who uses crystals in her curings the ancient way,
not like the white New Age people. My grandmother told me of
the "double-faced dreamers," powerful shamanesses of the old
days. I think she was talking about women who had dreamed of
Anung-Ite, the two-faced supernatural whose face is beautiful on
one side and horrifyingly ugly on the other. Double-faced dreamers were powerful sorceresses. Dreamers possessed any man they
met and caused men to go mad. One could hear them singing in
the night. They inspired fear, but they were also great healers and
the most skilled of all in doing fine bead- and quillwork; everything they made was beautiful. That's what Grandma told me.
Unfortunately, there are also a lot of fake female shamans, pre-
tending to be Indian, ripping off the gullible. For me our Lakota
ceremonies are as necessary as breathing. When I take part in them
I am at peace with the universe and all living things.

CHAPTER TEN

The Granddaddy
of Them All

I knew an old medicine man who called the sun dance the grand-daddy of all our ceremonies. It is the foremost, the most solemn, the most sacred of all our rituals. It is a celebration of life, of the sun, the buffalo, the eagle. It is a self-sacrifice, a suffering for someone you love, to take his or her pain upon yourself. It is not an initiation rite or a way to prove one's courage as was shown in the movie *A Man Called Horse*. That was a misrepresentation of what the dance is about. I don't want to talk here about the innermost meanings and details of rituals of the sun dance. That should be for a respected medicine man to do (or not to do). I want to talk about the basics as I have experienced them, year after year, at Crow Dog's Paradise, such down-to-earth aspects as the part I played as a woman and wife of the sun dance director. I'll start with the everyday things going on during a sun dance, the work and the never-ending tasks, and not the things directly involved with the ritual. First of all, people going to the sun dance, even if they are not dancers themselves, should refrain from sexual intercourse, drinking, smoking weed, and from all common pleasures. They should refrain from all worldly things for two weeks before the dance until four days after it is over.

The hard thing for me was maintaining the kitchen and caring for the people who would come around and camp. Some of them would stay to help build the arbor and get things ready for the sun dance. So I'd have to get wood, cook outside, haul water, feed them, do all the dishes, and fry bread over the hot fire. I was constantly getting that black soot all over my clothes. It took a pretty good toll on me—by the time you got one meal finished and got things cleaned up, it was already time for the next meal. This went on from sunrise to sundown. That took up all my time. On top of it I had to take care of the kids, getting their hair brushed, getting them cleaned up for the day. People would come and bring Crow Dog tobacco, or the pipe, and they'd want to talk to him, so whatever I was doing I had to put off, just to accommodate the people. There were always people arriving and you had to offer them coffee. Then I had to go to town, check the mail, run to the store, all these little things that took up my time. Crow Dog's daughter Bernadette was always helpful. I think she was as old as Jenny is now when I first met her. So we kind of grew up there together in the kitchen. She was usually the one who kept the coffee going, and she was always there when I needed help. I could always depend on her. Sometimes different women would come over and offer to help, but then we would have too many people in the kitchen and it would get to be a mess—people cooked different ways, which led to arguments. Every day we'd make two big old pots of soup, and we'd put beef in one pot and vegetables in the other. And every day we'd feed everybody in the camp. We'd make frybread over the open fire constantly. So the sweating was going on constantly, and the eating, too. The kitchen was constantly open. Sometimes I'd have the morning meals done when the sun was up. We'd cook on an open fire and make things like cornmeal, or pancakes. Just when you thought you were through, somebody would show up from a long way off, so you'd have to cook for them.

Then I had to care for the sick. A lot of people drink from the little river that runs through the Paradise and they come down with a tremendous case of the shits. They think because they are on Indian land the water must be pure, but it was already polluted from way upstream outside the res. Others wander off into the woods and they get a bad case of poison ivy. We always have a case or two of sunstroke to deal with. Last summer a white woman went to the outhouse and there was a big, fat rattlesnake coiled up on the seat. That was one encounter the lady could have done without. There's never a dull moment.

There's a lot of preparation for the sun dance. A lot of work goes into making the arbor, which is built around a circle, with a door to the east where the people come and sit, and usually on the west side there's a place where the dancers rest. Then we have to put up the sweat lodges, which are made out of fresh willows. There are at least two main lodges—one for the men and one for the women. Another major task is bringing in a lot of firewood. The main fire is lit before sunrise on purification morning. There's always someone there, the main fire person, to watch it and to keep it burning until the last day, the last sweat lodge. Then there is the sun dance tree, which is sacred. It is the tree of life. In the old days scouts were sent out to pick a flawless cottonwood. The scouts would count coup upon it as if it were a brave enemy.

Then there is the ceremony of putting up the tree. The way I know it, the tree, which has been left standing for a year, is taken out of its spot to be replaced by a new tree. They put the old one in a place where nobody will bother it, because it still has the offerings from the previous year on it.

On the last day of purification—the sun dance usually starts on a Sunday and ends on Wednesday—the old tree is taken out and the dancers are asked to clean inside and under the arbor and to get their things ready. Then the dancers go and get another tree, sometimes accompanied by their families. The only people who stay behind are the old people. So they go and get a tree, which is usually picked ahead of time by a medicine man or elder, who then marks it with the four directions, with wasé, red paint. A young girl, who has to be a virgin before her puberty, is given an axe, and she'll cut the tree, to mark it, in each direction. After that each sun dancer takes a turn chopping, with one swing each, until it comes down. Usually the men do this. It goes pretty fast. When the tree is down, they catch it and make sure it doesn't touch the ground. Then they trim it just a little bit from the bottom. When the tree is ready to go up they carry it with the leaves toward the front to the sun dance ground. When the dancers enter the camp, there is usually a warrior who will make a yell, the ageesha, and he'll do it four times by the time they get to the arbor. Then they bring the tree in, and that's the only time it is set down, very carefully. Then somebody puts the chokecherry branches in the crotch of the tree, along with the figure of a man and a buffalo made out of buffalo hide. From there they'll put on the flags in the Four Direction colors. Then the dancers all put their offerings on the tree. Before they bring the tree in they sing songs to greet its arrival. When all this has been done, they put the spiritual food into the hole in the ground into which the tree will be planted. We feed the tree with water, corn, papa, and chokecherries. Some use buffalo and kidney fat in the papa. Then they place the tree in the hole and the dancers raise it by pulling on ropes attached to its top. They have to steady the tree with the ropes, because it is big. In the old days a song was chanted after the tree had been raised:

> *At the center of the earth*
> *You stand,*
> *Looking around you,*
> *Beholding the people,*
> *Who stand in awe.*
> *They wish to live.*

During the purification days you're asked to get fresh sage. It's used for the wreaths around the dancers' heads, wrists, and ankles. They line the sweat lodges with sage, and they also put some under the tree. Whoever is piercing will lie on that bed of sage. So it takes a lot of people to gather all the sage. People get their eagle-bone whistles ready. And they get the last-minute things they need on their sun dance outfits. During purification, sweat lodges are run constantly. So a lot of rocks are needed. Then there's the water—you usually have to go to the tribal headquarters and get a water truck so there'll be enough. Also during this time, a lot of people are taken up on the hill to fast. By the time they come down they go right into the dance, so some dancers fast for four days and go into the dance, making it an eight-day ritual. During this time, also, campers are coming in, setting up tipis, and settling down.

Now the four days of the dance start. If there are many dancers, they'll start piercing from the first day on. Usually the dancers have made a vow the year before to pierce.

At the time of the piercing they ask that any women on their moon stay away from the arbor, or the sweat lodges, or any sacred things. Last year they asked women on their moon to leave the camp. When women on their moon come around the dancers, the dancers get real sick. Most women respect the rule, but sometimes there's young girls who don't realize this.

It's the dancers' choice how they want to pierce. I've seen some that were pierced with eagle claws. I've heard men say that they pierce because women have pain during childbirth; so they pierce for their children and their families and the women who've suffered bringing the generations into life. It's an honorable thing to do, to offer oneself in sacrifice. Some people pierce on their chest or on their back, and they'll pierce not from the tree, but they'll put the rope through the tree, over the crotch, and the horse will pull them. Women pierce now. Some do flesh offerings, some will pierce with feathers in their arms, some will pierce and drag a buffalo skull. I remember a sun dancer from Pine Ridge, Loretta Whirlwind Horse. Her father was sick and couldn't move his legs, so she danced for him. He later told in a meeting that while she was dancing for him, suffering, he could move his legs, and feel them, where he couldn't before.

When the women pierce with a feather, they pierce their arms and tie the feather on with a piece of sinew. Some will keep it on for four days. On the last day they'll make their last prayer. Then they'll have it pulled off. I have old scars where I've been pierced on my arms—Bill Eagle Feathers did the piercing, and he cut my arms for flesh offerings. That year I pierced with wooden pegs. Bill is one man that I really miss. At the sun dance he'd always make a coyote yell. Usually eagles come and circle around the arbor and the camp, as if they know they are wanted. They hear the dancers' eagle-bone whistles. It's our belief that Tunkashila communicates with the eagle, our relative. When you're given a whistle you're supposed to take care of it.

All of the dancers' pipes have to be smoked in one day. When one dance round is over, all the dancers face south in rows, and the first row will go and get their pipes from where they put them in the morning on the west side of the arbor, where all the pipes are laid when the dancers first come in. So they go over there and they pick up their pipes from the racks, and they go around the tree, and then back in the row. At the same time there'll be helpers that will pick out certain people from under the arbor to accept the dancers' pipes. The dancers will go back and forth four times, and the fourth time they'll give those people the pipes. When they hand them their pipes, the singing stops. The round is over, and the people who were picked will go back, in formation, to their place under the arbor where they smoke the dancers' pipes. The dancers have to keep their pipes real clean, so the people who smoke the pipes for them won't have any problems lighting them. I was sitting under the arbor with Rocky, and she said: "Why are white people dancing this year?" I said: "This is the year for reconciliation." There are some real sincere, dedicated people there, but I'm worried that once you let them in the door, they might try to take over, or to exploit it.

Different women will take turns running the sweat lodge. The guys sweat all the time, constantly, at late-night and early-morning sweats. We have children's sweats, too. The little boys will have sweats. My kids always sweat. June Bug said: "I'm going to sweat, but it's going to be a man's sweat. I'm not sweating with any girls." He was at that age. But it's really nice to see kids sweating and praying. They run the sweats themselves, and they'll say their prayers and express themselves. They conduct themselves in a good way.

After the last round of piercing, when it's time for the sun dance to end, they'll put some water on the buffalo skull, our altar. The helper will get the flags from each direction and all the dancers will gather their pipes. The leaders go out first. They dance in formation toward the east door, stopping four times. It's a beautiful sight. People will gather outside the arbor to shake the dancers' hands as they leave. The dancers go to the sweat lodge to do their last sweat. During the breaks in the dance there are ceremonies that go on too. Marriages are performed, girls' ears are pierced. After the dance, the feast begins. During this time, if a family has someone who has danced four years in a row and is finished with his four vows, they'll have a giveaway in his honor. Sometimes naming ceremonies are going on too, and we have special songs for that. Also during this time, people who want to dance the next year are asked to make their vows. And we honor the singers and drummers. From the time when they bring in the tree to the end of the dance they've been singing the songs. And if they do an honoring song, money is donated to them. It's hard to sit there and sing for four days straight.

When I danced, I suffered for my children, for the Lakota people, for my Diné friends facing relocation at Big Mountain. They cut my flesh from where I had pierced, and I put it in a little tobacco pouch and offered it to the tree, to the spirit. After having pierced for the first time, I was asked to speak. I spoke about my friends who had gone to another world, about Annie Mae Aquash, who had sun danced, who believed in the pipe and the sacred medicine.

I wanted to dance last summer at the Paradise but was still too weak from my car accident. I went to the drum to sing along in the wicaglata way, echoing the male singers, and I grew faint and had to sit down, but I am sure that, sometime in the future, I will dance again.

Good things happen during the sun dance, you could maybe call them spiritual. There were two men who had been bitter enemies some twenty years ago, and one of them had shot the other and nearly killed him. Then two years ago, in the spirit of the sacred dance, they not only forgave each other, but became friends and even pierced each other. It really touched my heart.

There is a Chicano who walks hundreds of miles on foot, all the way from Mexico, to come to the sun dance. They call him "So Happy." Years ago, he was a survivor of that horrible incident where a train car full of wetbacks were tricked out of their money and left in the car to suffocate.

At the last sun dance, in 1991, they flew the Stars and Stripes right-side up for the first time. That came as a shock to me. The only way I had ever seen the flag used by AIM people was upside down, the way ghost dancers used to wrap themselves in the flag as a sign of distress and mourning, and the way AIM used it as a sign of protest. But things are changing and getting more mellow. They flew the flag the right way to honor our own veterans who have fought in every war the United States was involved in— World War I, World War II, Korea, Vietnam, and Desert Storm. Sioux men were fighting in all those faraway places, though some who had been in Nam said later that they felt like the Crows and Arikaras scouting for Custer, scouting for the whites against non-white people. Still, many Sioux gave their lives in distant lands and so now we have a respect for the American flag. In a way it's good to come to an understanding, particularly as those flags last year were flown to honor Francis Primeaux, an old veteran and roadman of the Native American Church, who had died a short time before.

Also at the last sun dance, Archie Fire Lame Deer allowed some heyokas, the contrary, "forwards-backwards thunder dreamers," to dance. That was the second time they came and pierced. Being heyokas, they dress different than the other dancers. One was painted with black and white polka dots; another had his face hidden by a shawl; a third had a sort of fantastic many-colored outfit on and a bunch of feathers from various birds on his head. Everyone dressed according to his vision. They were very strong dancers.

And at last year's sun dance people encouraged me: "Sister, hold your head up!" We embraced and laughed and cried together. And there was the cry: "All you Wounded Knee veterans, stand up!" And so we stood there—Clyde and Crow Dog, Carla and Ron and Carter and myself—and they sang the honoring song for us. They say the movement is dead, but it isn't. We're still working for the people; we are still here. You can't stop us now. When they sang the honoring song for me and my sisters and brothers, I felt really good.

CHAPTER ELEVEN

Big Mountain

I am still part of the movement. I'm still involved in Indian causes and will stay involved until I die. But I've slowed down. I have given birth to five children. I am a thirty-six-year-old grandmother, and I have grown tired of the old roaming gypsy life, have grown tired of having to camp out for weeks in a tipi during a long South Dakota winter.

For a number of years after Wounded Knee, and after I moved in with Crow Dog, we took part in the fight for Big Mountain. It is an area within Arizona's huge Navajo reservation, which is so large that it takes almost a whole day to drive from end to end. Within the southwestern part of the Navajo reservation lies the smaller Hopi reservation. Some of the Big Mountain area lies in Navajo land and another part is within the Hopi reservation. The boundaries were not made by either the Hopis or the Navajos, but, in 1891, by some white government types who, as they always do, took a map of Arizona, drew a big square on it with the ruler, and said: "Okay, what's inside the square is Hopi, and what's outside is Navajo." Then they probably slapped each other on the back and went to the nearest bar to have a drink. As long as no white

119

rancher or farmer had any use for country that was looked upon as a wasteland, this "boundary" stuff didn't matter.

Big Mountain was called a "Joint Land Use Area" and the people of both tribes pastured their sheep on it, side by side, as friendly neighbors. They probably didn't know about these white man–made boundaries and where they run. Things changed when certain outfits, like the Peabody Coal Company, became aware of all the coal and uranium buried in the land and decided to reap the profits from it. That started the so-called "Navajo-Hopi land conflict," which really never existed as far as the traditional people were concerned. Tribal politicians were bought off and phony suits were started. Peter MacDonald, the dictatorial and very wealthy Navajo tribal president, had a hand in the business. That's why many Navajos call him Peter MacDollar. He was once hailed as the "most powerful Indian in the world." I hear that he's doing time now on various corruption charges.

The government finally decided that all the Navajos on the "Hopi side" had to be driven from their ancient lands and relocated somewhere else, mostly in white off-reservation towns like Holbrook and Winslow. The Hopis on the "Navajo side" were also to be relocated. The whole relocation plan was really just a scheme to clear the area for exploitation by the energy mafia.

I recently got a printed brochure from the Hopis that put the whole matter in perspective. It reads in part:

> The recent division of our land with the Navajos, which the United States enforces through its courts and police, is clearly a means to seize total control, even of that land supposedly granted to the Hopi. Those Hopis who are relocated onto new areas are only allowed to lease that land from the Hopi Tribal Council.
>
> With the discovery of mineral resources in that area came the passage of Public Law 93-531, which was not requested by the true Hopi leaders, but promoted by lawyers through

the Hopi Tribal Council, creating the illusion before the world that the Hopis have traded certain areas of their land over to the government on approved mineral leases.

We want everyone to know that the Navajos are not the ones taking our land, but the United States. The Hopi and the Navajo made peace long ago and sealed their agreement spiritually with a medicine bundle.

For generations more than ten thousand traditional Navajo people have lived on Big Mountain, supporting themselves by sheep raising and rug weaving. They lived in old-style hogans, moving with their herds from pasture to pasture. They had little contact with the outside world. Their forced evacuation has been going on for several years and "relocation" is supposed to be finished in 1995. Already over eight hundred families have been driven off their ancestral land and "resettled" in Winslow, Holbrook, or Flagstaff, many without ever getting their relocation money. They are penniless and desperate. Some got a little money and some miserable house to live in, but they are desperate too. They were used to living in self-built hogans. Now they have to pay rent. They used to heat their hogans with old-fashioned wood stoves and the wood they gathered cost them nothing. Now they have to pay for gas and electricity. They used to run their sheep and weave their own clothing. Now they are unemployed ghetto dwellers in a strange, hostile, and frightening environment. All this happened to the Navajos before, in 1863, when Kit Carson and the army laid waste to their land. He and his men destroyed crops, cut down fruit trees to make their country uninhabitable, and forcibly herded thousands of Navajos to a place in the desert hundreds of miles away called Bosque Redondo, where most of them died of disease and malnutrition. It is still remembered with horror as "The Longest Walk."

The Navajos on Big Mountain, facing relocation, called for help. That is where we came in. In 1980 Larry Anderson, an old friend and leader of Navajo AIM, contacted us. He was with us at Wounded Knee during the siege in 1973. He and some Navajo elders brought a pipe and asked Leonard to hold a sun dance at Big Mountain. They sought to attract support from other tribes throughout the country, and a sun dance would serve as a focusing point, a signal for help and for tribal interdependence. The elders told us: "We don't want to pick up the gun, or have any kind of bloodshed. We want to handle this with spiritual power. We need your prayers. We think your ceremonies might reinforce ours."

That's how we got involved supporting the cause of the Diné people on Big Mountain, spiritually, physically, and politically. *Navajo* is a white man's word. The people there call themselves Diné, and their country Dinetah. We drove out there. I got there with a group a few days ahead of Leonard, who had to finish the sun dance at Rosebud. That first year we went to Big Mountain we set up camp close to the sweat lodges and the arbor. Howard Bad Hand and Leli Takoja were supposed to sing. But that first morning there were no singers, just myself, Fred Wapapah, and another guy. And they didn't know any sun dance songs. So I had to lead the singing. It's hard work to keep that pace up, and about the second or third round Howard and Leli showed up. All that time they were lost in Black Mesa.

The sun dance circle was part of a large survival camp. The people there had collected a lot of cedar and sage for the ceremonies. Different support groups had come—"rainbow people" from different countries, black, white, yellow, Orientals, Latinos, and, as always, a few Buddhist Japanese monks. Some people had to set up a cookshack and brush shelter. They had an arbor and fire pits. Women joined together to do the cooking and there was a great deal of food donated by various organizations and individuals. Wherever you looked people were working, chopping wood, bringing in rocks for the sweats. Leonard arrived in good time with Jerry Roy and his family. They are old and true friends and always help out when there's work to be done. Navajos formed the security guard at the gate. There was a tremendous feeling of unity between all these different groups, though it was not shared by everybody. A few of the Diné objected to the sun dance, feeling that it was not one of their ways and did not belong in their country. But the Big Mountain elders persuaded them otherwise. One year Ernie Peters came from L.A. with his Chicano wife, Jessie, and insisted that white people stay out of the ceremonial area, which included the arbor. During the sun dance there was a big conflict over that. It was decided that the white people could stay under the arbor but couldn't participate in the dance. So Ernie Peters got up with all his people, his whole support group, and left. He said he was a sun dance chief and he was never going to support Big Mountain because of that decision.

Everybody had their own campfire at night and they'd pray for the about thirty-five dancers we had that year, including Larry Anderson and Clyde Bellecourt. Flesh offerings would be going on. From the camps you could hear the peyote drum in the distance. At night you could see the light in the tipis and hear the singing and praying until dawn. The dancers then would have meetings with the support groups and the elders, and talk about the struggle and how the Diné could stay on the land.

Many of the people at the sun dance didn't speak English, so some of these meetings went on a long time with interpreters. The elders talked about how there was no dispute between the Hopis and the Navajos over the land because of the many intermarriages that had happened. A lot of the traditional people had relatives among the Hopis. During all these generations they had always shared, and the elders said that they had given the Hopis the land where they were now meeting. Some of the elderly Navajo women would talk, and they'd start out by saying things like: "Hello, my grandchildren." And then they'd talk about the land, and the generations, about the centuries they have lived up there and raised their sheep. These talks went on for days on end. I noticed that the women seemed to have more pull, more of a voice than they do in our tribe. They spoke with anger about the white government telling them how many sheep they could have in every grazing area, forcing them to kill those that exceeded the number.

The white support groups did a lot of good work there. Besides bringing in donations, they did a lot of physical labor. A lot of them would go out and herd sheep for different families. That first year I camped there, an older Navajo woman named Katherine Smith came up to me. She must have been sixty or seventy years old. She had one arm in a sling, broken when her horse threw her as she was herding sheep. She insisted upon chopping wood for me with her good arm and, later, making a cooking fire. When some white men came to fence off the land, Katherine came galloping up on her horse and chased them away with her shotgun. Leonard, myself, and others from our support groups also staged protests to prevent the traditional Navajos from being forced to relocate and to keep coal companies out. We took down the fences where they were going to strip-mine the area. We put our bodies in front of the bulldozers. We were arrested and charged with obstructing the mining operations. We had a support committee and legal help in Flagstaff and they bailed us out. I said to Leonard: "Here we go again, just like old times." We had some potentially dangerous confrontations, but never firefights like at Wounded Knee.

The Big Mountain country is worth fighting for. It is beautiful, high country—hills dotted with piñon, cedar, and juniper trees. In summer the landscape is covered with many wildflowers, particularly Indian paintbrush, along with cacti, cholla, and tall sage. There's also a lot of wildlife—bears, bobcats, coyotes, deer, and mountain lions—but the lions you never see. They are too shy and wary. Enchanting are the nocturnal big-eyed, ring-tailed cats, which are not cats at all, and a special type of squirrel with big, long, bushy ears. Everywhere you look, the views are breathtaking. Tuba City is the largest town of any size nearby, and Oraibi the closest Hopi pueblo. When you go up in the mountains it's all dirt roads. I can understand why all Navajo families have four-wheel-drive pickups. The roads are rough and go for miles and miles until, finally, they come to a trading post. The locals didn't mind our support groups at all because we brought some extra business to these posts in an impoverished area. One time there was a big rainstorm as I was trying to get back to the camp. My truck was swimming through these dirt roads. I tried to turn around and got stuck in a sea of bright red mud. Only about the upper half of the truck was above this mess. A Diné family helped by pulling me out with their pickup and a lot of muscle power involving shovels. Then these newfound friends steered me back to the camp on another, much longer but drier road. For the Navajos, it is a blessing if it rains during a ceremony. It means that the Creator will answer your prayers.

We herded sheep for Pauline White Singer. She's one of the traditional women and like all of them always dresses in the old-style Diné way—pleated skirt, velvet blouse, high orange-brown moccasins, with plenty of silver and turquoise jewelry. She doesn't speak English, but we managed to communicate in sign language. Pauline lived in an old-style hogan, a small octagonal structure, almost round, built of logs and covered with sun-hardened mud. Inside, slightly off-center, stood an ancient iron stove on which she did her cooking. The stovepipe went straight up through the ceiling and stuck out from the roof. Most of the space was taken up by her loom, on which she wove her beautiful rugs. She did her weaving sitting on a sheepskin spread over the floor of smooth, hard earth. She had an iron cot and mattress to sleep on, and an old trunk that contained everything she owned in the world and also served as a table or bench. Otherwise she had a kettle, a few pots and pans, a coffeepot, a ladle, and a few knives, spoons, and forks. And that was all. She made frybread for us and a delicious mutton stew, red with chili. Mutton was the staff of life. She knew how to find wild food—edible roots, berries, and something that looked like a tiny orange carrot, which she pulled from the earth to show us.

Like all the traditional people on Big Mountain, Pauline believed in witches, particularly zombielike evil beings called "skin walkers." These sometimes appeared in animal disguise, similar to werewolves. Some of her beliefs resembled ours. Just as some Lakotas believe in wapiyas, conjurers who can make people sick by "shooting something into them," invisible quills, feathers, and whatnot, which a medicine man can "suck out" and so make the ailing person well, so the Navajo have a wizard who can "shoot" bits of bone or teeth from a dead person into someone they want to bewitch, or maybe grains of sand, ashes from a "ghost hogan," that is, a dwelling that has been burned because somebody has died in it. The Diné people on Big Mountain were also careful that none of their hairs, fingernails, and, to put it bluntly, shit would fall into the hands of a witch, who could make a poison out of these things to bewitch or even kill you. A witch might also feed a person "corpse food," a tiny bit of flesh from a dead child hidden in a piece of frybread or a bowl of lamb stew. Also, the Diné take sweats as we do, but their sweat lodge is a tiny wood-and-mud structure for a one- or two-person purification. They also have medicine men, so-called "singers" and "hand tremblers," who cure the sick. The singers do this by reciting a long chant, like "beauty way," or "blessing way," which is like a long, healing prayer. The patient usually sits on a sand painting, which will be destroyed after the ritual is finished. So we learned some of our Diné friends' ways, and they learned some of ours. We have something else in common—a majority of Navajos are members of the peyote church, just as we are, though there are some slight differences in the manner in which we run our meetings.

Well, it had been decided that it would give a big boost to the Big Mountain people to hold a sun dance there every summer. Crow Dog and Archie Fire Lame Deer began running sun dances every year at Big Mountain, starting in 1981. Over the years we had dancers from everywhere, some Chicanos and some Orientals. We never had any white dancers but they were allowed to sweat, to "humble themselves," and to be on the work crews. Some years airplanes would fly over the dance ground real low, buzzing us, making a terrific noise—air force jets, navy jets. I am sure they were spying on us, taking pictures.

Of course, wherever there are some "Indian doings," we have weirdos, groupies, and New Age people. One year on Big Mountain there was a woman, a "crystal channeler," who came to the sweat. She claimed that in Los Alamos they had gotten hold of a piece of the Shroud of Turin and with that were able to clone Jesus, because of his DNA on the shroud. But she said: "I'm channeling this, but this is the Antichrist, and the real Jesus is mad, and he's going to come back because he's mad at those people in Los Alamos." Whew, she should be a science-fiction writer. I started really pouring water on the rocks, and that slowed her down. That was a very strange sweat.

In 1987 a marine named Lone Tree was doing time in prison on a charge of espionage. He had been posted to the U.S. embassy in Moscow and was accused of having let himself be seduced by a Russian woman who induced him to spy for the KGB. His father is a Winnebago from Wisconsin, his mother a Navajo from Arizona. She was present at the sun dance and addressed the crowd, saying that she needed their prayers and that her son was just a scapegoat, unjustly imprisoned because he was a Native American.

One problem we had sun dancing at Big Mountain was the heat. The ground is all sand. When the wind blows you wake up in the morning finding your bedroll completely covered with fine, powdery sand. That sand is hot when you dance barefooted. It's like putting your feet on a grill. One year it was so hot—115 degrees in the shade—that the dancers had blisters on the soles of their feet. One guy was putting grease on our feet and that made it worse. Crow Dog and Lame Deer took pity on the women. They made a little artificial pool of water for us to put our feet in. They also let the women have a little water, but not the male dancers. Some fainted. Crow Dog dipped sage into water and moistened our hair with it. One of the Diné ladies came around with her fan.

She lifted our hair in the back and fanned our necks. They also
fanned sage smoke on us. And the Diné women sang for us. Some
of our Sioux songs had been translated into Navajo and so they
could sing our songs in their language.

I ran women's sweats at Big Mountain, because the Navajos
don't have mixed sweats. I had already been roped into leading the
purification because I was the only woman there who knew how
to do this. I experienced something like stage fright. I had been in
many sweats before, but always as a participant, not as a leader. It
went very well, except that some of the older Diné ladies thought
that I had been making it a little too hot for them. I thought I had
gone easy on them but forgot that our Lakota sweats are the hottest
of all—hot as hell. One year later there was this woman, Jessie,
who was already running sweats for the elders. She'd let them
come out after every round. But there were all these supporters,
women who wanted to learn and be a part of it. So they asked all
over for someone to run a sweat for them, and I was the last choice,
the bottom of the barrel. So I said: "I'll do it." Then I ordered fifty
rocks for that sweat lodge. The white women were real strong, but
the two Sioux who were in that sweat ran out of there, crept out
of the lodge. It kind of embarrassed me, because I thought Indian
women were supposed to be strong. What had happened—and I
had not realized it—was that underneath the canvas someone had
lined the lodge with plastic trash bags. They then caught fire and
burned the two Indian women. We just tore that plastic off and
threw it out the door. A couple of days later the Navajo elders
wanted me to run a sweat. I took it pretty easy on them, and got
the heat up slowly, but it ended up hot. And then they prayed for
a long time and that made it even hotter. They came out of there
really happy. They said: "You're the first woman to run the sweat
where we really benefited from it." Those were very strong
women.

In 1985, one Navajo dancer stood in the circle for four days and
nights, pierced, his skewers connected to the tree with long ropes.

When he broke loose on the last day, his skewers flew high up into a tree. When some men climbed up to retrieve them, they found them in the crook of a branch together with a fresh peyote button. This caused great excitement and was considered as something supernatural. So all the Diné peyote people brought their rattles, gourd boxes, and feather fans to the tree to have them blessed and to pray, telling me: "What happened is very sacred."

I danced at Big Mountain in 1987 and 1988. It was the first time I had pierced since I was twenty-six years old. I was thirty-two at that time. I kept dreaming all year about sun dancing. I dreamt that I was hanging from the tree, and I'd think and pray about this all the time. And I dreamt about my grandma, and about the Diné people, that we were all in a concentration camp with barbed wire around it. Inside, all the men and women were being separated, and the children taken away to foster homes. I kept dreaming this, and I thought maybe I was meant to do a pierce hanging, to suffer for the people. Even when I stayed away from home for a couple of weeks, I continued having these dreams—they kept bothering me. I finally went back home when it was time for Big Mountain, for purification day. I walked into my bedroom, and everything was there laid out for me—my sun dance dress and my sweet grass—and I knew I had to go back there to Big Mountain. The children were real sad that I was going. They said they were going to pray for me to come back. Leonard even bought me a new car, a Camaro, to get there. We went up to Big Mountain and made it in time for purification, and right away the women wanted me to run a sweat. I ran a real hot sweat, and the elderlies were in there. There were some real strong prayers in there. I was thinking about my dream and praying all that time. When I danced I ate medicine continuously just to keep my strength up. I kept dreaming and thinking about its meaning. Finally I asked Archie for advice. I told him about my dreams. I asked him if it was all right to do a pierce hanging from the tree, because I couldn't get away from that dream. He said it was all right, that I should do it. But when they were taking me to the tree, I got very scared and felt like telling them to forget the whole thing. But I could not back out of it because I had made a commitment, a solemn vow. They took me to the sacred pole and I stretched out beneath it, facedown. A Big Mountain Navajo woman, Sarah Katenay, pierced me with a skewer on one side, high up on my back. A young mixed-blood guy, my own age, pierced me on the other side. They pierced me real deep. They attached ropes to the skewers in my flesh and threw them over the crotch of the tree, and men on the other side pulled me up, ever so slowly. I was hanging there for a while, suspended in the air, about seven or eight feet above the ground. I had an eagle wing in each hand and fanned the air with it, hoping that the movement would make me break free. Suddenly, the skewer on my right side broke and I was spinning around wildly, like a tumbleweed in a whirlwind. Finally the other side broke. I was pretty high up in the air and all I could think about was to try landing on my feet.

They brought one girl to me after I broke. She took one look at my back and fainted. I had to fan her off with my eagle wings. I was hugging my family and everyone. I was still in a trance. I was happy. I was laughing and crying at the same time. I was proud to have kept my vow. Then all the elderlies came up to me just to touch me, praying and crying, telling me that I had done a great thing for the people. After that the helpers took me around the circle again, back to my place among the dancers, while all the women under the arbor yelled out the ululating, shrill, high-pitched "brave heart cry" for me. Later, we went over to Sarah's hogan and sat down in a circle on the dirt floor, wolfing down her wonderful chili stew.

In the following months I dreamed again but this time a red horse appeared in my vision, and I knew that I had to renew my vow and sun dance with a horse. So once more I put on my fringed deerhide outfit and went to Big Mountain to be pierced. Again I stood in the circle. The cedar man came around, from one sun dancer to another. He had cedar burning in a large seashell, so that we could fan ourselves off and get strength from the cedar. They also burned sage for us and its strong fragrance filled the air. As always, I had also eaten the sacred medicine to help me get through my ordeal. Again I was taken to the tree and pierced deep on the back on both sides, this time by my son Pedro. Again the ropes were thrown over the sacred pole's crotch, but now they were attached to a horse ridden by a young warrior. As he walked the horse off a little distance away, I was slowly lifted in the air. The rider has to know his job so that the horse dancer does not slam into the tree. Again I had in each hand an eagle wing. The rider kept walking the horse maybe fifty feet or so off, toward the east, and would then gallop quickly back to the tree, thereby jerking me up and down in order to make me break free. I finally called to him to come real close and he did, gathering the ropes in all the time to keep me hanging above the ground. When the horse was at the tree, it started dancing. That was strong medicine. I fanned the horse off myself with both eagle wings and it raced away with its rider toward the east and I broke loose. Some of the skin off my back was then put on the tree as an offering. I was glad to have been allowed to suffer spiritually for the cause. My body bears the marks of sacrifice. I have four scars on my back from Big Mountain, two from hanging at the tree and two from when I was pulled by the horse. And I have two deep ones on my arms, right below my shoulders, from my first sun dance, and the scars from flesh offerings when old Bill Eagle Feather cut forty little squares of skin from my arms. And two more scars on my wrists where feathers had been stuck through at a sun dance. Then I have four piercings on each ear that were ceremoniously pierced by Fools Crow's daughter. I also have scars from different accidents and confrontations, and I'm missing a few teeth as the result of too many fights. I call them honorable scars.

The fight for Big Mountain was led by the women, the strong-hearted Diné mothers and grandmothers. They were at the core of the resistance. Sarah Katenay, who had pierced me, and Mary Shay formed the Weaving Project, made up by a group of traditional women weaving rugs to get funds for the struggle. They sold their rugs, through white supporters in California, for amounts raning from sixty to a thousand dollars apiece. They raised a lot of money that way for Big Mountain. This project also had a spiritual side. Weaving was taught to the Diné by Spider Woman, the female supernatural who had saved the people of the First World when they were engulfed by a big flood. She made a raft out of spiderwebs, a sort of Noah's ark, upon which the people climbed and survived. Spider Woman also made the Thread of Life for the hero called Monster Slayer. Some women sing and pray while they weave. They always leave an imperfection in a rug, because nothing made by humans should be perfect. They likewise leave a little opening on the rug for the spirits to escape. In October of 1992, some thirty women elders from the Weaving Project led a protest, saying that driving them from their sacred land was a violation of Navajo religion.

The fight for Big Mountain is being lost. The forced relocations are continuing. I fear that the beautiful country there will become a great black hole made by the strip miners. But I do not think that our fight has been in vain. One day it will bear fruit, and our years of support for the Big Mountain people have cemented the bond between the Diné and the Lakota people, particularly between the peyote church members of both tribes. It was like one long, long alowanpi—a seven-year-long relation-making ceremony.

CHAPTER TWELVE

Under the
Tempe Bridge

I had tried to run away from the Paradise before I finally left Leonard Crow Dog for good. I couldn't take the life there anymore. It was killing me, mentally, physically, spiritually. We were so much inside a pressure cooker that our nerves were raw. Bleeding nerves, you might say. We blew up over little things. We no longer shared the same bed. So I gathered up the children and ran. I could make a very bad pun and say that I went from Crow Dog to the dogs. I was alone, penniless, without a roof over my head, and with four children to take care of. I was vulnerable, without protection. I was abused verbally and physically. At a party that, as usual, included some hard drinking, a man for no reason beat me within an inch of my life. He was blind drunk and in a state of wild rage, which he took out on whoever was most vulnerable and female. Somebody smaller and weaker.

For a very short time I lived in a shack out in the boondocks. There was a lot of violence going on in the area—you could hear the yelling and shouting of drunks all night long. I was utterly depressed. I had an icebox with Jack Daniel's in it, and I'd get up in the morning and take a shot as an eye-opener. I could not even get up the money to pay rent for this miserable hovel and had to leave. Once more I had the sky as a roof. My heart muscle cramped, and I went to the hospital for an EKG. They gave me some muscle relaxants and told me to take them. I felt like downing the whole bottle. I wanted to get it over with. I wanted to die. I gathered up all my stuff and went to my mom's place with all the kids, but she couldn't handle it. There were already two of my sisters parked there with their babies. Then I got a job with the medical records department at the hospital. I was at the very bottom of the ladder and the pay was not enough to keep body and soul together. On the other hand, if I saw in the records that a man had the clap, or genital herpes, I could warn my girlfriends: "Stay away from him."

I had a real close friend. Her name was Norma Brave. She had been gung ho for the movement. She would have gone to Wounded Knee, but her parents stopped her. Later on she married a much older man, a relative of mine in the extended Sioux family kind of sense. Like me, she had to spend so much time with their children that she didn't have time for anything else, such as going back to school. She had a hard life. She had twins, a girl and a boy. One of them was brain damaged and the fluid had to be drained away with a tube. Anyway, Norma and I were buddies on account of having both been in the movement and being sun dancers. We'd talk about our troubles and try to get strength from each other. She told me that she wanted to get back to school and hoped to get some form of public assistance so she could learn a trade. I had been working at the hospital only a short time when they brought Norma in—dead. Somebody had battered her so that she looked like a rag doll somebody had thrown in a trash can. I went to see her with her family before her body was cold. I looked at her and was petrified. I saw myself lying there. They said it was a stroke that killed Norma, but I think it was abuse. It is a real problem. The man I was staying with at the time, whom I had just moved in with, was already hitting me. One day he had beaten me pretty badly and I was all black-and-blue. Just then Norma's sister, Mary Ann, dropped in together with my sister Barb. I wouldn't let them turn the light on because I didn't want them to see how I looked. So they came in and we talked about Norma. Somebody turned the light on anyhow. Mary Ann stared at me and said: "My God!" Then she told me about the White Buffalo Calf Society and their shelter for abused women. "You should go there," she said, "it is sad for you to be living like this. Go to the shelter. Look at me, I don't even have a sister anymore. Don't go on being a baby-sitter for this man. Go, do it for yourself, do it for your kids."

So I ended up going to the shelter with all my children. It's a big building outside Mission. They are very strict there. You can't be loud, you can't yell at the kids. You have to watch them and make sure they don't run around or be wild. It's hard. You have duties and chores; for as long as you stay at the shelter you have to work and help keep the place clean. At least it was peaceful there. The people who ran it had created a peaceful atmosphere. You have to talk to the counselors, tell your story, and be honest. Tell them why things happened the way they did. One of the counselors assured me that the shelter would help me, but I was totally spooked. I was afraid to go out, even to the grocery store, even for half an hour. One day Archie Fire Lame Deer dropped in to visit me. I told him that I had left Leonard and he gave me a hug. Because he is a medicine man I asked him whether it was still okay to pray with the pipe, and he assured me that it was. The big problem was that Leonard would absolutely not accept the fact that I was leaving him. He wanted me and the children back. The pressure got so bad that I felt I had to get out of South Dakota altogether.

A lady from the White Buffalo Calf Society took me to Marshall, Minnesota, and left me at the shelter there. But there was a hitch. I had to get through all kinds of red tape before I could be admitted. Also, it would take a month before my ADC money, Aid to Dependent Children, could be transferred from Rosebud to

Marshall. So here I was on the street, in a strange town, without a penny, and with four hungry children on my hands. As usual, when I am absolutely desperate, I turned to Richard Erdoes in Santa Fe. Luckily I still had my notebook with the telephone numbers and I called him up. As always, he helped me out so that I could last until things were sorted out. Finally I got my ADC check and was admitted to the shelter.

Being in Minnesota didn't help much. In Rosebud they have a computer that keeps track of where the public assistance money is going, and through this, Leonard found out where I was. That alarmed me. I was determined not to go back to him. So I left Marshall and hit the road again. I went to Sioux Falls and then took a bus to Omaha. I parked the kids at the shelter there. As I mentioned before, I knew that my father lived in Omaha and looked up his address. It was Christmastime. I went to see my dad and felt bad that I had to tell him that I was at a shelter and had no money. He said: "I'd take you in but I have a family here." It almost broke my heart. After all, I was his daughter, but he never had any use for me or for my sisters. I guess he didn't need me there with my four kids. He gave me thirty dollars to save his conscience. This got me as far as Denver.

The shelter in Denver was a hard place. If you got edgy, or needed time for a cup of coffee, somebody would watch the kids for you. But if you wanted to go out for a couple of hours, to relax, to get away from it all, they wouldn't help with the children. They had very strict rules. The daily workshops they had were no help. And they had a lot of psychological counseling, which I didn't need. What I did need was a place to stay, school for my kids, a job while they were in school. So I went on to Tucson. I thought I might just as well drift toward the South, where it's at least warm. In Denver the snow was a foot high. Also, in the Southwest I had friends who were members of the Native American Church and I felt a great need to take in a meeting. In Tucson they wouldn't accept me at the shelter because I was "not within their jurisdiction." They sent me to the Salvation Army, which was divided into a men's side and a women's side. I met a lot of people there who were in the same situation I was in. I found that I was not the only one and I took comfort from that fact. The Salvation Army was not exactly the Holiday Inn. I was in a room with many other women. We got bunk beds—one for me, one for my two biggest, and one for the two smallest kids. They gave us sheets, blankets, and a towel. They got us up early in the morning and gave us a kind of vegetarian soup. The people who ran the place had better food. I could smell it. I had the kids with me—Pedro, Anwah, June Bug, and Jennifer, who was only two and wasn't talking yet. The whole thing was a nightmare. The Salvation Army people were on my case every minute—"Watch your kids! Control your children! Watch, watch, watch!" The kids were at that age when they get into things and run around. They did not want to be cooped up in a small chamber called the "playroom." They were forever running off in different directions and I had to chase after them. Clean up after them, too. It was like watching a paper bag full of fleas. At the Salvation Army you had to be out at six o'clock in the morning. Every day it was the same: "Can't I stay one more day? I have no place to go to." It was very hard on the kids.

It seems to me that the greatest difference between whites and Indians is the way that they treat those in need and their ideas of relationships. We might be poor, or even blind drunk, but somehow we take care of each other. If you have no roof over your head, you can knock on any door and somebody will take you in. They will give you their own bed or couch to sleep on. They feed you what they themselves are eating. And they won't make you feel that it's charity. It is just done automatically because there is a feeling that we are all in the same boat. There are no class distinctions. You might be only a sixth cousin but still be welcomed as a relative, part of the tiyospaye, the extended family. In New York, on a cold day, I saw an old homeless woman, in a flimsy dress, lying on the pavement in front of a fancy jewelry store. A well-dressed couple was stepping over her, going into the store to buy, maybe, a two-thousand-dollar watch. They treated that poor woman as if she had not been there. That could not happen on the res. We have our faults but at least we share, we still have feeling for each other. For us every Indian is a brother or a sister, welcome to sit at our table.

The Salvation Army finally kicked us out. Luckily, I had a friend in town, Ron Rosen, whom we called Doc because he was a volunteer doctor at Wounded Knee. I contacted Doc and told him I needed some help. He rescued us. Doc found me sitting at the bus station, on a cardboard box, with no money and all the kids whining for something to eat. So he took us to the nearest McDonald's. I had some other friends in Tucson—Ed Mendoza and his wife, peyote people—and they took me in. Then another friend came to help, Fred Walking Badger, a Papago. He is a medicine man who once went to jail after a big ruckus with a white man who kept a two-headed snake. Fred had heard about this and confronted the man because he considered such an animal sacred, not to be owned by a white man who might exhibit it as a curiosity. So Walking Badger went to get this snake from the white man, who refused to give it up. The result was a free-for-all with a certain amount of damage to all concerned.

Well, my welfare checks finally came in again, and I managed to make a small deposit on a run-down trailer home near a school. I always tried to keep the kids studying. Also, the Mendozas tried to organize their own Native American Church and I was again going to meetings. But then Crow Dog found out once more where I was so I packed up and hit the road again. In Phoenix, Leonard finally caught up with us, and so there we were, the whole happy family together again. We got a place where we all stayed together, though, in the case of Leonard and myself, not as husband and wife, but like brother and sister. Thus it came about that we all lived in Phoenix for about three years.

I gave up trying to run. Leonard and I had come to an arrangement: we were no longer lovers. He was performing his ceremonies all over the country. He wanted me to travel with him but I was tired of the gypsy life. I said no. We both had our faults and yet we tried. If it had not been for the drinking it might have been all right. We pissed away a lot of money partying. We did not have a regular domestic household where the parents work nine-to-five jobs. Leonard always made sure we had food and were taken care of. We stayed together but physically and emotionally lived apart. When the pressure on us became unbearable we turned on each other. I am sorry for that, and I am sure he is too. He was away for long periods of time. He was free to see other women. I went to bars and had a few drinks with the boys.

The switch from Rosebud to Phoenix was like jumping from the frying pan into the fire. In no time, the whole of Leonard's entourage came down from South Dakota and moved in with us. It was like living in an ant heap. Some were nice and helpful but the total lack of privacy just tired me out. Coming home, I always had the image in my mind of joining an arctic bird colony—a million gulls or terns crammed on an undersized rock. There were the usual, never-ending cries for help, the welfare money going to bail some drunk out of jail, the same incessant, night-and-day coming and going. The hardships of living in the Paradise were now added to in Phoenix.

We lived in different places. Mostly in the barrio. In Rosebud, during the winter months we had been freezing our asses off in temperatures of seventy below. In Phoenix, we were dripping with perspiration when the thermometer stayed at a hundred degrees in the shade for days on end. We moved around until we ended up in the same neighborhood where we started out, a Hispanic community that was Mexican and Indian. It was all right because you could walk around at night and no one ever bothered you. But they busted a lot of people because many of them came from Mexico illegally. There were also city ordinances—so many people per household—and they'd find ten people living in one room. Our last house was nice. It was one of the oldest in the city and it had a big porch with pillars in front, a pretty large Spanish-style adobe. It was on Van Buren and Fourteenth and the area surrounding the barrio was pretty rough. My oldest son, Pedro, was doing pretty well in school, and then, suddenly, he started changing habits. He'd sleep all day and was up all night. He'd take off with gangs. I'm pretty sure he was doing drugs at the time. I thought about leaving, but I really liked Phoenix. Our neighbors were nice, but a lot of outsiders were moving in, gangs of drug dealers looking for new turf to conquer. You could get cocaine on any street corner. Pedro kept a knife at all times and he was not afraid to stick someone to save himself. He wanted a gun, and I said: "No. You think it will protect you. But if you carry a gun, you'll die by the gun." I was sitting on the porch one night and this guy comes up and says: "Hey, I got some good stuff, some crack." I said: "Oh, really? Let's see. . . ." He came up close and I grabbed him and hit him in the face. I said: "You'd better get out of my yard. I have children here, and don't you ever try to bring drugs around here." Later they told me I shouldn't have done that—"Don't you know most of those people have guns?" And there were a lot of hookers in that neighborhood, and a lot of drugs. And gang members—a lot of them moved from L.A. to Phoenix.

I did take classes at P.C., Phoenix College. I took home economics, nutrition, textiles, child development, cloth making. I was taking care of the kids during the day, so the evenings were the only time I had to go to classes. I really enjoyed it. I felt good about myself, and the teachers at P.C. were first-class.

But I went home one evening and Leonard was there and he was really mad. He wanted to know where I had been. I said I had been at class. He said it was a waste of time, that I'd be better off staying at home with the kids, being a housewife and mother. We had our agreement, but in a way he still felt that he owned me, if not as a husband then as a father or older brother. It was a difficult situation for both of us. We tried to leave each other but somehow couldn't let go. He has tried very hard, sometimes, to understand a woman's point of view and he even thinks that he is "pro-woman." But he comes from a male-oriented hunting and warrior society whose centuries-old ways are ingrained in him, a society with proverbs such as "Woman should not walk before man." He also comes from a tribe that has a great oral tradition. He is a wonderful and compelling speaker, but he cannot read or write. He inherited his father's and grandfather's contempt for the white man's books and schools. To him, book learning—ta-chesli, bullshit. I can't blame him. Schools of his and his father's generations were terrible. Old Henry went to the third grade for eight years because there was no higher grade in Indian schools. I know men and women who, as recently as twenty years ago, got their high school diplomas though they were totally illiterate. So I understood him, but that didn't help me. When we moved, I stopped going to college.

I wanted to buy a house but it didn't work out, so eventually we ended up back on Fourteenth Street right off Van Buren—that's where all the hookers are, the pimps, the drug addicts. But nobody bothered us. My friend Sharon always had some smoke, and we'd drink beer. Her boy ended up getting in trouble because he shot a cop. He was young but he was a gangster involved in drugs. It wasn't much help that our Indian and Mexican neighbors were kind, ready to lend a helping hand when needed, because the gangs from L.A. and Chicago were moving in. That we were living in a very dangerous part of town was brought home to us in a terrible, heartbreaking way.

Among our closest friends were the Roys, a family of Minnesota Indians. The father, Jerry, is a fine, good man who sun danced many times and hung from the tree. He earns a living by making and selling tipis. Leonard and Jerry were always together, as close as twins. The Roys had moved down to Phoenix to help Leonard, who needed somebody to do his organizing and handle the correspondence. Jerry brought his whole family. He was still selling his tipis out of Phoenix. They were always going with us to peyote meetings and sweat lodge ceremonies on the Salt River Reservation. Jerry has a number of kids. One son, John, is a very spiritual young man who has pierced at the sun dance and is heavily involved in Indian religion. His youngest son at the time was a sweet, friendly kid named Teddy Bear who didn't like living in a big city with a population of over a million. He didn't like the overcrowded schools, and he missed his old friends and classmates in the small city the Roys came from. So he went back to Minnesota to stay with his auntie. Teddy Bear was doing really well. He was on the honor roll and on the football team. Then he phoned that he'd come down to Phoenix for the Christmas holidays. His mother, Pat, was very happy. On Christmas Eve, Pat wanted to take us and the whole family out to dinner, but an older brother, Miles, was out shooting pool. It's his hobby. So, about nine-thirty, Pat got tired of waiting for Miles to show up and sent Teddy Bear and Mickey, another brother, to look for him and bring him back so that we could all go out to a restaurant. We were having a few beers when somebody knocked real loud on the door. When we opened it, there was nobody there. In our Indian way, that's a sign of death, a way of telling you that someone you love is dead. So Jerry was very concerned and went out looking for his boys.

About an hour later Jerry called, and he said: "Teddy Bear just got stabbed. He's dead." I couldn't believe it. They had been coming out of the bar around midnight—it was just a little bar off Seventh Street with a dingy little alley and a back-street parking lot—and some other guys came after them wanting to fight. I don't know how it started; I guess they were drunk, didn't like Indians, and just wanted to have a go at them. Teddy Bear was driving the car, and he got out to warn his brother that one of those guys had a knife, and he got it right in the heart instead of his brother. They took Teddy Bear in the car, and there was a hospital about four blocks away, and they were in such a hurry to get him there that they crashed the car right into the door of the hospital. By that time it was too late. That night they took him to the morgue. No charges were ever brought against these gang members because they couldn't find the knife. So the next night, Christmas night, we had a peyote meeting, and we just sat there not knowing what to do. Everybody was feeling so bad. We all wept. In the morning, as I was bringing in the water, the phone rang and it was Leonard Peltier calling from jail. Jerry told him the bad news about Teddy Bear. That was the last time I spoke to Peltier. Then we had a wake service at the mortuary for Teddy Bear, and we had the staff, the fan, and the drum go around, and we all sang for him and had a service like that. He was only seventeen, a handsome boy with his whole life ahead of him. Leonard buried him on the reservation next to Clear Water, who was killed at Wounded Knee. Jerry wanted it that way. After that night of tragedy I started to be more concerned about Pedro and my other kids. What made it worse was that Teddy Bear was clean, he didn't drink and he was really into his schoolwork.

I became more depressed than ever. When we first started living in Phoenix, I had told Leonard that I never wanted to go back to South Dakota. I was very adamant about it and he could not do anything about it. That's why he stayed. After all, he too loved the children. He met different relatives in the Native American Church there. He'd go to sweats. He'd go on speaking tours and then come back only to travel again when some university would have him come and speak. I stayed behind, alone, with the kids. I started drinking heavily.

There were two places Indians in Phoenix liked to go to get drunk. One was called Mr. Lucky's. On the weekends they had bands upstairs, playing country music. Downstairs was a disco with rock 'n' roll. Thursday was ladies' night. Sometimes, on certain nights, Mr. Lucky's would have musclemen, male strippers, for the women to gawk at. At other times they had go-go girls for the men to make eyes at. The other favorite Indian watering hole was the Cancan on Fifteenth Street. It was a huge place that once served as a warehouse. Over the bar they had the *Playboy* poster of Sacheen Little Feather in the nude on a double spread. Very inspiring. Sacheen is a friend who once, years ago, made headlines when she received an Oscar for Marlon Brando. The Cancan was the place for country music. It had a huge dance floor and the place was always packed with Navajos from wall to wall. And, boy, could they dance! There are a lot of Diné in Phoenix. They come in winter to work. I met many friends from Big Mountain there. I preferred Mr. Lucky's to the Cancan. Most bars in Phoenix closed at 1:00 A.M., but Lucky's stayed open until 2:00 and steady customers would get a complimentary margarita after the last dance.

There was still another bar with strippers. I went there with Bull Bear and another skin, an Apache. I was still parking my car when these two were already at the front table. They already had a load on. There were signs—DON'T TOUCH and HANDS OFF. It meant that they did not allow the customers to touch or fondle the go-go girls. One of the girls came over to our table. I told Bull Bear: "You're supposed to tip her," but he had no money left. I gave him five bucks and he tried to stuff it into her bikini. The Apache already had his hands between her legs. They had this big heavyweight bouncer who came running, yelling: "No touching! No touching!" The Apache was fighting Bull Bear over the girl, yelling: "I'm going to take her away from you!" She didn't want to have anything to do with either of them. Luckily both passed out before things got really rowdy.

One night I was at Mr. Lucky's. I was downstairs, and I'd dance if someone asked me to. Then this guy came up to me and said: "Guess what tribe I'm from." I said: "Apache." "Right," he said. I said: "Guess what tribe I'm from." He said: "Sioux," and I said: "Right on!" He said: "Let's show 'em how!" So we went and danced the last dance. He was with a Pima guy named Moran and two other guys. I was going to my car when they came over and said: "Do you want to party? Let's go to the Tempe Bridge." I agreed to go. We went down a back road and came upon a place where a lot of cars were parked. Everyone was just sitting around listening to their ghetto blasters under the bridge, drinking, cruising around, meeting people, checking it out. It's near the university. Everyone just parks and parties up. If the police come everyone has to take off, because you're not allowed to be there.

I was partying with Moran, and we took this Navajo fellow back to his apartment. Then we went to Moran's apartment. It was already eight in the morning, and it was about a hundred degrees. I then realized that I had lost my car keys, probably at the Navajo's place. He said: "My cousin has a truck," and so he took us around. The problem was that I couldn't remember where we'd dropped that guy off. We bought some more beer and jumped in another car and went back under the bridge to look for the keys. By then it was evening time and we couldn't find the keys. I had to go to the bathroom, so I went behind some bushes and fell into the canal with my pants down. Oh, man, it was a drag. I was in the water, trying to get out, but I couldn't because it was too steep. Pretty soon I started yelling and Moran and another guy came over. By this time I was all buzzed up from the alcohol and I said: "Come on in, the water's fine!" They helped me out. I never did find the keys. I ended up calling a locksmith to come and make a new key. We had another twelve-pack. The whole thing turned into a long, forty-eight-hour drunk. We kept on drinking under the bridge, one beer after another. My head was swimming. I could no longer stand up. Moran took me to his apartment in the Wild Winds complex. He dropped me on a couch and threw a blanket over me. I was dead to the world. A disheveled woman clutching a beer bottle was hunkered down in a corner. No one knew how she had gotten there. I woke up when somebody was shaking me, yelling: "Who's that?" It was Moran's old lady, a young Arikara woman. She kept yelling: "Who's that?" and "Are you fooling around with my man?" Moran was yelling from the other room: "It's just a Sioux gal, sleeping it off. Nothing's going on." Then we all burst out laughing. After I got dressed and sobered up I found Moran sitting in the swimming pool they had there, in his shorts and boots. He grinned and said: "Jump in!" I did. Then the woman with the beer bottle suddenly emerged, crawled into the front seat of Moran's car, and tried to take off. He ran and stopped her by jumping on the hood. Later, they took me back to my place. I introduced Moran to my kids and to Brad, my sister's husband, who was baby-sitting. Then I had a shower, cleaned myself up, and put on a new dress. After that I behaved for a while. For a week, to be exact.

Next weekend we were going to go to San Carlos, the Apache reservation. That's where Geronimo's tribe is from. First a bunch of us went to shoot some pool and have a few. I was drinking Jack. Moran's house was only two blocks down so we went down there, and we met another guy, who wanted a ride to the liquor store. So he hopped in. We were in the Camaro, and it was really packed—a whole carload of guys. That's when I got stopped. Right away they gave me one of those sobriety tests. I failed miserably. They handcuffed me and threw me in a car. It was hot and I was sweating and crying—tears were streaming down my face. It took them eight hours to process me in a holding tank, where I almost got into a fight with a big old black hooker and a Mexican one. They were talking about how they could fight, and about their old men, yakking away. I had a hangover and told them: "Why don't you just shut up? Is that all you talk about is how you fight? I'm tired of listening to that shit." They said: "Girl, you're in the wrong place to get sassy. Who do you think you are?" I said: "I'm from the res. I'm not from your jungle. I wasn't raised in a city. What are you going to do about it?" The hookers kept bragging about what big fighters they were, and how mean they could be, daring me to get it on, but there was a full-blood Indian girl with us in the cell and she backed me up. She was a warrior woman for sure, and after one look at her, the hookers cooled down. Then Moran came with a bail bondsman and got me out.

I was arraigned, and that was a drag, because they fined me six

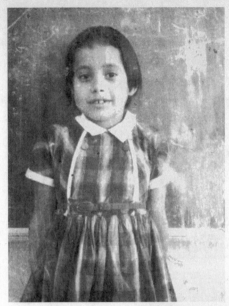

Mary in school. This is the only photograph taken of her as a child.

Mary's great-grandfather Thomas Flood (Indian name Cheki Paw) at age twenty-seven. He was born in 1863 and died in 1906 at the age of forty-three. He was a tribal delegate to Washington and a tribal interpreter. He was murdered, shot to death. Nobody knows by whom.

A meeting of the Native American Church at Crow Dog's place, Alex One Star doing the drumming.

A Sioux sweat lodge. The participants are inside, taking their vapor bath in the dome-shaped lodge.

After Crow Dog's release from prison in 1977, a great honoring feast and dance was given for him and Mary.

In 1971, at Crow Dog's Paradise, a man undergoes the self-torture of the sun dance.

A buffalo skull serves as an altar during a religious rite.

Sioux women participating in a sun dance at Pine Ridge, 1972.

At Rosebud and other Sioux reservations, many Native Americans still live in substandard houses, without modern facilities.

A scene on the Pine Ridge Sioux reservation, part of Shannon County, S.D. According to a recent article in the *New York Times*, Shannon has the lowest per capita income of all the more than 3,000 counties in the U.S.A. The people of the Rosebud reservation are not much better off.

During 1976, Mary made many impassioned speeches in support of her husband at the time, Leonard Crow Dog, imprisoned for political "offenses" in the aftermath of Wounded Knee.

At a ceremony held at Rosebud in 1977, Mary, as a special honor, was given the name Ohitika Win—Brave Woman.

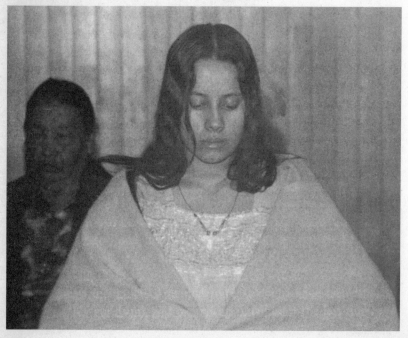

Mary's mother, Emily, with one of the grandchildren.

Mary and her new husband, Rudi Olguin, at their wedding, in Santa Fe in 1992.

Mary in Paris in October 1992. She was invited to give a lecture at the Musée de l'Homme, on the occasion of the opening of the Discovery of America exhibition.

hundred dollars. There was a city program so that you could work off your fine. In my case that meant working for twelve days. There was a whole crew—you'd meet early in the morning and there was a bus that would take you to a park, or wherever you were going to work that day. They put us in the dirtiest part of the city. There was shit all over the streets. But the men had to do that, shovel up the shit. I had to clean bathrooms in the parks and tidy up the whole area. The toilets had to be really clean because the inspector would watch us and check out our work. Later we cleaned the city streets. Everything from picking up trash, pulling up weeds, to landscaping in the parks. It was a pretty strict program. You couldn't mouth back and had to behave. The crew was mostly wetbacks. Hardly anybody spoke English. I made a lot of friends there. We'd sit in the back of the bus and talk about things, those that could speak English. The others gossiped in Spanish. One black guy was especially nice to me, helping out when the work was too heavy for me. Every morning we got a break for about twenty minutes. We sat around in a park and these two guys went behind the hill to smoke a joint. They had to pee and went behind a bush and got promptly arrested for indecent exposure. They were kicked off the program. They didn't even get a ride back—they had to walk.

We went out and celebrated the last few days. Had our first Bud in twelve days. Even the program director said: "Drink and drive. Get arrested and fined. Keep this program alive!" I had a Bud Light T-shirt on and this guy, Alberto, asked me more than once: "Hey, Bud Light, you want to have a drink after work?" I finally said sure. So I went to a bar with Alberto and we had a few beers. He tried to teach me the finer points of playing pool. Then we decided to cruise around. We stopped in at a park. You are not supposed to be in the park after hours and, of course, the police checked us out. Alberto had a warrant out from Mesa, for some old traffic tickets, so they took him to jail. He gave me his money, two hundred dollars, and said to hold it for him and take a cab home. I couldn't

OHITIKA WOMAN

find a cab and had to walk home. The park was on the other side of town, so that meant hoofing it for sixty blocks—through the worst part of Phoenix, downtown. It was dangerous, and I was scared. Some seedy characters came running after me, yelling: "Hey, girl, stop!" I kept walking. My heart was pounding. One of those men ran around and in front of me. He wanted me to give him a blowjob for ten dollars. I said: "Are you kidding? I don't do that stuff." The situation didn't look good. I could see out of the corner of my eye that these creeps had a companion slowly following in a car. On a sudden inspiration I told the guy crowding me from the front: "I can't do what you want, but I know where there are some hookers, close by where I live. You'll drive me, I'll show you." That satisfied them. So I caught a ride home with them and I pointed out some hookers to the one who had crowded me. He was happy and I got a ride home. Crazy!

Alberto had given me his sister's phone number. I called her up and she got him out of jail. I went to their place. I told Alberto: "I still have your money," and gave him his two hundred dollars back. He said: "Are you kidding? Anybody but you would have spent that money." We became good friends after that. Alberto is from Nogales. He'd go to Mexico sometimes and always brought me back a little present, a trinket or a curio. Meanwhile, Bernadette, Leonard's daughter, who was baby-sitting for me at the time, got tired of my partying and moved out.

I still remained on my "liquid diet." One of the people on that cleanup crew, an Indian woman, had told me about Mexican bars: "Go downtown. There's some good bars with nice-looking men who have money to spend." She told me about one place only one block from where I lived, with the best margaritas in town. It had a mellow atmosphere. Everybody was having a good time, jawing and dancing. It wasn't rowdy. I'd sit at the bar, sip my margarita, and check out the scene. Then I discovered another bar across the street. I went over there one day and, lo and behold, sitting in a booth was Albert Two Hawk, from Rosebud, son of Webster, a former tribal chairman. It's amazing in what strange places you meet old acquaintances from home. I was shooting pool with him. I won a game, and when I jumped for joy my foot went out from under me and I broke it. I wasn't even drinking. It was just clumsiness. I went around in a cast for a couple of weeks but still went dancing in the nightclubs. I was irrepressible, on a continuous tear.

One day there was a knock at the door. It was Moran, my Apache friend from under the Tempe Bridge. He drove me to the top of South Mountain to see the sunset from Lookout Point. It was very romantic. The view was magnificent. Then he took me out to dinner and fed me real good. Moran is from Salt River. He is a roofer and gets up every morning at four to go to work—when he's not under the bridge, that is. He gave me a good-bye kiss, saying: "If you ever need me, I'll be there." On that nice note I ended my stay in Phoenix. I had gotten tired of the scene there and of the life I was leading. I packed up the kids and went home to Rosebud.

CHAPTER THIRTEEN

Living on Beer, Commodities, and Love

When I came back to the res after Phoenix, I had what the
wasichu call culture shock. Things were even worse than
before. Rosebud looked like an area ravaged by war. I had seen
poverty before, in my youth, but now we seemed almost well off
in the old days of twenty-five years ago. Most of the little businesses we had then, the timid attempts to make it in the white
man's way, were gone. Gone was the ancient movie house, crum-
bled years ago into a ruin. Gone was the little café with its pool
hall, the little shop where Barb had made fancy western shirts, a
space she shared with an Indian jewelry maker, and even the great
Abourezk's trading emporium—everything gone, gone, gone. The
whole res stank of poverty. You could see it in the listless way
people were moving. If a tourist car stopped you usually saw a
zombielike wino emerging from the shadows trying to panhandle.
Everybody was on welfare—GA (general assistance), ADC (Aid
to Dependent Children), food stamps, commodities.

Just as I am going over this manuscript with Richard for the last
time for final proofreading, somebody hands me the *New York
Times* from September 20, 1992. It has an article on the front page,

150

headlined SAD DISTINCTION FOR THE SIOUX: HOMELAND IS NO. 1 IN POVERTY. The article is subtitled "Life at the bottom. America's poorest county." It describes our reservations as "mean and despairing places." It says that Pine Ridge, our neighboring res, with which we have a common border, is the poorest of all the 3,141 counties in the USA. Well, if Pine Ridge is the poorest, then Rosebud must be a close second. The average income on our res is about $3,100 with 65 percent of our people living below the poverty line. We are the leftover, surplus folks.

Most people live on GA. You go out and apply for a job so that you have that on record. But there's no jobs, so it's automatic that you'll qualify and get into the welfare system. You go to the Bureau of Indian Affairs (BIA), to the social services. You tell them your situation—your income, what bills you pay, how many people are in your family. Even if you're a single person you'll qualify. You get very little—maybe a week's worth of living expenses, after paying the bills. A lot of people do crafts, beadwork, or quillwork, which they sell privately or to the trading post. Sometimes you can hock something there, but there are so many people doing stuff that there aren't enough places to sell them. You end up underselling yourself. If you're on GA you can get food stamps too. You can get either commodities or food stamps, but not both. Commodities are still bad. It's the same old stuff, government-issued staples— powdered milk, powdered eggs, dried meat, dried potatoes, and pork—which Sioux just don't care for. You get some good stuff, rice, flour, and cereal, but there's much too much cheese and butter. Many middle-aged or even young people are obese. But it's not the healthy, muscular kind of obesity that comes from good, nourishing food. It's just flab. It's just not healthy. Also you don't get everything I listed here. You must make choices. If they give you one thing, there's another thing you can't have.

I prefer food stamps because you can buy fresher food. In order to get food stamps or commodities you've got to go through a lot of red tape. You have to prove that you have a low income, or no

income at all. That's easy. It's the general condition of almost
everybody on the res, but processing is slow. By the time you get
your food stamps your GA money has already run out. A few years
ago I was on GA. They'll allow you rent and utilities, and that's
it. Nothing for clothing, gas, phone, or a great number of other
things you can't do without. You get thirty dollars per person
besides the food stamps, which doesn't last very long. So what do
you do? People are desperate for money, so they sell their food
stamps for half price, or sell their commodities at a big discount.
You have to make a choice whether to have decent meals or buy
clothes so your children can go to school. Of course, it is illegal to
sell food stamps or commodities, and people get busted for it. The
authorities also try every way they can to cut your welfare. There
is one lady bureaucrat who, if she sees someone win a couple of
bucks at bingo, reports you right away and your welfare check is
cut. When my sister Barb started a tiny burrito business, cooking
up burritos and selling from house to house, the same woman
immediately reported her. Every effort to start something, to in-
vent some kind of tiny business to earn a little money on the side,
results in a smaller GA check. Some people give up trying to work
and just get drunk instead. The winos will sell their food stamps
to get booze. They'd rather go hungry, or see their children starve,
than go without their wine. And some women on ADC, when they
get their checks it's a joke—they'll give their children some junk,
some candy to keep them happy, and then, right away, they'll start
partying. But faced with such poverty people drink to forget their
misery. Life is hard, and many people are just unable to get
through the month without selling, or swapping food for something they must have. I wish we had food co-ops like they have in
cities, but that's just a dream. There is no money to translate
dreams into reality. And it is the same in all the little hamlets and
settlements that make up the res, places like He Dog, where my
mom lives, or Black Pipe, Upper Cut Meat, Soldier Creek, Grass
Mountain, Two Strikes, Ring Thunder, or Bad Nation.

Eighty percent of the people are unemployed. Tribal chairmen and politicians, mostly half-bloods, hand out the few jobs there are to their relatives. The others are out. The name of the game is nepotism. But can you blame them when they give a much-needed job to a brother or nephew?

The bureaucrats give us vocational training—carpentry, shoe-making, and auto body repair. Both Leonard and I, at one time, were trained as car mechanics. That comes in handy, because our cars are so old and decrepit that we have to keep fixing them all the time. The old car cemeteries are always full of people trying to find a part that still works. It is one business that thrives on the res. But how many carpenters, shoemakers, or mechanics do you need on the res? Very few. In the Black Hills, some white entrepreneurs provide a few jobs—staging mock attacks upon phony stockades and forts, working in phony Indian villages along the main highway with billboards like: INDIANS AT WORK: SEE HOW THEY LIVE, or SEE REAL SIOUX INDIANS MAKING MOCCASINS, or GIANT REENACTMENT OF THE CUSTER BATTLE; REAL SIOUX BRAVES ON HORSEBACK EVERY AFTERNOON FROM MAY TO OCTOBER. This kind of work pays very little, is demeaning, and forces people to live all summer long some seventy or a hundred miles away from home. Ben Black Elk was a highly gifted and intelligent person, the son of the man about whom the book *Black Elk Speaks* was written. The only job Ben could find was sitting on a bench in Keystone, in full regalia, under the shadow of Mount Rushmore, posing for tourists, being photographed with his warbonnet and fringed buckskin shirt, his arm around a grinning tourist lady or with some white brat on his lap. He used to get twenty-five cents for posing and, after a few years, ended up charging a dollar—this a man who had it in him to become a scientist or doctor if given half a chance. Some people get jobs picking spuds or wrangling cattle on a ranch. This, too, is slave labor, usually at a good distance from home. The government tries to solve the modern "Indian problem" by relocation, which means dumping large numbers of Lakota men and women in faraway cities. There are sizable numbers of Sioux in L.A., Denver, Chicago, Rapid City, Cleveland, and St. Paul, where they form their own ghettos, as out of place as a crocodile in Manhattan's Times Square. Relocation often means loss of identity. Here, far from the res, some people cease to be Indians without ever being accepted by whites. They sit, as one of my friends put it, with one ass between two chairs, a red and a white one. Then there is the problem of "itching feet." People, particularly men, get sick of living on the res, where there is nothing for them and nothing goes on, so they start drifting from place to place in the hope of finding a better life, and when they do not find it, they go on the road again. That is why you find Lakotas in the strangest places—Seattle, Tacoma, Vancouver, Manhattan, Dallas, Santa Fe, Tucson. Wherever you go, you'll find a Sioux.

On the res you have an ongoing feeling of helplessness and insecurity: Will I be able to pay next month's rent? Will they turn the electricity off for nonpayment? Will I still have a phone? You never know from one moment to another where you stand. You live from day to day, and that affects your life-style. We live in a culture of poverty mixed up with our Indian ways. There is no orderly, predictable march of events. You can never plan ahead. You are totally dependent on your car for transportation, so when you run out of gas money you become like a prisoner. You can't go anywhere. You can't do errands. I see men becoming resentful of women. The man has no job. He can't provide. In the Sioux way, you are supposed to be generous, to make gifts, but the guys have nothing to give. The woman becomes the "breadwinner" with ADC money and the little she might make on the side with beadwork. Sometimes the man can't stand it anymore and he splits. Like my father used to say: "I've had enough of that baby shit." There are emotional outbursts, explosions of anger. Every week somebody gets killed. And women fight over petty things, just like the guys. They hold grudges over little incidents that happened years ago. I watched a fight between two ancient, doddering couples. They all looked as if they were eighty years old. They could hardly walk. They had been drinking. The men were accusing each other of making it with their old ladies, screeching at each other in feeble voices, trading feeble blows. And the old women were pulling hair, yelling: "You tried to take my man away!" It was grotesque. I doubt whether these great-grandfathers could still get it up. I used to be good at fighting when I was young, but I don't fight anymore if I can help it. I have learned my lesson. Yet I do like to have a gun or numchucks around for self-protection, just in case.

Drugs are a problem on the res and in neighboring Pine Ridge. There's a little bit of everything. People are being sent to prison for possession and distribution of all kinds of stuff, ranging from marijuana to cocaine. And there's acid, speed, uppers, downers, and heroin. Not too much crack, so far. People like pej. The Sioux word for *grass* is *pejin*. So they call pot "pej" for short. It's so expensive people smoke it as an extra treat. People grow it, too, but you have to do it in a safe place, because somebody will find it and make off with the pej. I knew a guy who had grown a huge plant of high-quality weed, but a friend of his stole it, ripped it out by the roots. He was running around Mission screaming: "That asshole stole my weed! I'll kill him!" People are hungry for good pej and pay any price for it if they have the mazaska, the money. There are dealers everyone knows who have dealt for years but are never busted. Maybe they have friends in high places. Then again, one of the main dealers in Pine Ridge got busted this past winter. He was big-time and they were after him for years until they finally found a way to get him. His own cousin turned him in for a measly reward. He was facing years in prison but managed to plea-bargain it down. They found twelve Harley-Davidsons at his place, which they took away. Agents try to trap people. Two guys came to my place and knocked on the door. When Pedro opened it they told him: "Takoja, we hear you can get some good-quality pej here. We've got the money." Pedro told them: "You got the wrong place. Look somewhere else." He knew what they were about. The word is out that some people are wired, that the heat is on. I think that weed should be legalized and the government should concentrate on the hard stuff.

The young addicts on the res don't have the money for pej or other expensive drugs. So they are "huffing gas," that is, inhaling gasoline. Or they sniff Wite-Out, the white plastic stuff you use to correct typing errors. They put it, open, into a paper bag, stick their head into it, and sniff. One teenage girl was in a coma from this for weeks and then died. Then there's hairspray. You puncture the can, depressurize it, shake it up into a foamy mass, and then drink or inhale it. It has a great kick, like a mule kicking you in the head, opening your skull. Shoe polish can be cooked up into a nice soup that gives you a great high and an everlasting hangover. People will drink anything if they can't have regular booze—perfume, cough medicine, hair conditioner—whatever. The big thing now is "Montana gin"—one bottle of Lysol to a gallon of water. It's a mighty potent brew. One guy, who reversed the ratio, bloated up, turned black, and died. You can also strain Lysol through bread. It will get you blind drunk, but you don't stagger, so they tell me. Whatever bad things go on in New York, Chicago, or L.A. eventually find their way to the res. Many people on the res are on drugs and alcohol at the same time—cruisin' and boozin'. I was lucky and never got into hard drugs. I smoked a little pej once in a while, but that was all.

Housing is one of the biggest problems. There's new housing, but rents start at $190 and go up to $500—depending on how many people there are in the family and how many rooms you need. If you are on GA or ADC you can't afford it. Then you look for somebody to rent you an old shack or trailer. I went through a dozen "homes" during the last few years. You scrape together enough for the first month's rent. Then you stop paying. You hang on for as long as you can while the owner tries to get rid of you. In the end he succeeds. Then the same circle of looking for a place you can afford starts all over again. When we had to camp out, with a tipi, a propane stove, and a brush shelter, the kids loved it. They had a large area to explore and play in, and a stream for swimming, but I had gotten too old for it. Whenever it rained you had to run and pack everything away. There was water in the tipi—it was dripping through the smoke hole on top—and outside, the mud was ankle-deep.

Last summer we stayed in a run-down trailer at Antelope. The plywood floor was so rotten you could stick a finger through it. As soon as you entered there was a big hole in the floor. I put a little ratty rug over the hole, praying nobody would step through it and break a leg. Electricity worked only in the living room. In one small bedroom was a red light, which made it look like a photographic darkroom being used. You had to be an Einstein to make the toilet flush, which posed a highly technical challenge. Over the front door I nailed a sign: THIS PROPERTY INSURED BY SMITH AND WESSON. This seemed to help, as nobody ever tried to break in. As usual we failed to keep up paying the rent and had to move again.

We got another trailer house in Antelope from an Indian lady. It had a phone, and even cable TV, but it didn't have hot water and the kids had to bathe in a little tin tub filled with water heated on the stove. Also, the trailer was located in a "too friendly" neighborhood, meaning that we were overrun with people coming in with one or two twelve-packs, guzzling beer into the wee hours, so that we got nothing done.

For two months last summer I lived in what I called "my little home on the prairie," a hundred-year-old log cabin with an earth floor and no electricity. There was a pump outside, at some distance. It also had the standard outdoor privy with a million buzzing flies, and a big wood stove inside. And that was it. As long as it was warm, it was not a bad place to live. We were out in the rolling hills. The only thing you could hear were two magpies who came around during the day. We ate commodities and I baked my own bread. Of course, if the car broke down, which happened all the time, I was marooned, cut off from the world. As soon as it started getting cold, I had to move again. You could not live in that place during a South Dakota winter.

Things are going from bad to worse. Nowadays, if you want to get a place you have to apply to the housing board in your old community. Then they'll look at your finance records, and if you have any bad credit with the board, you won't get the place until you pay up. Most people owe so much back rent that they'll never be able to pay it all. So some folks live in abandoned car wrecks or even prehistoric-style earth lodges.

When things get absolutely desperate we move in with Mom. She has a "normal," that is a white-style, lower-middle-class, home, very nicely kept. She has a steady job at the elementary school in He Dog and my stepfather is a retired teacher with a pension. They are part of the minority that has a steady income. As a result, everybody is hitting them up for money and a place to stay. Recently everybody was camping out at Mom's—myself with Rudi and the four children, my sister Sandra with her baby, another relative with one more baby, and one of my brothers. My brother is a computer technician with a bachelor's degree, but there's no job for him. He is overqualified. If there is a position to be filled, you're always overqualified or underqualified, unless you are a relative of one of our big shot politicians. There's only one bathroom at my Mom's place. Well, use your imagination. We all try to have our own places and not drive my mother crazy, but sometimes we are still like little chicks crawling under the wings of the mother hen for a little warmth.

At the moment we have a trailer for ourselves. Everything in it breaks down—the fridge one day, the stove another—but Rudi is a good fixer.

The health service is not too good either. A lot of people don't trust doctors and would rather go to a medicine man for help. A lot of infants die of something called "infant diarrhea." You have to have a 106-degree fever before they'll admit you to the hospital and anything really serious they refuse to handle. When I had my major car wreck they flew me to Sioux Falls. The same thing happened to Bobby Leader Charge when a white drunk ventilated him with an AK-47.

Then there's the problem of race relations. A lot of people try to forget about it, but there are a few who have been hurt by the eternal wrangle of how much Indian blood you have—one-half, one-fourth, one-eighth—or whether you are tribally enrolled or not. I was often put down because I am an iyeska, a half-breed. I felt at home in AIM because they just identified themselves as red people, not as full-bloods or breeds. They accepted you for your attitude, not for your bloodline. When I moved to the Paradise, some of Crow Dog's relations gave me a hard time. Sometimes, when I disagreed with Leonard, he'd say I had an "iyeska attitude." On the other hand, I think that the ikche wichasha, the full-bloods, have some reason to be prejudiced against the breeds, because they and the whites control everything. It is hard for a full-blood to get a job or a loan. The iyeska call the full-bloods "stupid, uneducated back numbers," while the full-bloods retaliate by calling them people who identify with the white man, money grubbers who've forgotten what it means to be an Indian. There are many good iyeska who are grass-roots people, keeping the old tradition, but both sides often stereotype each other. And there's the land problem. Years ago a tribal chairman started the TLE—Tribal Lands Enterprises—which made it legal to lease reservation land to white ranchers. Once a year the people get their lease money, often their only income. But some haven't gotten any money for years because it is caught up in the usual red tape connected with everything having to do with government. The res is now like a checkerboard with half the squares owned or leased by whites. Relations between full- and half-bloods, however, are improving. Our little local Sinte Gleska College (Spotted Tail College in English) has helped a lot and done some good things, such as getting the two sides together and reviving the use of the Lakota language. Once a person speaks Lakota he or she is accepted by the full-bloods as one of theirs. At that college they learn to help each other instead of working against each other. Lionel Bordeaux started this program and deserves the credit.

If I had my way, people would be more self-sufficient, not dependent on Washington. They should have cheaper, better housing and more space to plant some trees and have kitchen gardens. Women should get together and talk about how to change things for the better. There are programs for women who are trying to get their families together, but there are not enough social workers getting out to the people. And many women cannot go to these meetings because they have no car or gas money. The Native American Church has a women's auxiliary that does good work. They encourage us to do traditional crafts. Many people do beautiful bead- and quillwork but have to travel far to find an outlet. I myself make beaded and feathered earrings that I have no trouble selling in Phoenix or Santa Fe, but for which I have no outlets on the res.

Things are not all bad. The land is beautiful. Life is laid-back and we do not have the all-American rat race. The days pass slowly, on Indian time. Uptown, young people are cruising or parking, talking to old friends, or meeting new ones. They have a beer or two. They joke. The boys make eyes at the girls. The girls giggle. They listen to rock 'n' roll or country music. They sing forty-niner songs. You go to the club and there is a line of white cowboys with their big hats on, having a Coors. They have their rodeos and watch their livestock, mostly keeping to themselves. They don't mingle much, but there's no friction. We have "sobriety dances." You go dancing on the weekend. You sip soft drinks. There are nice snacks, but no alcohol at all. And you'll ask someone: "How long since you quit drinking?" And they'll answer: "Since yesterday." And some guy will tease me: "Don't do anything I wouldn't do," and I tell him: "I've already done everything."

I'm forever bouncing back and forth between the white and the Indian world. When I'm on my "white and middle-class" binge, I get up, turn on the radio real loud, put on my face, even paint my nails and tease or frizz my hair with a rouche on top. I can't exist without constant music. Rock 'n' roll, hit songs, country music. I am addicted to modern Sioux songs by Jackie Bird. I put the same tape of hers on again and again. I eat junk food and get fat. I drink margaritas instead of Bud. The TV is on all day, even if nobody watches. And then, one day, I look at myself in the mirror and say: "Shit, what is going on here?" And let my hair hang loose, Indian style, put on a choker, go to a meeting, take medicine, go to the yuwipi, sing forty-niner songs, eat wasna and wojapi, happy at being Indian again. I guess my "white man" binges are due to having been exposed to middle-class comforts in New York.

And then something very bad happens. Today, the fight for Native American rights is, above all, a fight for our land and environment. The land is a living part of ourselves. Once it is gone, we are gone. The fight is not merely preaching against Styrofoam, aerosol, and Pampers, which are all bad, though I do that too. Or fighting against trash being burned in open dumps. Or trying to stop trucks with uranium waste from the Edgemont area driving through the res. Now some entrepreneurs from Connecticut, and the East generally, want to turn our reservation into a garbage dump. The wasichu have already given us smallpox, measles, and whiskey, and now they want to bury us in their waste. The tribal government has sold us out, making deals without a referendum and against the will of the people. The waste disposal firm will send us the crap and filth from Minneapolis, Denver, and other big cities and will bless us with an Everest of garbage on five thousand acres of our most beautiful land situated near some of our most sacred places and not far from Wounded Knee. I have fought for a sovereign Sioux Nation, but in that battle we have been defeated. But when it comes to hazardous waste it is suddenly all right to be a "sovereign tribe," which can be exempted from protective environmental laws and regulations. So now these firms come to us with their garbage. They do so not only to get around laws that protect white Americans, but because it is also so much cheaper. "Those benighted Indians," these people reason, "are so desperate for money that they'll accept any terms offered."

The contract our tribal leaders signed reads in part: "In no event shall any environmental regulations or standards of South Dakota be applicable to this project." On top of that, these polluters shall have the sole right to decide what kind of shit, poison, toxic or hazardous waste they will dump on us. If, at some later date, the tribe should adopt stricter standards for waste disposal, then we must compensate those bastards for the costs arising from the new rules. And, of course, we will have to live with whatever they dump on us forever. For allowing them to do this to us, they will pay to the tribe the magnificent sum of one dollar for every ton of waste. I do not know if and what our great iyeska leaders got paid under the table for selling us out, but if we find out that somebody has been bribed, there will be a sharpening of scalping knives. In the meantime, we'll struggle against an incoming tide of the white man's offal. Most of the tribal council people now agree with us.

Every year some two hundred thousand motor bikers hold a huge powwow at Sturgis, South Dakota, at the edge of the Black Hills. With their shaggy beards and tattoos, they are often called rough, barbaric Archie Bunker types. But many of those bikers offered to help us fight the waste dumpers. They came down to Rosebud wearing T-shirts with slogans printed on them: REMEMBER WHEN SEX WAS SAFE AND BIKERS WERE DANGEROUS? This country must really be going to the dogs when even bikers turn environmentalists. We found them to be nice, jolly, concerned men and women. They wanted to hold an antidumping demonstration on the res, in Ghost Hawk Park, but the politicians forbade it. After reading this chapter, it won't surprise you that I sank into a deep canyon of depression and tried once more to find consolation in a bottle.

CHAPTER FOURTEEN

On a Tear

I was drinking again, doing some very heavy boozing. I was on a big tear and it went on for a long time, from the summer of 1990 to the spring of 1991. This whole period of my life I spent in a haze, in a fog. I think that during all that time I was hardly ever sober. AIM and all the other Indian rights organizations recognize alcoholism as our number one problem and they try all kinds of approaches, but nothing seems to work. You can't solve the drinking problem without getting rid of its causes but you can't do this either, because it is the government and white society that are at the root of the problem, and both are beyond our power and influence. That goes not only for our Sioux reservations but for nearly all tribes in the United States. It is the whites who manufacture the booze, who transport and distribute it among us, who profit from it, and who make the laws governing the sale of liquor. It is the neglect of society at large that makes it impossible for us to rise from our abject poverty. So we drown our misery in cheap wine and whiskey.

The possession or sale of alcohol used to be illegal on both Pine Ridge and Rosebud. The result was that many Sioux men became bootleggers in a small, you could say family, way. Last summer they opened up the Rosebud Reservation to liquor and now it's everywhere. Anyone who has the money and the right connections can open a bar or a "club." There is one outside Mission. It enforces strict rules because they've had too many fights in there. If you cause trouble more than once, you're banned forever. We have a liquor store, the R & R, just outside Mission. Other places on the res have bars, too. The reasoning behind the new law was that if liquor was made legal, we'd have fewer accidents. Before, if you lived in Mission you had to go all the way down to Nebraska to get smashed—a ninety-mile round trip. If you lived someplace else on the res you might have to drive even farther to get your favorite poison. You got drunk in Valentine, forty miles south of the res in Nebraska, or Murdo, outside the res in the north, and then wrecked on the long way home. Allowing liquor on the res, close to where you lived, was supposed to prevent injuries and deaths caused by drunken driving. Personally, I have a hunch that as many people as before are DWI, driving while intoxicated, and that the number of accidents is more or less the same. On neigh-boring Pine Ridge, booze is still outlawed. You get arrested, jailed, and fined if the tribal police find just one single can of beer in your car. But alcoholism on Pine Ridge is still about the same as on Rosebud. Right now, the people from the Ridge go to White Clay for their beer. It's only two miles outside the res. They drink quarts, mostly Old Milwaukee or Busch, whichever is cheaper. If you want hard liquor, you have to go farther down the road, maybe all the way to Gordon, Nebraska. White Clay is notorious for fights. People are trying to hustle money for beer. You can bring in a diamond ring and they'll give you a case for it. Whether a reservation allows liquor or not does not seem to make much difference.

We are a socializing, gregarious people. We like to visit back and forth, to get together, chat, gossip, and joke. That's the chief pastime. In fact, the only one. But there's hardly a get-together without drinking. The favorite activity is playing quarter pitch and spinners. To play quarter pitch, you try to bounce, or rather ricochet, a quarter into a glass of beer. The loser has to drink it. There are a lot of other rules, but that's the basic thing. And, after a night of quarter pitch, forget it! Then you can play spinners, where you spin a quarter and pick heads or tails with other players. The loser then has to drink continuously while the quarter is spinning again. When playing either quarter pitch or spinners, you can go through a case of beer in twenty minutes. It's fun and it's deadly. It costs a lot of money to go out drinking at the clubs, so a lot of people will just buy their beer and go home to play quarter pitch. Everybody gets caught up in the fun and excitement, and everybody gets drunk. My resistance to alcohol is much lower than it used to be, because I hardly touch a drop now, and Rudi doesn't want either of us to get soused. But when we got married our Indian friends in Santa Fe threw us a big party at a public campground, high up on the mountain, halfway to the ski basin. And, of course, they had some big coolers full of beer and started a game of quarter pitch. And they picked on Rudi, because he was new at the game. To please them, he drank like a good boy, but he wasn't used to drinking, and he passed out on his bed. When I went in to kiss him I missed the bed altogether and wound up on the floor. Well, that was our only relapse since we got together.

While I was on my gigantic binge I still had enough awareness left to know that I needed help, that I should get into treatment or counseling. Leonard got on my case about it. His answer was always: "We have the medicine, we have the peyote, we have the pipe, we have the sweat lodge. There are elders here you can talk to." That's good, but in retrospect, I am sorry I did not seek professional help at the time. It might not have worked, but it would have been worth the try. I brushed with death many times during that nine-month binge, totaling no less than five cars.

One time, my sister Barb and I were partying, when things got rowdy and ended up in a drunken orgy. So Barb said: "Let's go while the going is good," but I was in no mood to quit. Barb gave up on me, saying: "I've had enough of this shit," and took off. Finally, I decided to go look for my sister. I got into the car and went after Barb. I still had a full bottle of Canadian whiskey, and I was drinking it. I was barreling down the road, almost blind drunk, taking big swigs from the bottle with one hand, driving with the other. I couldn't find Barb, so I went heading west toward Parmelee, and then everything started spinning around—my head, the car, the whole world. And that's the last thing I remember. After that there was nothingness. I woke up the next morning in the passenger's seat, wondering how I had managed to get there. I noticed the whiskey. There was still some left, so I drank it. I got into the driver's seat and tried to start the car but couldn't. It was probably out of gas, but in my state of confusion, I couldn't be sure of that. I crawled out of the car to investigate and found I had stopped an inch from a steep ravine. One little inch more, and that would have been that. I stumbled to the road and tried to hitch a ride. I saw a big prairie fire going on nearby, the wind whipping up the flames. For a moment I wondered whether this was just my imagination, or whether the fire was real. It was, because there was a fire truck, which picked me up and dropped me at the junction. I walked home from there, slowly sobering up. I told my friends: "I almost killed myself," but they just laughed it off.

I was still on my binge when my first book came out and I had to go to New York and Washington on a publicity tour. In Manhattan I stayed part of the time with my coauthor and his wife, and part of the time with Marilyn, a white lady friend from the old civil rights days. I had been out with some friends partying and when I arrived at Richard's place, he said: "Mary, you're totally out of it. Jean has to put you to bed. You've got to sleep it off and stay sober. We'll be interviewed tomorrow." Jean bedded me down but as soon as she and Richard were asleep, I got up, dressed, and sneaked out of the apartment. It was on the West Side, on Eighty-ninth Street. I found a bar open and went in there, ordering some margaritas. The barkeep said: "You're too drunk. I won't serve you." I got rowdy, and probably obscene. I got into a cab and asked the driver, who was a Puerto Rican guy, if he knew where to get some pej, some pot. "Sure," he said. "Let's go for a ride!" He turned the meter off and drove straight to Harlem. There he took me to the house of a dealer, a black guy with whom I got into an argument about the price. The guy got ugly and threatened me with a knife. I said: "Go on, you're just a pussy!" The cabdriver pulled me back into his taxi and took off at high speed, tires screeching. He almost had a heart attack. "Jesus, lady," he said, "are all Indians that crazy? Do you want to get us killed?" He gave me a talking-to. He drove me around for two hours, showing me New York at nighttime. He didn't even charge me. I'll be eternally grateful to this man. He could have robbed me or raped me, instead of which he acted like a father. I don't know how I could have remembered the way home, or Richard's address, but somehow I made it back. I didn't need a key to get in, because I'd never locked the apartment door. In the morning I was all innocence. Jean and Richard had not even noticed that I had been out and on a night ride. I later told them as much as I could remember. "You don't know how lucky you are," was all that Richard managed to say.

Then we all went to D.C. on the Metroliner. I was on my best behavior. We had good interviews. I was as sober as a judge. At the Larry King show, all went well. Then disaster struck again. At the fancy hotel our publisher had checked us into, Jean and Richard had one room, I the other. There was a sort of square nightstand with a lamp on it. I noticed at once that it was really an icebox full of bottles of beer and the most delicious hard stuff. I started to work on it. When Richard came to wake me up in the morning he found me totally wasted and the room in an unimaginable mess. He had a similar icebox in his room. You are supposed to take one of these little bottles for a nightcap and the hotel later charges you for it. Richard and Jean were too straight to take it for anything but a lampstand.

How they got me into a cab to the railroad station I don't know.

The driver was a young man from Ethiopia. I climbed into the front seat with him and tried to steer his taxi and we had quite a tussle. On the train I got into an argument with a ticket collector, calling her all kinds of names. She almost had us put off the train at Wilmington. Richard pushed me into a corner and said: "Let's sing peyote songs!" This distracted me enough so that I caused no further disturbance. The rest of the way to New York we just kept singing, to the wonderment of the other passengers. I was still pretty much buzzed during the next few interviews at our publisher's. I don't know what my emptying that lampstand icebox cost Grove. It must have been a nifty sum, because on subsequent stays to publicize the book in a number of cities, the publisher made sure that I was not led into temptation. As far as Richard and Jean are concerned, I can only say that they are very patient.

Back at home after my tour, I went on as before. When you are drunk you do the craziest things. At the Rosebud Fair I met a kid who was half my age. We were drinking beer and tequila. It was hot, a real sizzler, which only heightened the effect of the alcohol. I was grounded, meaning I had no car. Or, rather, the last one I had wrecked was in the repair shop and I did not have the money to get it out. I felt caged, a bird without wings, restless, impatient. The kid said: "I'm supposed to break horses on the Wind River Shoshone Reservation in Wyoming." I said: "What are we waiting for? Let's go. Hiyupo!" The kid didn't have wheels either, so we hitched rides, guzzling beer all the way, from Kilgore to Valentine, to Pine Ridge, to Everett, to the Wild Rice Festival. We even stopped at the Long Horn Saloon in Scenic, a dark, gloomy place that still has five inches of sawdust on the floor. In the old days it had a sign saying NO INDIANS ALLOWED, but now it only had a cage for locking up rambunctious skins. Every now and then, as we drove along, I would sing out: "Stop, stop! A neon, a neon!" Meaning a package store with a neon sign reading "Bud," "Coors," or "Miller." It was a mad ride from neon to neon. We fell in with Dan and Orville White Butterfly, who offered us a ride. It was not exactly where we wanted to go, but at least they were going north. What the hell! They dumped us in Lame Deer, Montana, on the Northern Cheyenne Reservation. The kid and I were so out of it that we forgot our stuff, which was in the White Butterfly's trunk. We were standing there, freezing, when a typical derelict "Indian" car came wheezing up. Inside were two Cheyennes, two cases of beer, and two bottles of Jack Daniel's—two of everything. They took us to their shack, way up in the mountains, and we stayed there the whole night through until "two of everything" was gone. Our new companions got us back to the highway, but while we were waiting to thumb a ride, someone reported us to the local police. We were arrested for public intoxication. The cops took us to the nearest jail, telling us: "We are doing you a favor. In the state you're in, you're a danger to yourself." They threw us into the drunk tank and didn't release us until six the next morning. I had nothing left. The only thing I had on me when we were arrested were my numchucks, which I carried for protection but the cops seized as a dangerous weapon.

The weather had suddenly changed, as it often does in the mountains. We were left standing on the road without jackets, freezing. Whatever money we had set out with was long spent—for beer mostly. I had only enough left for a phone call to get some friend to wire us some mazaska, but the only phone I could find was broken. We were shivering and our teeth were going like castanets. The ground was covered with frost. At 7:00 A.M. the jail door opened as they let out another wino, a Cheyenne who owned a car without a heater. He took us to his place in Lodge Grass, Montana. At least it had a stove and some wood to get us deiced. The walls of his cabin were covered with *Playboy* triple-spreads. He treated us to some pan-fried bread and luncheon meat. He invited us to have some Montana gin, that is to suck up Lysol through a slice of bread, but we had just enough sense left to decline. The Montana gin soon had him lying on the floor, open-mouthed, his eyes bulging, but, thank God, still breathing. We stumbled around in the wilderness but finally got a ride with some Crows. We were now in Crow country. Our new friends took us to their home in the Big Horn Mountains. They gave us a hot meal, hot coffee, and coke, which got us sober. They also gave us all the money they had on them, nine bucks—Crows, our former arch-enemies! It got us to Landers, Wyoming, and from there we walked ten miles to the kid's uncle, who was half Shoshone and half Sioux.

After it turned out that the kid wasn't particularly good at breaking horses, and instead almost broke his back, we decided it was time to go home. I was still without wheels. I found a used-car lot where they had a clunker with a five-hundred-dollar price tag. It was a mess but the motor was still in halfway usable shape. I phoned Richard, who was by then back in Santa Fe, for help. He wired the money. The car lasted exactly one day before the kid totaled it. Richard called all this a "remarkable odyssey, a real anabasis," whatever that meant. As I said before, he has a patient heart.

When you are drunk, you get into fights. You tie one on, and then you look for your enemies. If there are no enemies, you fight with friends. You get into free-for-alls, even if that's the last thing you want. I went partying in Valentine, Nebraska, forty miles south of the res, with two friends, George and Ron. I was drinking Everclear, grain alcohol, 150 proof, and was lila itomni, real drunk. George called me into the back room and said: "I don't really feel like going back to the res." I said: "Me neither. At least not for a while. I'll party a little bit more and go back later." I was admiring a cute little baby and when the mother, who was also far gone on Everclear, showed up she thought that I wanted to steal her baby. I told her I had enough babies of my own. It just turned into a big old-fashioned bar fight. Her whole family got into it, and George and Ronny, too. There were more of them and they got the better of us. That woman went berserk. She went outside, got hold of a hammer or rock, and was smashing up the windows of our car.

Before she could finish the job, we just jumped in and took off. It was about 1:00 A.M. and freezing. We got out of Valentine and as far as the cemetery when the car broke down. We were all booze-blind and beat up. A trucker stopped and took us all back to Mission. I should have called my sister Barb and Jim, her husband, but I didn't think of it. I was beat up so bad that I went into shock. I could hardly talk. My face was so black and swollen even my best friends could not recognize me. They took me to the hospital. The police came, took pictures of my face, and wrote down my statement. After that I hyperventilated. I couldn't breathe. I thought I was dying. That went on for some two hours until a nurse came and gave me a shot. When they let me out, Jim had one look at me and was ready to load his shotgun to do some damage. He only calmed down after somebody told him that the people who had beaten me up, the whole family, were medically insane and suffering from delusions. That was the first and definitely the last time I drank Everclear.

I got into a fight at Irish's bar with a close friend of mine named Tina. We were both pretty drunk and I said: "Those are my beers." We started shoving each other, and she pushed me over the table. I fell and hit my head right on the corner, which gave me a big shiner. We hugged and made up at once. She is one of my best friends, but when you are soused you don't know who you are and who everybody else is. That is why friends, even brothers, sometimes kill and maim each other in a red haze of drunkenness.

While I was in Santa Fe to do taping for this book I got some money from my publisher and used half of it to buy a fancy-looking secondhand car. Then I set out for Rosebud, about eight hundred miles away. Richard was very dubious about my driving alone. But I can be stubborn and insisted there was nothing to it. He said: "For God's sake, don't drink while you are on the road. Don't drink at all. Drive straight home to the res." I promised. I should have listened, but I stopped at Pine Ridge to see an old girlfriend who had been at the Knee with me. Liquor is a criminal offense on the Ridge, so I should have been careful. I was just going to stay over one night and then drive on to Rosebud. I was almost home. But when we ran out of booze we went to a bootlegger who sold us two pints of Canadian Lord Calvert whiskey. I said: "Let's go to the dam at White Clay and watch the sunrise." So we parked up there and got into the Lord Calvert. But after someone reported that I had almost run into somebody, two tribal police guys showed up. They told me to get out of the car. I had been sitting on a dime bag of weed without knowing it. I don't even know to this day how it got there. I was in a jam. Trouble always finds me. Or I find it. Drug possession being a federal offense, the FBI came down from Rapid City. They searched me and found the sixteen hundred dollars I had left from the publisher, money I hoped would last me three months. "Aha," they said, "drug money." They were convinced that if an Indian woman had that much cash on her, it had to be drugs. It was all my own doing. Nobody had put me in that situation. I had put myself there. The FBIs asked me whether I wanted to talk and I said no, an automatic answer ever since my old AIM days. They put me in the can and kept me there over the weekend. I had not even seen my kids yet. I was arraigned on Monday and they let me out on self bond. The judge was a woman and real nice to me, I think because of *Lakota Woman,* which was already out. Of course, they had me on DWI—driving while intoxicated—a mandatory thirty days. Then they charged me with possession of pej. I never went back to court because I did not want to serve the thirty days. I had a hell of a time getting my car back, which was full of presents for the kids. My money had in the meantime gone from Rapid City to Pierre, the state capital. Richard and the publisher had to make innumerable phone calls and send documents that proved that this was honorably earned money. I had to drive ninety miles to Pierre to get it back. For the first time in my life the FBI treated me with a modicum of respect. It was almost as if I had been white. They told me: "You have a book out, and it's good to see somebody from the reservation making something of herself." But they also threatened me: "Don't kid yourself. This won't be swept under the rug."

I climbed into my yellow, fancy-looking car, which already had started crapping out on me, and went home to my mom's, where I dropped off all my stuff. After spending a week in jail I wanted to go to the club and kick back. Most of all, I wanted to be alone with myself. I told Mom: "I have to go to Mission to get something I really need." Then I went to the club. I ended up by buying a case of beer and getting a room in the Antelope Motel. As it snowed outside I sat there, all alone, drinking myself into oblivion—out of disappointment and because of being bone weary of the gypsy life, forever staying in other people's places. I wanted a home where I could raise my kids. I wanted to put down roots. I had a good cry and felt sorry for myself, particularly after the case was gone.

I don't even remember how often I landed in jail in connection with my drinking. Once you get caught up in the scene it is hard to get away from it. There was a point when I just wanted to turn myself in for treatment, because I was aware that it was hurting my kids to see me partying. Whenever things got too bad I'd jump in the car and cruise around drinking. Three years ago I spent New Year's Day in jail. I had been partying, drinking Martini and Rossi, using beer as chasers. Out of the blue, I don't know what drove me, the devil I guess, I said: "I want to go to Parmelee, I want to go to my hometown." On my way to Parmelee I saw a car by the side of the road, broken down or out of gas, and some unhappy guys standing next to it. So I stopped and took them into town. One of them, a young man called Blue Horse, was an old acquaintance of mine. We got to talking and I said: "Hey, you want to go onto Norris and get a twelver?" And he thought that was a great idea. We got the twelver and got back to Parmelee, where I parked the car to open the case and celebrate. That was very stupid, because I parked very close to where a police car had placed itself strategically to watch out for itomni New Year's revelers. Right away there was the cop charging me with reckless driving. He said:

"Your car was seen running into Alonzo Smith's yard, doing considerable damage." I assured him that it wasn't me, that it had to be another car that looked like mine, which was the gospel truth, but I got the heat from that anyway. They took me to jail, and here I was in the drunk tank again, and it was packed. I said: "Happy New Year to all!"

And only two weeks after that incident I, along with my friend Tina, got thrown in again for "public consumption," that is, for drinking beer out in the open, on the street. So that was another "sleeper." They put you in for your own protection and release you after twelve hours. I was sick of myself after that.

Even after my big wreck in March 1991 I was not at once ready to quit. Mom doted on me and did everything she could. I was still in pretty bad shape, but I was also restless and mad because I wasn't able to move around. Mom's place was so crowded that it made me itchy. I felt imprisoned so I got a place of my own. But after I was taken off medication I started to drink beer to ease the pain. I started drinking steadily. Mom got tired of me and said: "You're still in shock. You need to go back to church, you need to see a psychiatrist, you need to go back to the hospital. You don't have a wreck like that and walk away from it and go back doing what you were doing before." But for a good month the drinking helped me fight the pain. Then I didn't need it anymore because there was less pain.

Then one Sunday I went to Debbie's "night club" with some friends of mine. I grew up with Debbie and it was in front of her house that I had my bad car accident. We were sitting around having a few rounds when Debbie came over to our table. She said that if I wanted anything it would be on the house. So I went for it, having double shots of Jack on the rocks, and got pretty loaded. The friends I was with wanted to leave. I said: "I'll just have one more round, I'll find my way back." So they took off, leaving me still downing double shots. Debbie told a friend of hers to take me back to town. He took me back in his van, but he didn't know where I lived, and I was in no condition to show him. He took me to his home in downtown Mission. I was completely gone and only wanted to sober up a bit. He said I could either come into his place or lie there in the van. I told him: "I'll just lie outside for a while." After about fifteen minutes I got up. I did not want to run into any cops, so I just walked around the side streets, but the police found and stopped me anyhow. They said: "Where are you going?" I told them: "I'm just going home. I live right over there. I'm almost home." "Get in," they said. I knew they were taking me to jail for a sleeper.

Again, Mom knew about it from her scanner. And she was upset. I almost got used to that, being in jail. They won't let you make a phone call for twelve hours. If you're intoxicated they'll put you in the drunk tank. While in there I'd meet people I knew. At least if you're in with other people it's better, you can talk, and it helps pass the time. You can sing together, sing the AIM song or forty-niners. There's not many fights in there; we'll talk and joke—"I wonder what we'll be eating." And we know what we'll be eating—a little bit of oatmeal with cold, bitter coffee. That'll be your breakfast. The food is terrible. But one time we got thrown in the jail at Kyle, on the Pine Ridge Reservation, for a liquor violation, and they fed us good! But the Rosebud jail is bad. The drunk tank is just a toilet, a floor, a sink, and a camera so they can keep tabs on you. No beds. A cold tile floor. When someone flushes the toilet it's so loud it echoes, and the whole building shakes as in an earthquake. You'll hear keys jingling outside, followed by voices: "Jailer, what time is it?" "What time do we go to court?" "Can I make a phone call?" But you don't get to do anything. You can rant and rave but it doesn't do you any good. Then they put you in a cell, with usually four beds. You have to carry in your own mattress, and they have sticky, itchy, old wool blankets, but by then you're grateful to have them, after being in the "chill tank." They are pretty cold-blooded in the Rosebud jail. It has a sign over the entrance reading HEARTBREAK HOTEL, and they aren't kidding.

Of all the different groups and races that make up the so-called melting pot, we Native Americans have the highest suicide rate. And that again is linked to despair, which, in turn, leads to drinking. One could even say that driving while intoxicated is a form of Indian suicide, because so many die from it, or are maimed for life. One suicide, committed two years ago by a close friend of mine, still haunts my sleep. His name was Pewee Leader Charge. He was a kind and gentle man, immensely talented, a fine artist and gifted poet. He was in Vietnam and received a terrible wound that left him with a bad limp. He had been a member of AIM and was at Wounded Knee during the siege. He was also an incurable alcoholic. For a time he was married to one of the most beautiful full-blood women I ever met, a Navajo whom he had met while in college. They had a child, a lovely girl named Anpo-Wichahpi, meaning Morning Star. His wife's mother ran an antialcoholism center at Fort Defiance, in Arizona, and she was always after Pewee to make a solemn oath in the presence of others, promising to quit drinking. And always he refused, saying that he was not ready and did not want to make promises he could not keep. His wife finally left him when she saw that she would never be able to stop his drinking. So he came back to South Dakota.

He tried many things, but always alcohol messed up everything. He was thrown in jail, again and again. Sometimes his own mother called the cops on him. You couldn't blame her altogether. She could not handle it anymore. She just got tired of bailing him out, time after time, and paying his fines.

I had great love and respect for Pewee because he was very much involved in the ancient beliefs of our people. I grew up with him and it was he who took me to my first sun dance and showed me its beauty and meaning. The summer he returned to South Dakota he wanted to pierce at Joe Eagle Elk's sun dance, but his mother told him not to do this because he was not worthy, because he drank too much. And that hurt. It might have been the last straw. He got drunk and wound up in jail—for the last time, as it turned out. His mother would not bail him out. She had long ago given up on him. And it was true, he was hopelessly tied to the bottle, and all his intellect and talents could not help him. Two veterans from Nam, Bill and Jack Menard, tried to get him out of jail. They went to the tribal judge and asked him to release Pewee because he was still suffering from his old wound as well as damage from Agent Orange and Vietnam stress syndrome. The judge refused to let him go.

I was sitting under the arbor after the sun dance, at Crow Dog's Paradise, when Pewee's youngest brother, Bobby, came up to me with tears in his eyes, telling me that Pewee had hanged himself in jail. They have TV cameras in the cell and the jailer is supposed to watch them all the time, but nobody was watching when Pewee died. There was a rumor that the jailer was making it with one of the girls who take the calls. There are always rumors. I was stunned. I felt a cold hand squeezing my chest. Then the tears came. Pewee was me, was all of us.

Bobby showed me Pewee's suicide note, addressed to his sister, Rita. He said that he was just tired of it all, tired of being always a scapegoat, tired of the life he was leading. He wrote that he loved his family very much, but that they all could go to hell. He asked that Crow Dog should bury him in the traditional way, not in a coffin, but in a star blanket after being put for a while on an old-style funeral scaffold. He wanted to be with the old people who had died a hundred years ago. He did not want a Christian burial. Neither did he want his body to be transported in a car. He wanted to be driven in a wagon drawn by horses. He named who his pallbearers should be, the ones who would carry him in his blanket. He wanted only Vietnam and Wounded Knee veterans to bury him. He wanted to be laid out in a tipi, and they used one of Jerry Roy's for that. Being a good artist, he made drawings of what his funeral should be like. At his grave he wanted a buffalo skull, his sun dance outfit, his pipe, and all his sacred things. I felt so bad when I went to his wake. All the traditional people came, the whole town of Parmelee. My mother came and was overwhelmed by the beauty of his old-style going to another world. Everybody prayed—in Lakota and English, in a Christian, or peyote, or Sioux religion way. When they buried him in Grandmother's bosom, an eagle circled overhead. People said that it was Tunkashila taking Pewee to the spirit world. After that I had a kind of breakdown. I said to myself, over and over again, why did he have to go like that? I got a case of beer and just drank.

But by his death, Pewee made me a great gift. His suicide was one of the main reasons I finally quit drinking for good. I knew I was depressed but that drinking only made it worse. I thought: "Pewee is gone, but what about myself? Alcohol almost took me to the other side, where Pewee is now." I wanted to commit suicide myself. Mom said to me: "Don't even think about this. You have a family. You think you're alone. You are not alone. We are all praying for you, worrying about you. You have a life to live. Choose life over death. You have been away from us too long. You'd better go to church, or to your peyote church, or to a doctor, or to Uncle Fool Bull, who is a medicine man. You have to straighten up and get well." So one morning I got up, smiled at myself in the mirror, and poured the last bottle of Jack down the drain.

I do not want to give a wrong impression. There is good beside the bad on the res. Nature is beautiful, and there is bravery in the face of adversity. There is goodness and people helping each other, poor people sharing what they have with those who have even less. We have stouthearted women and great pow-wows, songs and ceremonies. We have our sacred medicine and eagles are still flying over the sandhills. But drinking is a great problem. I would like to dedicate this chapter to the Pima Indian Ira Hayes, hero of Iwo Jima, holder of the Congressional Medal of Honor, who, being drunk, drowned in a ditch. He was one more victim of a country that has no use for its heroes if they happen to be Native Americans.

CHAPTER FIFTEEN

Bleeding Always Stops If You Press Down Hard Enough

In 1973, inside Wounded Knee, during the siege, volunteers set up a clinic. Mostly this was the work of our women. There were frequent firefights and as a result we had a number of people with gunshot wounds. I remember a sign tacked to the wall of our homemade "hospital": BLEEDING ALWAYS STOPS IF YOU PRESS DOWN HARD ENOUGH. This was meant literally, but for me it was symbolic—in my mind Indian women are always pressing down hard to stop the bleeding of their hearts. It is not easy to be a Native American woman. In 1977, during a big honoring feast for Crow Dog, I was honored too. Two medicine men, Bill Eagle Feathers and Wallace Black Elk, gave me a new name—Ohitika Win, meaning Brave Woman. They painted the partition of my hair red and fastened an eagle plume to the side of my head. But I have a feeling that most of the Indian women I know are Ohitika Win, are very brave. You have to be to live under this government, in the shadow of poverty, scratching out a living and raising children amid the disintegration of so many of our old ways, the falling apart of our reservations.

There has always been a contradiction between two different

views our men hold in regard to us women. On the one hand, Lakota society was male-oriented, as is usual among tribes of nomadic hunter-warriors. It is among the sedentary corn-planting pueblos that society is women-oriented. In some ways we have overromanticized the good old days when the "red knights of the prairie," the proud, hard-riding warriors, the "noble savages," ruled the land west of the Missouri River, when millions of buffalo were there for the taking. Women held a place of honor then, but even at that time there were many customs that were not romantic at all. A man who got tired of his wife might step into the dance circle and throw a bone into the air, singing: "Like this I throw this woman away," leaving her helpless and unprotected. A jealous husband could cut off the tip of his wife's nose for adultery, to make her less attractive to others. But if he took a girl behind the bushes there was no cutting off *his* nose. Women did almost all the work. While young women and girls wore hair ropes between their legs, as a sort of chastity belt, to preserve their virtue, a young man might make a name for himself as a seducer, as if he had done a brave deed in war. Women gathered the wood, sometimes bent over under the weight of their burden. Early white settlers were astounded to see that Indian women could carry heavier loads than white men. Our women were up earlier than the men, fetching water from the stream. It was the women who put up or took down the tipi. There was a communication gap between male and female. To "speak with a woman" did not mean having a conversation, it meant wanting to make love. Some of this attitude is still expressed today through supposedly funny posters like: "Before the white man came, there were no taxes, no telephones, no jails, no nuthouses. Women did all the work. And the dumb white man thought he could improve upon a system like that."

The warrior's excuse for letting the women do most of the work was that at all times he had to have his hands free to hunt, if there was an opportunity, or to defend his family in case of a sudden attack by enemies. There was some truth in this, though the men overdid it with their "must have my hands free" business. Yet a white man was wrong when he made this poem:

> *Pity the poor squaw,*
> *Beast of burden and slave,*
> *Chained by tribal law*
> *From girlhood to grave.*

Women were more honored among us than among whites. During much of the nineteenth century, many American women did not have the right to own property. Our women always did. The tipi belonged to the wife, just as in the southwestern pueblos the house belonged to the woman. Among whites, even the upper-class lady could take no part in politics. American women did not get the right to vote until 1920. Compare this with the women of the Iroquois Longhouse, who elected the tribe's chiefs.

If the Sioux of old were male chauvinists on one side, they were feminists on the other. They prayed to Wakan Tanka, whom they also called Tunkashila, the Grandfather Spirit. But the most important supernatural being in their mythology was Ptesan Win, the White Buffalo Calf Woman, who brought the sacred pipe to the Lakota, taught them its use, taught them, as a matter of fact, how to live as human beings. To emphasize her power, there is the tale that she first appeared to two young hunters, one of whom stretched out his hand to possess her physically. For this lack of respect he was burned up and reduced to a little heap of charred bones and ashes. This is a strange sort of mythology for a tribe whose young men boast of their sexual conquests. Our old tales also talk of Wohpe, another great supernatural being, whom a white person might call a goddess of love and beauty and purity, a woman and a shooting star at the same time. And there is the mystical woman who, in times long past, got pregnant by swallowing a pebble, giving birth to Iyan-Hokshi, the Stone Boy, heroic slayer of an evil witch. Unlike Wakan Tanka–Tunkashila, who, like the God of the Christians, never appears as a person, Ptesan Win and Wohpe are beautiful female beings. It is said that the White Buffalo Calf Woman dazzled humans with her unearthly beauty. In some tales, she appears to the hunters as a young girl in a shining white buckskin dress, and in others as naked, clothed only in her flowing raven hair. When she leaves the tribe, after teaching them all they need to know, she transforms herself into a white buffalo calf, symbolizing the close relationship between the people and this holy animal, who gave of itself so that the humans could live, whose skull is our sacred altar. And just as Ptesan Win instructed men and women in all the different aspects of life, so the buffalo gave us all the physical things we needed to survive—its flesh nourished us; out of its fur and hide we made robes and blankets; and out of its bones knives, needles, shovels, awls, even play sleds for the children. While it is impossible to imagine how Wakan Tanka–Tunkashila looks, if indeed he has a visible form, Ptesan Win and Wohpe appear in human shape. So the macho Sioux have what the anthros call a "culture heroine," but no real culture hero.

The contradictions go further still. While the men try to dominate women, they are actually afraid of them. The power of a woman on her moon—that is, while menstruating—is believed to overwhelm the power of even the greatest medicine man. Also, in old Sioux society the woman, the proverbial "burden carrier," won honors for doing the finest beadwork or making the most beautiful cradleboard, honors equal to a man counting coup upon an enemy. Bearing a child was looked upon as being the equal of a warrior's great deed in battle. Even a little girl having her ears ritually pierced during a sun dance earned as much respect as a man who had hung from the tree, or pulled buffalo skulls. A girl was given a lavish feast when she was on her first moon and, when a little older, was honored again through the performance of the ball-throwing ceremony. Finally, a hunter was looked down upon if he did not share his catch with the helpless ones, the widows and orphans of the tribe. It is sad that these two great rituals that celebrated a girl's transformation into a woman are now only seldom performed and almost forgotten. I think it would help us a great deal, and make for more harmony between men and women, if these ceremonies were revived. In those rituals that have withstood the suppression of Indian religion and are still performed throughout the reservation, we still have a lot of symbolism that puts women in an exalted place. The sweat lodge was the female universe. The little sacred mound represented Maka, the Earth, the nourishing All-mother. The earth was also called Unchi—Grandmother. The impregnating sky was male, the conceiving earth female. One reason for the Lakotas' aversion to becoming farmers was their belief that "you should not cut Grandmother's hair, or rip up her bowels," meaning that you should not dig up and plow the earth or cut the plants growing out of the soil. Woman was the firekeeper, the bringer of the water of life. Woman stood for continuity, creation, and survival.

Similar views and symbolisms are found in almost all Native American tribes. Among the Pueblos, Navajos, and Iroquois, descent was always traced through the women. In some Pueblo tribes, children are given their mother's family name. Sons join the religious society, the kiva, of their maternal uncle, not that of their father. In the old days, if a Pueblo woman wanted to divorce her husband, all she had to do was put his moccasins outside her door. Then he had to leave. Among the Navajo the posts holding up the hogan represent supernatural female spirits, again symbolizing that it is the woman who holds a family together.

The Navajo also have a woman supernatural being, Spider Woman, who is also a part of Hopi mythology. Called Kokyang Wuhai by the Hopi, she is a most powerful being. She is one, but also many. Her powers are both positive and negative. And among the Keresan-speaking Pueblos, a goddess called Tse Che Nako brought the world into being, along with the animals, the plants, and the spoken languages. There are many female gods in the mythology of almost all tribes.

There have always been strong women among us. As a Cheyenne proverb puts it: "As long as the hearts of our women are high, the nation will live. But should the hearts of our women be on the ground, then all is lost." Centuries ago, Iroquois women had become sick and tired of the eternal warfare between the tribes and went on strike, refusing to sleep with the men, or bear children, until peace was made. And they won.

In the ancient tribal life of the Sioux there was some ugliness in the relations between men and women, but it was overshadowed by beauty. There was some putting down of women, but much more uplifting of them. There was hard work for the women, but hunting was also hard on the men, and at least the tasks of both sexes were well defined. Everybody knew where he or she stood. Men and women had definite rules and responsibilities. They knew what was expected of them and lived up to these expectations. A wife abuser was an outcast, as was the no-account man who acted upon the whims of his penis rather than upon the urgings of his heart.

Under the outside pressure of white power and suppression, the old ways were destroyed. The tiyospaye, the extended family, disintegrated. Much that was positive among our traditional society was wiped out, and much that was negative was not only preserved, but enhanced. White society, until very recently, ran according to male values. Only think of the many white families who are proud of their little Cherokee great-great-grandmother. But where is the good old Indian great-great-grandfather? Nowhere, because for a frontiersman, taking a native woman to his bed was acceptable but an Indian man having a white woman was not. The whites' attitude of male superiority rubbed off on us. The dominant culture forced its values upon our tribes.

Among our Lakota tribes the contradictions between two opposing values are not only a collective experience but are deep inside all of us. I remember how touched and thrilled I was when Crow Dog described to me the essence of Ptesan Win, the White Buffalo Calf Woman. He has a mind and language of his own when he talks about sacred things. It is very deep and wonderful. He described Ptesan Win as the Holy Woman, the fire-bringer, the bringer of flint, of the stone knife. He said: "She had the power, she brought the pipe. She was the Red Woman of the Red Nation, she was three-dimensional." And he went on telling me: "The Holy Woman was young and beautiful. She was born in the womb bag of the generations, the universal birth bag. She was the Creator of Creations. She had a back carrier containing all the medicines we have, the healing herbs, the roots. She was the all-knowing teacher. Power was given to her. This woman was the center of the universe. She brought the seven stones, the sweat lodge, the seven sticks to start the fire. She was given the chanwaluta, the red wooden dish, in which she brought the sacred food—Indian corn, chokecherries, timpisila—the wild turnip. She brought these things to the people. This should be taught to our women." He could speak so beautifully and with so much understanding, and yet, at almost the same time be very macho, very man-centered, you could say. The one seems to go hand in hand with the other. There is still another female supernatural in our mythology, Anung-Ite, the Two-Face Woman. One side of her face is indescribably beautiful; the other is uglier than anything else in the world. So we have all become two-faced when another culture was imposed upon us from the outside.

Our women have been touched by it too. In the old days they were proud to be virtuous. The "one-man women" were honored. There was a ceremony where women bit the isan, a sacred stone knife, at the same time proclaiming that they had been with only one man, the one to whom they had given children. Today the whole res is full of unwed mothers, often with children from different men. I am no exception. I am not ashamed of that. Giving life is always a great thing. It is just that the old values have disappeared and our old world has broken apart.

I have a feeling that many of our men resent women, and I know the reason. The men can't hunt anymore, can't find jobs, can't provide. There is nothing they can do. A woman can still make beadwork to sell to tourists, or wait on tables in the tourist traps along the highway, or clean up in the many motels. The women get the welfare checks, the Aid to Dependent Children. Often the husband has to leave because his wife won't get her welfare as long as there is a husband around. So the roles are reversed. In many cases the woman is the provider now, and a very poor provider, usually. If she finds work, she has to leave her kids for the grandparents to raise. There is a whole generation of reservation kids raised not by a father and mother, but by grandma.

Poverty is now worse than ever. The poorest counties in the whole USA, Shannon, Mellette, and Todd, are in the Rosebud and Pine Ridge reservations. We have cradle-to-grave everlasting unemployment. Dependence on the meager government handouts is destroying the soul of our people. Poverty, dependence, and misery breed anger. Anger, which cannot vent itself upon its causes, turns against itself. Those who are powerless often work off their frustrations upon those who are even more vulnerable.

There is nothing for the men to do and they are unable to care for their families. Some men take it out on the women. I was raped when I was fifteen years old. I was told that it was my own fault because I was walking on a lonely road alone. Because I didn't carry a knife, because I was just too dumb to know better. You can kick, you can bite, you can scratch, but he is bigger and stronger than you, and that's it. I didn't feel good, that I can tell you. I was ashamed, too embarrassed to tell my mom. I didn't go to the police because that's a no-no. After that I carried a knife, even slashed some tires of guys who tried to snag me. At age seventeen I got pregnant. He was a nice-looking Indian guy with long braids. Maybe it was the braids that did it. He was popular. He took me way out into the boondocks. Later, I found out that he was only interested in having his pants fixed and his shirts mended. I wouldn't do that. So I went to Wounded Knee to have my kid.

One man told me when I indicated that I was not interested in him: "I can get any woman for a case of beer, a dime bag, and a little rhetoric." The nicer ones say: "Warrior woman, let's make a little warrior." Nine months later the woman is nursing her little warrior, but the big warrior is over the hills and far away. There is that attitude that all a woman is good for is lying in the sack and watching the kids. There is a lot of wife beating going on. I know women who were beaten. It's the same old story. They get beaten up, but they stay with the man because, in spite of everything, they love him. Or they stay for the sake of the children. That's all they've ever known in their life. To many it seems normal. A lot of women can't comprehend the fact that they can live their lives without being dependent on a man who is going to beat them. Mostly these guys will take off with the welfare money, or take the food stamps and sell them, or sell the commodities, and have a party. There is a lot of abuse. A man will want to go out and party. And if he wants to party, that's what he is going to do. If the woman gets mad about it, she'll eventually get a whipping and it will end up with a big fight, which the man will win almost every time. And the children will get caught up in it. They have to watch while their mother gets a beating. That's the way things are. There is no way to build a life for the people. You'll see women with black eyes and fat lips trying to hold on to their marriage. I couldn't and wouldn't do that.

Years ago my sister Barb lived with a wino who got violent when drunk. They lived way out on the prairie and it was actually his mother who called my mom and told her: "You better come after your daughter. She's in a bad way." Mom got there and found that Barb had lost so much weight she was down to ninety pounds. That man had beaten her with a tire iron and poured whiskey down her throat. As usual, Mom kept her and nursed her back until she was her former self again. I told Barb: "You sure know how to pick them, all right." She answered: "Look who's talking."

Annie Mae Pictou Aquash was my friend. She was one of the strongest and bravest women in the movement. She was beautiful and gifted. She married Noo-Ge-Shik Aquash at Wounded Knee, during the siege. He was a big hero there, an elegant, slim full-blood with a tiny black beard and a stylish low-brimmed hat. Their ceremony was beautiful. Wallace Black Elk performed the marriage in the old, traditional way. They burned the cedar, they smoked the pipe. Four men and four women made flesh offerings to make their future happy. People crowded around them, singing the AIM song. Like myself giving birth to a son at the Knee, this first marriage inside the self-proclaimed Independent Oglala Nation was looked upon as a lucky omen. Two years later, Annie Mae moved in with us at Crow Dog's Paradise—*alone*. Noo-Ge-Shik was a warrior, a fine artist, and seemed to be a right-on, sensitive man. But he had a dark side where women were concerned. Annie Mae told me that he had treated her badly, that he was very possessive and insanely jealous, that he would not let her have any friends, that he held her like a hostage for weeks and beat her. She was not the kind of woman to stand for this and left him.

When men get insensibly drunk they go "monstering," they give you the "death look." There was a man and his wife, I won't mention their names. They seemed to have a good marriage and to be happy together. One day he got into drinking the hard stuff, more than usual. He went berserk and killed her. He doesn't know why he did it, doesn't even have the slightest remembrance of it. The day before, I saw them laughing and joking together. Another friend of mine was found dead in her home, strangled with a nylon stocking. A young woman, Nellie, was discovered early one morning, lying dead among some trash cans at St. Francis. She was badly beaten up. I used to be good buddies with her. She had a brand-new baby. On the res, death is a way of life.

Sometimes it is the man who dies. One girl I knew, she was with this man who drank a lot. He was always partying. She had a good job in the tribe as a secretary. One time they had a party. She was in the kitchen and he came up behind her and started choking her. She grabbed a knife, stuck it into his heart, and killed him. She is now in a halfway house in Sioux Falls. And we had the case where a woman, out shopping in her car, caught her husband in another car making love to a woman. She revved up her vehicle and rammed them at full speed. Everybody was killed.

In 1984, a famous case of woman battering involved a Northwest Coast lady, Paula Three Stars. She had lived with a man, Sonny Evening, for a number of years. He was a wino who beat her into a bloody pulp every time he got drunk. He did it once too often, and Paula, tired of being hurt, killed him in self-defense. Now, men have always had the right to kill, if necessary, in defense of themselves, or their families, and of their property, but this same right was not always given to a woman. Paula was originally sentenced to ten years for first-degree murder. She felt "stunned, betrayed, and outraged." Thanks to intervention by a number of courageous Native American spokeswomen and organizations, her sentence was later changed to three years' probation, and she was released. Another famous case was that of Yvonne Wanrow, a Colville Indian, who shot and killed a white man, William "Chicken Bill" Wesler, a known child molester. Wesler burst into Yvonne's home in the wee hours of the morning totally drunk and lurched toward the bed in which Yvonne's three children were sleeping. The day before, Chicken Bill had tried to molest Yvonne's nine-year-old son, Darren. He had threatened the boy with a knife and bruised his arm but Darren had managed to escape. Chicken Bill had also previously raped the seven-year-old daughter of Yvonne's baby-sitter. When he broke into her house Yvonne was still on crutches, with one leg in a cast, the result of a fracture. She took no chances but let Chicken Bill have it point-blank, defending not only herself but also her kids. In spite of the fact that the intruder had been arrested many times for similar offenses and was well known to the police, Yvonne Wanrow was indicted for murder and had to fight for years to preserve her freedom. There are many similar cases, but these two will suffice to highlight this problem.

We have to struggle against domestic violence. Women are now beginning to fight this situation. They go into tribal politics. They are not afraid to put a restraining order on violent men. They give strength to each other. We have the White Buffalo Woman Society at Rosebud, and the Sacred Shawl Society in Pine Ridge. The White Buffalo Woman Society was founded in 1979 by Tillie Black Bear, herself a victim of domestic violence. She has also started a drive to have all the Medals of Honor given to the soldiers who massacred our women and children at Wounded Knee in 1890 revoked.

If a man hits a woman, she can turn around and put him in jail for domestic violence. A tribal judge might release him even if he cannot make bond, but he can't go back to his house or go near his wife and make trouble. And the court forces him to go to domestic violence counseling. They have all kinds of programs for that, both for men and women. They can take a couple's kids away for child neglect. They can make you go to alcohol addiction counseling. There is a halfway house in Antelope called Little Hoop. You go there for thirty days' counseling and you can't have any letters or phone calls. Many children are taken to foster homes because of domestic violence. Some men, when ordered to have counseling, will just say: "To hell with it," and split, going to Denver or St. Paul, living in Indian ghettos, leaving their women and children to fend for themselves. But some guys, who care for their families, will admit their mistakes and try to make a go of it.

In some tribes we have had instances of incest. This is something absolutely new, the result not only of alcoholism, but of too much contact with white America's "civilization." In the past, incest and child molesting by close relatives were unknown because this crime violated the most important taboo among Native Americans. The fear and abhorrence of incest was so pronounced and widespread that it led to so-called avoidance taboos, which made it impossible for a mother-in-law to speak to or come near a son-in-law, or for a father-in-law to even have a conversation with his daughter-in-law. But now, the vices and crimes of the white, dominant society trickle onto our reservations as the result of the suppression of our old religion, which formed a bulwark against them.

Another problem we are facing is the removal of children from their mothers because the father is drinking, or on account of "primitive living conditions in the home." Children are torn from their families for the flimsiest reasons, to wind up in white foster homes or orphanages. We also oppose the many attempts by white childless couples to adopt our kids. A child adopted out of its tribe is lost to us. Our kids are our greatest hope for the future and we cannot afford to lose them.

I remember that in Michigan, Indian women formed the Native American Child Protection Council (NACPC) to prevent the "wholesale abduction and adoption of Indian children." They pointed out that because of the shortage of white babies available for adoption, and because nobody wanted black babies, there was now a sort of gold rush stampede to adopt Indian infants. They pointed out that adoption agency scouts were going into Native American homes, telling the residents that their place was unfit "because two or three children were sleeping in one bed." Hell, in most Indian families I know, there are two or three kids sleeping in one bed. We don't have the white-style "nuclear families," with a limit of two children, and our houses, mostly shacks and trailers, are too small for more than one bedroom.

The NACPC got together with other Indian women's groups and there was, and is, a shared feeling that our children should not be adopted out unless at least one member of the couple is a Native American. We are also of the opinion that children should not be given in adoption until there is a guarantee that the child will not lose its Indian identity. In this fight to keep our little ones, to preserve for us a future generation, we run again and again into those whites who want to convince our families to give up their kids for either monetary, racial, or religious reasons.

Among the worst offenders is the Mormon Church. The Latter-day Saints build some of their churches on Indian reservations. They have a program to place our children in Mormon homes, luring the parents with promises of a better life for their children, saying: "Your kids will get a better education, better food and clothing, and better living conditions than you are able to give them." They even try to bribe the children with gifts of candy and toys. The Indian women are pestered and badgered to sign papers for a "voluntary placement program for one year," meaning forever. They say: "We will make your children 'shining with light and delight fulsome,'" whatever that means. Well, it means child stealing. Hand in hand with that kind of stealing goes a theft of land in a grand manner, particularly in the Southwest. We are all hell-fired up to fight this alien church.

Another fight I was involved in was trying to prevent the forced sterilization of Indian women. My sister Barb was sterilized without her consent. Mom thinks that Barb needed a hysterectomy for reasons of health. She always says that Barb might have died without it, but Barb and I don't think so. There was at that time, some fifteen or twenty years ago, a trend among white BIA doctors to sterilize Native American women, either by taking out their wombs or by tying their tubes. The prevailing attitude among the white people running our lives was: Those damn Indians, breeding like rabbits, living in substandard conditions, existing on welfare, are being a burden on the American taxpayer. And most of them are not even legally married! Let's prevent those squaws having more papooses!

Many women were unmercifully harassed by white social workers and hospital people, who told them that they were bad mothers since they were always drunk, their homes were unsanitary, and they didn't have money enough to raise children. Again and again, Indian women were told: "Wouldn't it be better for you not to have more children rather than have them wind up in a faraway foster home?" As an example, in July 1974, in one small hospital in Claremore, Oklahoma, no fewer than forty-eight sterilizations were performed on Native American women. One of the strongest fighters against this form of genocide was Dr. Connie Uri, a Choctaw-Cherokee medical doctor who lived in Los Angeles and supported Indian civil rights causes. Altogether, several hundred essentially illegal sterilizations were carried out during those years. Chicano women were also targets of the sterilizers. Barb went to a conference on this subject in Europe, describing what was going on.

Women on the res generally like *Lakota Woman*. They tease me, calling me a star. They tell me: "It's about time someone had the guts to tell the truth, to write about what's going on. Everybody talks about it in private, but nobody has the guts to go public with it." Many Indian women have told me that they are real proud of the book. There are even some guys who have come up to me on the res, saying that they like the book, asking me to autograph it for them. They even tell me: "Right on, sister! Let it all hang out, tell it like it is! It's important." They even have the book up at the college. But there is a negative side to it too. Some say that I destroy the romantic image of the noble Indian. One of my aunties criticized me for the personal stuff I put in the book. She is a fundamentalist Christian and just does not understand how I could have put such embarrassing things on paper, mentioning things that should never be spoken of. A lot of women come to me for advice and I tell them: "I am not an elder. There are grandmothers who have been in the world longer than I, who have a long life of experience, who can tell you a lot more than I could." I just tell the sisters: "Be strong for yourself and each other." I suddenly have many white women admirers. Some are New Age people and they send me crystals as gifts. They are beautiful and I like to look at them, but I do not know what to do with these wonderful sparkling things that seem to have a rainbow at their core. I know that there are some people who have a gift to use crystals, but I am not one of them. I have gotten many letters from women who have read the book. Some wrote me: "I can feel for you, because I have been through the same things," or: "I remember those days, you brought it all back for me," and: "Truth is always beautiful, even when it is ugly." Some white women wrote that they did not even know that Indians still existed, that they are still struggling for survival. One black woman wrote: "I love you, sister. I live in an urban slum, you live in a rural slum. That's the only difference. What you experienced, we experienced." Some writers want help, others want to help. One woman in California wanted to come and live with me. She wanted to get into Indian spirituality and have visions. She wanted to live in a tipi. I wrote her that living in a tipi wasn't all that great, especially in winter, and with children. I advised her to stay close to the hot and cold water, the gas stove, and the flush toilet. I hope that my book did some good. I agree with the woman who wrote that truth is beautiful, even when it is ugly.

I am proud of our Indian women, proud for their courage in adversity, for holding the tribes together. I think of them often, and I remember. I think most of all of *ANNIE MAE AQUASH*. She stayed with us for a while. She was a Micmac, but she learned our Sioux ways. She took medicine with me in meetings of the Native American Church. Wherever Indians were mistreated or had problems, there you could find Annie Mae, in the middle of it. She told me: "If any of my brothers are shot at, or being killed, I'll go and fight with them. I'll defend my sisters, if they are in trouble. I'll die for my people. I do not care for living a long life. I'll put my body on the line. Better to die young than stand aside and see others fight." She died young, her frozen body lying in the snow. I think she knew that hers would be a violent death. Her spirit lives. She was a very special friend to me.

I feel particularly close to the sisters who were with me at the Knee. There is *LORELEI DE CORA*. She was our "pistol-packing mama," who at only nineteen years of age ran the medical clinic inside Wounded Knee. A Miniconjou Sioux, she had been involved in the movement since she was sixteen. She was for some years married to Ted Means, brother of Russell. I remember her telling the crowd at the Knee: "This is where it's at, the fewest and the poorest making a stand here. We are the grass roots." She was one of the founders of Women of All the Red Nations. Several of our women took part in the firefights. And when someone was wounded, our nurses—Lorelei DeCora, her sister Mary, Madonna Gilbert—would go out and bring them in amid a hail of bullets. Now she works as a nurse at our tribal hospital, where she runs a program fighting AIDS on the res. I recently asked her: "Did we really do all those crazy things way back?" She just laughed: "We thought they were the normal things to do."

And there is *KA-MOOK*. Once known as Darlene Nichols, she's an Oglala from Pine Ridge. She was, until recently, married to Dennis Banks, one of our leaders and a founder of AIM. Ka-Mook was arrested in 1975 on a firearms charge and taken to jail in Wichita, Kansas, where she gave birth to her second daughter, whom she named Ta Tiyopa Maza Win, or Iron Door Woman. She wrote from jail at the time: "Iron Door Woman is the perfect name for her. She has been behind iron doors for 2½ months and her name tells it." Ka-Mook was held in solitary confinement under maximum-security conditions. Shortly before she gave birth a guard poked his finger into Ka-Mook's belly, saying: "Are you sure that's a baby in there, and not an M-16?"—his idea of a joke. She also wrote from her cell: "The feds are putting us behind bars to hold us down, but they can't keep us in jail forever. One of these days we'll all be out again and we'll be that much stronger. Maybe then our children won't have to suffer and go through the things we're putting up with now. And by shoving us behind bars they're also making our people on the outside stronger. And I'm here for a reason and that reason is my children and all the children of my people."

I owe much to *GRANDMA JOSETTE WAWASIK*, an Ojibway

lady who acted as the chief midwife for me when I gave birth to Pedro on April 11, 1973. She helped deliver my baby with bullets flying through the air and the pigs' armored personnel carriers churning around real close to the perimeter. She went on calmly, pressing on my belly, lifting the newborn out, cutting the umbilical cord as if this was a routine birth in a peaceful city hospital. She was holding my baby up at the window for everybody to see, and there was drumming outside, and the singing of the AIM song, and tears and laughter, and hugging all around. "I am here at the Knee because I believe in life," Grandma Wawasik told me. I will remember her forever. After I had my baby they made a big meal for me, but the boys were so excited they ate it all up, so I had tea. Carter Camp, one of the AIM leaders, claimed Pedro as his nephew. He said: "I'm going to be his first uncle." Dennis Banks made him a birth certificate from the Independent Oglala Nation. I still have it.

And I will also never forget *GRACE BLACK ELK*, Wallace's wife, who, sadly, has gone to the Spirit World. At the Knee she told us: "They can't do anything to us but kill us and, if they do, others will come up after us to finish this fight."

One of the bravest women I ever met was *GLADYS BISON-ETTE*, from Pine Ridge, who always stood up to the goons who had murdered so many of our people, and who told our mini-Hitler, Dicky Wilson, to his face that he was a killer, a crook, and a drunken fool. It was Gladys, and a few other women like her, who, shortly before the takeover, at a meeting in Calico, told the men: "Let's make our stand at Wounded Knee, because that place has meaning for us, because so many of our people were massacred there. If you guys don't want to do it, we women will, and you men can stay behind and mind the kids."

After the marshals opened up on us, Gladys spoke to the women, saying: "There were bullets coming out of the night, whizzing around our heads, our chests, our legs, bullets over and around us, but none of those bullets found their way into our bodies, because the Great Spirit protects us. Don't be afraid of those bullets—pigs' bullets, I call them."

Beside Gladys stood *ELLEN MOVES CAMP,* a Lakota, who had been fired from her job with the health service because she stood up against the oppression that was going on. She remembered: "There were only two men from AIM at the meeting in the Calico community hall, but there were three hundred of us women, and elders, old chiefs, and all of our medicine men except one. He was too old and sick to come. It was there and then that we made the decision to make our stand at the Knee. It was the women who came forward and spoke out and who first came up with the idea to take over the Knee. The men were hanging back, worrying about the consequences. It was the really old people, the grandfathers and grandmothers, who agreed with us, saying: 'Go ahead and do it!' " At the Knee, Ellen ran around with a headband reading IMPEACH NIXON. Like most of us, Ellen has mellowed out. She has to stay home now, at Wanblee, South Dakota, minding the grandchildren, our common fate.

A third strong Sioux woman was *LOU BEAN.* At the head of some three hundred demonstrators at Pine Ridge she faced seventy-five heavily armed marshals. One of the marshals told Lou: "The seventy-five of us could whip the shit out of the whole Sioux Nation together with the entire AIM crowd." She answered back: "That's what Custer said. Why don't you come over and try us? We are ready to fight." Well, they stayed put, busying themselves with eating sandwiches out of their little lunch boxes. Lou also told them: "I'd rather hug a rattlesnake than anyone among you."

A special friend of mine is *MICHELLE RICHARDS,* whom we call Mickey. She was one of the strongest women at the Knee. Then, when she was big with child, she and another Wounded Knee sister dug Annie Mae's grave. She did something truly heroic by refusing to testify before a grand jury against a brother who had shot a vicious drug dealer—in Valentine, Nebraska, of all places! She said that as a traditional Native American woman she could not be made a tool of the white criminal justice system. For refusing to testify, she was held without charge for three months. She went on a hunger strike, going without food for thirty-nine days. Then she refused to take even water. They took her to the hospital to force-feed her, shackled to her bed, and placed her under round-the-clock surveillance, but they could not break her will. They finally gave up and let her go. We admired her for what she did. Mickey just shrugged it off. Mickey hates the goons, and for good reason: They shot her mother through the butt and her young nephew through the arm. She is a grandmother now, still living on Pine Ridge, married to a Sioux from the Standing Rock Reservation.

And I remember a Lakota woman named *IRMA,* who sneaked in and out of the Knee with her heavy backpack bringing food into the perimeter. You had to come in from Porcupine, which meant each time doing a nine-mile hike through terrain infested with trip-wire flares, marshals with infrared sniper scopes, and attack dogs. And there was *MILDRED,* who, when surrender was discussed, gave the warriors a pep talk: "The same ravines they massacred our women and children in a hundred years ago, we are now in, the same place, the same gullies, the same chankpe opi wakpala. They want us to come out and give up our guns. We are not that crazy!"

Among the brave-hearted women who came from the East was *CARLA BLAKEY.* A Salteaux Indian from Canada, she was for some years married to Art Blakey, a black jazz drummer. She grew up in a place where you ran into polar bears on the street. She came to the sun dance last summer and was honored, being given the little rainbow-colored patch that all Wounded Knee activists are proud to wear. With Carla came *TRUDY LAMB* and *CHARMAINE LYONS.* Trudy, who is from a tiny New Jersey tribe with a tiny reservation, brought her flute. Charmaine was a Cherokee from North Carolina, and from the Six Nations. I also remember a woman from the Northwest who told me: "You are fighting for your land. You've got a special relationship to the buffalo. Well, I came here to fight for our brother, the salmon."

And what about *SAHRA BAD HEART BULL?* Her son, Wesley Bad Heart Bull, was knifed to death by a white racist, Darold Schmidt, at the little hamlet of Buffalo Gap, on the edge of the Black Hills. The trial began just a week before the occupation of Wounded Knee, in the town of Custer, deep inside the Black Hills. We all went there—AIM people and Sioux from Pine Ridge and Rosebud—to see that justice was done. Custer calls itself "the town with the gunsmoke flavor." It sure lived up to its name, because when we found out that the murderer would go free on a second-degree manslaughter charge, we set fire to the courthouse and the chamber of commerce, which was in a sort of phony log cabin. This, as one of the guys put it, "sent up a hell of a smoke signal." Sahra, the victim's mother, was stopped from entering the courthouse. When she tried to get in some pigs with helmets and face shields pushed her so that she fell down the stairs. When she tried to get up, one of the troopers choked her with his long nightstick. Then all hell broke loose. I remember that big fracas vividly.

I was outside with all the AIM people, while Dennis Banks, Russell Means, and Leonard Crow Dog were inside the courthouse. They had only a handful of guys in there. We were trying to get in and the riot squad was blocking the doors when all hell broke loose. The pigs were beating up on the people. I saw two of them dragging a young girl through the snow. They had ripped most of her clothes off so that she had only her bra and pants on. There was a girl next to me who hit one of the troopers with a hammer and broke his face shield. When Russell Means came out of the courthouse, the pigs clubbed him down, hitting him on the head with their big hardwood sticks. I saw him sitting in the snow, handcuffed, with a dazed look on his face. I was pregnant at the time and big as a hippo, or rather, as a whale. We were making Molotov cocktails. Carter Camp, Dace Means, Stan Holder, and Victorio were taunting the riot squad guys: "Come on out. What are you hiding behind the bushes for?" but those pigs stayed put. They didn't want to die, seeing those AIM guys were for real. It was just like a war zone, like a Vietnam movie. They were throwing tear gas grenades at us. Then Dennis came around in a big, old propane truck, driving right through the flames. It freaked out the state troopers. It was funny because at the same time those buildings were burning, everybody was lining up at the gas station filling up their tanks—free of charge. We took a back road out of Custer, back to the Mother Butler Hall in Rapid City. The cops tried to stop us, but Crow Dog told them: "You can't search this car. We have sacred things in here." Strangely enough, they let us through. Later, in Rapid City, everybody was jumping into cars to go downtown and confront the rednecks. A whole busload of us got arrested. Somehow, I was overlooked. That's when I cut a white woman's face. She screamed at me: "You fucking dirty Indians, why do you come here where you're not wanted? Get your fucking red asses out of here!" I took one of those glass ashtrays, broke it, and slashed her face.

Well, for making a nuisance of herself on the steps of the courthouse, and protesting her son's murder, Sahra Bad Heart Bull got three to five years. Although she was an elderly lady she was strong, fighting the riot squad guys like a wildcat. Her son's murderer got two months' probation. Nothing unusual about that.

I had two other friends from the Knee. *TONIA ACKERMAN* was in her early twenties while at Wounded Knee. She grew up in Montana, worked her way through several years of college, and became a teacher and counselor at the Little Red School House in St. Paul, an alternative AIM school for Indian kids. Tonia was a real scrapper. She had triangular steel points at the tips of her cowboy boots, so-called shit-kickers, and she sure knew how to use them. *MADONNA GILBERT* was already the mother of three children when she came to Wounded Knee but it was not her first siege. She had spent nine months on Alcatraz Island during its occupation from 1970 to 1971. She worked also as a teacher in survival schools and became prominent in the Indian women's movement. She's into powwows now, a champion jingle dancer.

LIZZIE FAST HORSE was one of our strongest older women at the Knee. In 1971, already a great-grandmother, she climbed all the way to the top of Mount Rushmore, stood on top of Teddy Roosevelt's head, and joined a demonstration led by Lehman Brightman to reclaim the Black Hills for our people. They stayed up there on top of the mountain with John Fire Lame Deer, about a dozen Sioux men and women from Rapid City, and our white friends Richard and Jean Erdoes. Also among this group was *MINNIE TWO SHOES,* an Assiniboin Sioux. She later came to Crow Dog's Paradise to have her first baby. Leonard's sister Christine acted as the midwife. I saw Minnie not so long ago up in Montana. She has more kids now and has her hands full raising them, so she can't be so very active anymore in the cause.

It is not necessary to have been at Wounded Knee to have been a fighter for Indian rights. My husband's sister Rocky became involved in the movement when she was in her mid-teens and she has been very active ever since. She is well known in Colorado for her fight for the civil rights of both Indians and Chicanos. She teaches both Native American and Hispanic studies at a college in Denver. She is also a curandera, a healer with herbs. In her home she has racks of plants, roots, and berries. And she knows them all. She is also into helping the homeless. A real close friend of mine, she takes part almost every year in the sun dance at Crow Dog's Paradise.

I met Rocky in the summer of 1974, at the sun dance, when Pedro was still a baby. We really got together during the time when I had to do a lot of cooking, and she always helped in the kitchen, and with the tobacco ties, getting sage and other things that needed to be done. She really contributed. Later on, we got to be real good friends. We ended up sun dancing together. When we were traveling through Denver, she'd always have her door open for us.

A very great leader is *JANET McCLOUD*, a Puyallup from Helm, in Washington State. For many years, Janet has been in the forefront of the struggle for Native American rights—fishing rights, women's rights, all kinds of rights. She is now the head of a large family because her husband, Don, a wonderful man, died some years ago. They are a close-knit family, mostly fishing folks. To them the salmon is what the buffalo was to us Sioux. Janet, the founder of the Northwest Indian Women's Circle, keeps herself busy with lecturing, giving interviews, and editing her newspaper, *Moccasin Line*. At an Indian women's conference in New York she said: "They call this a feminist meeting. I'd rather call it a strengthening. Indian women have to be strong. They have no choice. So much rests on their shoulders. Can you understand that?"

At the same conference, *SHIRLEY HILL WITT,* an Iroquois anthropologist and one of the founders of the National Indian Youth Council, spoke about the stereotype of the "bronze nubile naked 'princess,' a child of nature or beloved concoction of Hollywood producers. This version is often compounded with the Pocahontas legend. As the story goes, she dies in self-sacrifice, saving the life of the white man for whom she bears an unrequited love, so that he may live happily ever after with a voluptuous but high-buttoned blonde."

Shirley Hill Witt's talk about Hollywood stereotypes reminds me that we are not all that happy with *Dances with Wolves*. While the movie was visually breathtaking, it was also the same old story—the hero and heroine were, as usual, white.

Talk about Hollywood also makes me think of another friend, *SACHEEN LITTLE FEATHER*. She made headlines in 1973 when Marlon Brando persuaded her to be his stand-in at the Oscars. After it was announced that he had won the award for his performance in *The Godfather,* he had Sacheen go up and tell the audience that he was rejecting the Oscar because of the shabby, stereotyped image Hollywood habitually presents on the screen. On that occasion she made a passionate speech about the plight of Native

Americans, denouncing the injustices done to her people. As a result she was blacklisted by an outraged movie industry and her career as an actress was ruined. Brando did nothing for her. She told me recently that she had not heard from him in more than a decade. She was homeless for a long time. She said to me: "When I really needed help, Brando ignored me. I was just a pawn in his game." They really exploited her. They twisted her arm to pose in the nude for *Playboy,* "to show the beauty of the Indian woman." She was young and naive then and fell for this crap. I met her again in 1991, when I was in California to promote my book, and Sacheen is still gorgeous. She was really happy about my book, telling me: "It's about time Indian women started speaking out for their rights. We've been oppressed too long." She has never stopped being an activist and working for the people, fighting alcoholism among both Indians and whites, giving lectures on health, trying to help the homeless. Sacheen's brother died of AIDS and now she is active in the fight against this dreadful disease. She goes around to the street people, handing out needles and condoms and giving out information about how to avoid getting infected. While I was in L.A. she cooked a dinner for me. We sat around the table—Sacheen, her boyfriend, a guy from the American Indian Treaty Council, and myself, and it turned out that we were all left-handed. It was really funny because as my mother has told me: "You know what the traditional Sioux say about left-handed people—they get into mischief all the time." That is certainly true for me. Trouble always finds me. I agreed with Sacheen when she told me: "First you have to get angry for what happened to you before the healing can begin."

Through Richard and Jean, I met *BEVERLY HUNGRY WOLF,* a woman from the Blood people, who are part of the Blackfoot Nation. She is also an author, like myself, and has written books about the ways of her people. In her tribe, if a woman dreams that she will be a medicine person and healer, then she can become one. Many religious rites were given first to the women by the sky dwellers, not to the men. Dreams often come to women rather than to the men. Many ceremonies cannot be performed without women playing a part in them. The Bloods have women's as well as men's societies and in some cases a woman can even join a man's society. They have holy women who put up the sun dance lodge and who fast to fulfill their vows. People go to a holy woman for prayers and to get face paint. It was good to learn how highly respected such women are in Blood society.

Last year I found a new friend in *YOSSI RAMOS,* who is half Mexican but has a classic full-blood face. She now lives with her daughter in Santa Fe, but she also spent years in New York and sun danced both at Crow Dog's Paradise and at Big Mountain. She was part of the Indian civil rights movement back in the seventies, long before AIM.

In front of the Museum of Natural History in New York stands a big statue of Teddy Roosevelt on horseback depicting him as the macho conqueror of the West. On either side of Teddy walks an African tribesman and an Indian with bowed head. It is a real Lone Ranger and Tonto monstrosity. I have seen it a few times myself. Yossi and her group decided to do something about it. They were mad because the feds had just stormed Alcatraz and driven out 150 Native Americans who had held the Rock for nineteen months. So on July 15, 1971, Yossi and six others went to the museum with buckets of red paint and did some "ornamenting," paying special attention to Teddy's nose. They splashed red paint all over that bronze cowboy. On the socle they wrote: "Return Alcatraz" and "Racist Killer." They had done their paint job in the middle of the night, but around 2:30 A.M. they were spotted by some cops from the Central Park precinct and arrested. Yossi and the others were taken to court on a charge of second-degree criminal mischief. Besides Yossi, who was only seventeen at the time, the other women were Janice Kekahbah, representing the National Indian Youth Council, Blanche Wahnee, Marie Helene LaRaque, and Charmaine Lyons. Charmaine was later at Wounded Knee. Helene, I am told, now lives in Canada, near the Arctic Circle, fighting for the rights of the Northern Deneh people. Yossi says that it was a worthwhile experience.

On another occasion, inspired by the "liberation" of Alcatraz, a group of mainly Indian women decided to take over Ellis Island, which at that time was totally deserted and covered with rubble. They almost made it, but their boat started to sink and they barely got back to the Manhattan shore. Unfortunately, two guys who had come from Alcatraz were holding a press conference at the same time: "Indians have taken over Ellis Island." That tipped the feds off and from then on there was always a Coast Guard cutter hovering around the island. So the women gave up on that.

Another New York Indian woman I admired was *JEFFE KIM-BALL*, a wonderful Osage artist. She had an unusual life, having studied art in Paris and, for a while, running the Art Students League of New York. She "discovered" many young Native American artists and was tireless in furthering their careers. She was strong in defending Indian rights. She was involved in the attempt to take over Ellis Island. In the sixties and seventies, there were three places where Indians stayed when they came to New York—with Richard Erdoes on Eighty-ninth Street; with Stan Steiner, who wrote *The New Indians,* on the Lower East Side; and with Jeffe on Bank Street in the Village. Jeffe died of cancer in Santa Fe. At her wake a Pueblo elder appeared out of nowhere, releasing Jeffe's soul with corn pollen. Native Americans owe a lot to her.

Back home in Rosebud I have two friends, *APRIL* and *TINA*. Whenever some man tries to abuse me they get into it with him—or them—saying: "Don't fuck with our sister!" April is a big strapping girl who can fight it out toe-to-toe with any man. Even tough guys are afraid of her. They have battled at my side quite a few times. I could go on and on about strong sisters I'm proud to call my friends, but the list is so long that I better stop here. They are all ohitika win—brave women.

Many years ago I talked to an old woman who is long dead now. She was almost a hundred years old when she talked to me and I was fascinated by what she had to tell me about the old days when she had been young. She was born on the Rosebud Reservation, though some of her ancestors had been Canadian Indians who married into our tribe. She lived on her ancestors' original allotment north of Antelope Creek. She said that she could "see back five generations." She had known her great-grandfather and her great-grandmother. She complained that nowadays people don't know their great-grandparents because "they don't live that long." She complained that many kids no longer speak the Lakota language. She told me that her grandfather had to buy his wives with many horses and buckskin hides and that he kept two despite the missionaries always being after him for that. She had been forced to go to the nunnery school, where she had been beaten for praying the Indian way. And although she had little education she still had all her wits about her. She had been taught to be modest by her mother, who had forced her to wear long sleeves down to her wrists and to always have her hair braided in two. She had never seen a girl and a boy kiss in public until she was fifty, and then it had shocked her. She said that nowadays girls were "half naked." She also told me that in her youth she still had slept with a hair rope between her legs so that she could not be sexually molested.

Well, things have changed since her times. We are no longer that modest, and that "woman shall not walk before man" kind of bullshit doesn't go over well nowadays. Basically though, I don't think things have gotten that much better for women—white, black, or red.

It is to AIM's everlasting credit that it tried to change men's attitudes toward women. In the movement we were all equal. Some of the decisions were made by the women—for instance older women at Calico telling the men to take over Wounded Knee. And the men always put the safety of their women first.

When the bullets started to fly, Pedro Bisonette covered my body with his own, and a sixteen-year-old kid did the same, putting himself between me and the feds' fire when I was walking to the outhouse. After the big shoot-out at Oglala, on June 26, 1975, during which two FBI agents were killed, Joe Killsright Stuntz caught a rifle bullet between his eyes trying to cover the escape of the AIM group in order to give the women a chance to get away. So while I criticize some of our men for macho attitudes, I also have to remember those who put their bodies on the line for us.

We Indians have had some token progress but even that is being taken away from us by the government and Supreme Court. We're actually going backwards, economically and politically. I am sick and tired of all the bullshit that has been dumped on us by the wasichu for more than five hundred years after we were "discovered" by a fellow who was merely eight thousand miles off course and who thought he had landed in India. I am tired of being dominated by an alien and hostile culture. I am tired of the pressure to adapt to the white men's idea of beauty, which prods me to have an ivory skin, to be as thin as a rail but have big breasts, to spend money on all kinds of crap to have "glorious silky hair," to be manicured by a "nail artist," and to shave the hair nature made grow under my armpits. I am sick and tired of being asked to conform to standards that are not our own. I am sick and tired of being forced to live within a society dominated by money, or in the case of us native peoples, by the total lack of it. I am sick and tired of seeing our men driven by despair, boredom, and lack of anything meaningful to do to find oblivion in alcohol, to commit suicide, or to end up in prison. I am sick and tired of seeing Indian people being driven by prevailing conditions into violence against each other. I am sick and tired of seeing the steady erosion of our land base, because without our land we will cease to be. I am goddam sick and tired of being put down on account of my sex and my race. I am sick and tired of the newspapers read by Indians running ads that say: "Strong, willing girl sought as live-in baby-sitter and all-around maid. Must be sober and accommodating. Call collect." What's the matter? Could they be running out of our black sisters to do the shitwork for them? And I am also sick and tired of ads reading: "Loving couple eager to adopt cute, healthy baby boy." After five hundred years of being held in subjection, we are finally standing up on our hind legs. Together with my sisters from many tribes, I am a birth-giver, a rebirth-giver, fighting to ensure a life for unborn generations. I am a Sioux woman!

CHAPTER SIXTEEN

Moon Power

In one important aspect of their lives Indian women are very different from their white and black sisters. When a Lakota woman says: "I am on my moon," it means that she has her period, and that has a special magic and mythical meaning for us. Being on our moon is surrounded by ancient but ever-strong beliefs, by legends and mythology, by customs going back to the dawn of time. It is the widespread belief, not only among us Sioux but among most Native American tribes, that a menstruating woman has a special, overwhelming power that nullifies the power of the men, even that of the medicine men. By her mere presence, a menstruating woman can render any ceremony or curing ritual ineffective. I heard a medicine man, taunted because one of his attempts to cure a sick person failed, say: "There was a woman on her moon around. That's why. She did it on purpose." I truly believe that at the time of our monthly cycle some men are afraid of us. Leonard Crow Dog, in his vision of Creation, of the Sioux Genesis, has described the woman's part in it beautifully, poetically, and with words full of cosmic mystery:

"And then it was time for Tunkashila to create woman. There

was no moon then. It was still the period of sacred newness. The sun again called all the planets and supernaturals together, and when they had assembled, the sun, in a bright flash, plucked out one of his eyes. He threw it on the wind of his vision into a certain place, and it became the moon, and it was female. And on this new orb, this eye-planet, he created woman. 'You are a planet virgin, a moon maiden,' he told her. 'I have touched you, and made you out of my own shadow. I want you to walk on the earth.' This happened in darkness at the time of a new moon.

" 'How will I walk over that land?' the woman asked. So the sun created woman power and woman understanding. He used lightning to make a bridge from the moon to the earth, and the woman walked on the lightning. Her crossing took a long, long time.

"Now the maker of the universe had created man and woman and had given each a power of their own that has never been changed. Doing that, the sun had used up another million eons of creation time. He instructed the woman in her tasks, which she learned through her dreams, through her visions, through her special woman powers.

"The Great Spirit had created man and woman for each other, but not right away. They had to make contact slowly, get used to each other, understand each other for the survival of their caretaking. Tunkashila let blood roll into the woman. She walked on the lightning, but she also walked on a blood vein reaching from the moon to the earth. This vein was a cord, a birth cord that went into her body, and through it she is forever connected to the moon. And nine months of creation were given to her. And the Spirit told her: 'You are the caretaker of the generations. You are the birth-giver. You will be the carrier of the universe.' "

The power of the moon is also invoked in the legend of We Ota Wichasha, the Blood Clot Boy. Again, here is how Crow Dog tells it:

"So how was the Indian born? He was born from the sunrise and from the woman. This woman at first was all alone on this earth after it had been created. This woman was beautiful and no man had touched her. Then she met a spirit, a power from the moon, the shadow of the generation. It worked upon her so that she began to bleed in woman nature for the first time. And she used yellow bark and rabbit skin to put between her legs to contain the flow. And after she had encountered this power and woman's nature cycle had started within her, she went to sleep. When she got up the next morning she had an urge to make water. She took that yellow bark and rabbit skin from between her thighs and squatted and this little drop of moon blood fell to the earth. Mashtinchala, the rabbit, came upon that little clot of blood and started playing with it, kicking it into life. Rabbit did this with the help of Takus-kanskan, the mysterious moving power that quickens the fruit in the womb and gives motion to all living things. And being kicked around and around, the little blob of blood took shape, forming a little gut. The rabbit played with it some more, and the blob began to grow tiny arms and legs. The rabbit nudged it some more, and suddenly it had eyes and a heart. In this way the blood clot began to move by itself and grew into We Ota Wichasha, the first man." There are several versions of this story and there are also Blood Clot Boy legends among other tribes. They all stress the terrific power of women during their moon time.

Ishnati is the Lakota word for menstruation. It means "dwelling alone," because, in the old days, a woman was isolated in a special tipi, or moon lodge, for four days. When a woman has her period she cannot be around the pipe because she would have a negative influence on the pipe. She would also affect all other ceremonial objects—the eagle wings and eagle-bone whistles, the gourd rattles, the peyote fan—in a bad way. If a menstruating woman were present during a healing ritual, the incense, the sage, the cedar, the sweet grass would lose their power to cure. They might even harm the sick person. It is believed that a woman on her moon would pollute the medicine. When the men are singing, such a woman should not even be near the drum, because the drum is also sacred.

These are the teachings of our traditional people and everyone acts in accordance with them. It is not that menstruation is looked upon as something unclean, as in some non-Indian cultures, but that a woman's moon power is so great that it turns all other powers upside down. A woman should not even handle food, or cook for somebody, because that might cause stomach trouble. A man should not even talk to a woman who is on her monthly cycle for it could harm him, making him break out in boils or pimples. If a man should have intercourse with a menstruating woman, it could drive him mad. Moon blood can make flowers wilt. I heard an old man tell a white visitor: "Woman on her moon spits on a rattlesnake, rattlesnake dies." The visitor asked: "Did you ever make an experiment to see whether it's true, get hold of a menstruating woman and make her spit on a snake?" The old man answered: "That's not necessary. Everybody already knows it from way back." It is also believed that if a woman touches a weasel skin while menstruating, she will become sick and her legs will become disjointed, and if a man wears a weasel skin while making love to a woman on her moon, he will be struck by an illness that could kill him.

At a sun dance, I heard the announcer say: "The dancers can question any woman about whether she is on her moon, especially the young girls out there who don't know any better. If they're on their moon, they should leave the camp and not come back until they are finished with this." One year we had a separate "moon camp" across the road, out of camp, because everyone had their medicine out in the open. If you are going to the sun dance, you'd better know about your cycle so you won't interfere with the ritual. My friend Rocky, who has been sun dancing for years and years, noticed that this one woman was spotting, and the woman said: "No, it's just that my panties are dirty." But Rocky made the women security take her to the bathroom and be checked, and sure enough, she was having her period. So they made her leave the circle immediately. If the men hear about such things they get very upset. Menstruating women will make the dancers sick and weak, so that they fall down. It takes away their strength to endure the piercing. Even accidental contact with menstrual blood, according to some elders, can cause illness of the skin and genitals in men. It creates a tremendous negative energy. The first time I was at a sun dance, I had not planned to participate. I did not even bring my pipe, but one woman went on her moon and I took her place in the circle and danced for her.

Years ago, when the movement was in full swing, the girls were real strong, and there was a "moon watch" where we took the menstruating women to the moon lodge and we'd feed them and care for them but, at the same time, have security there to make sure they didn't go anywhere. As the years went on, it started to be embarrassing. Women didn't want to be asked all the time: "Are you by any chance menstruating?" And they did not want to be cooped up for four days and nights in the moon lodge. So we finally made a rule—if you're on your moon, just stay away.

And it is the same with all other ceremonies. There can be no woman on her moon participating in a sweat lodge purification. One old man told me that when a menstruating woman once came into a yuwipi ceremony, all the spirits present there took such fright that they stormed out of the room like a whirlwind, breaking all the windowpanes in the process. And even in a cross-fire ceremony of the Native American Church, run the Christian way, no woman on her moon is allowed to participate or touch the sacred morning food. And it is the same with a woman after childbirth because as long as she is bleeding, even a little bit, it is like her being ishnati, and she has to stay isolated. In the old days, very strict traditional men even avoided their wives as long as they were nursing, abstaining from intercourse for a very considerable time. Well, that acted as a natural kind of birth control, of childbirth spacing.

Women even have to be protected from their own moon power. A woman can become a medicine woman, but only after menopause. If a medicine woman were still menstruating, her moon power would clash with her medicine power and they would cancel each other out. There would be no power at all, and therefore no healing. Women must be careful that Iktome, the evil Spider Man, or a coyote does not get hold of or eat her menstrual blood, because they would then have absolute evil power over her. She must also take care that no wapiya, no conjurer, obtains even the tiniest fleck of her moon blood, because he could mix it with other medicines and make a love charm out of it that would make the owner irresistible to the woman. All this is part of Lakol Wichohan, the Indian way.

I have inquired and read up on what menstruation beliefs are common among other tribes. Among our old enemies, the Crows, a woman on her cycle was not allowed to come near a wounded man or a warrior going on a raid. They no longer have moon lodges, but in the old days, menstruating women had to stay in willow brush shelters for four days, abstain from meat, and live on wild roots or plants. When their periods were over, they purified themselves in the sweat lodge, smoked themselves up with cedar incense, put on new clothes, and resumed their normal, everyday lives.

In some tribal mythologies the female supernaturals menstruate. In Navajo mythology, I was told, their great supernatural godlike being, Changing Woman, first menstruated in the last quarter of the moon. Right away they had the Blessingway Chant sung for her and made a blessing so that the Diné people would have many offspring. Since that time, all women have their monthly period because Changing Woman has passed this on to all womankind. She also instructed the Diné how to perform a girl's puberty ceremony on the occasion of her first moontime.

In some southwestern creation myths, Earth Mother and Sky Father made love and in the fourfold Earthwomb created living things. Earth Mother then created the world waters and stirred them into life with drops of milk from her breasts. In the innermost of the four great wombs, the Womb of Generation, higher life emerged. It was still primitive, unknowing. Sun Father quickened the seed inside Earthfoam Mother and she gave birth to the Hero Twins. The godlike Twins then led all creatures up into the second great womb, named the Beneath the Navel Place. They ascended into it by means of a cornstalk or spiderweb, according to several legends. From this place people and animals ascended into the third womb, called Earth Vagina. And finally the Hero Twins led all living beings into the fourth and final womb, the Shining Sun Place. Now the people were formed as they are today, they had been given intellect, and the women began to menstruate. Creation was finished.

Among our old allies, the Cheyenne, a menstruating woman stayed in the moon lodge for four days. During this time she was not allowed to have any boiled meat, but only meat roasted over glowing coals. If the tribe was on the move, she could ride only a mare, not a stallion or gelding. If a man ate from a dish or drank from a bowl that had been used by a woman during her moontime, he was sure to be wounded or killed in his next fight. The same was true of a man who had slept with a woman during her period. Special care had to be taken not to have a man's weapons contaminated by moon power. An arrow affected this way would not hit an enemy, and neither would a gun touched by the hand of a woman on her cycle. Shields have magical male powers that protect the warrior in battle. If a menstruating woman accidentally entered a tipi in which a shield was kept, it would at once lose the power to protect its owner. In order to empower it again, the shield owner was not even allowed to reenter his lodge until the contaminated shield had been purified with incense of sweet grass and juniper leaves during a solemn ceremony. Also the tipi had to be partially dismantled. Only when power had been restored to the shield was the tipi completely covered and pinned closed again. Among the Arapaho, a woman on her moon had to stay away from sick persons in order not to make them worse. The woman would have to stay isolated, have her own separate dish to eat from and her own cooking fire. Girls would not put on clothing worn by a pregnant woman so as not to catch her pregnancy.

Among the Winnebagos, a menstruating woman had to fast for four days. She was not allowed to lie down and sat wrapped in a blanket the whole time. If they had to touch their bodies, they could not use their hands but had to use a stick. A menstruating woman was supposed to take the spirituality and power away from a holy man. The Winnebagos were, however, unique in believing that there is a power greater than a woman's moon power, namely the power of the war bundle. If a menstruating woman should come near it, she would not stop her flow but keep on bleeding until she died. For that reason a woman stayed as far away as she could from a war bundle ceremony. If she did not she could only be cured by the bundle's owner and keeper.

Among the Comanches, a women during her period had to stay in a tipi of her own, or else she would move in with her parents because the medicine of old people was "too weak" to be harmed. When something she had in her tipi was needed by someone, it was put outside because nobody was allowed to enter. She was not supposed to wash her face during her confinement because that would make it wrinkled, nor would she comb her hair for fear of becoming prematurely gray. After her menses she had to purify herself by bathing in a running stream, no matter how cold.

Among the Papago, no man dared come near the little shelters in which women stayed during their moontime. If a man stumbled upon one by accident he had to turn his face away. Here, too, the menstruating woman possessed a tremendous mysterious power, the power not only to menstruate, but to bear children, a power altogether different from the men's power to hunt or to make war. Both powers had to be kept apart from each other so that they should not cancel each other out. A mere look at a man from a menstruating woman supposedly took his power to hunt away from him forever. If such a woman stepped over a deer trail, the deer might go away. That could cause a famine. A woman often destroyed the dishes she ate from during her period. Even today, Papago women, as a rule, do not resent their days of isolation, saying that it is a welcome vacation from work.

Some Northwest Coast tribes believed that when going after whale or walrus or bear, some exceptionally brave men could actually use menstrual blood on some things, thus adding the women's power to their own male one. But this was a rather unique belief.

In most tribes, these customs are not designed to keep women down, but merely to escape from their power. Among the Sioux, a special puberty ceremony, called ishnati awichalowan, used to be held for a girl. The camp crier or herald, the ehayapa, would ride around the tipi circle, announcing that a young winchinchila had now grown up and was ready to assume a woman's responsibilities. She might be carried triumphantly on a blanket to her father's tipi. She would be dressed in a new, white buckskin outfit. Many presents would be made to her and horses given away in her honor. Sometimes a special and intricate buffalo ceremony would be held for her, with a buffalo skull altar to show her connection to Ptesan Win, the White Buffalo Calf Woman. The girl's first flow was carefully wrapped up and placed in the crotch of a wild plum tree, where no evil spirits could harm it.

The Cheyenne also had a solemn puberty ritual. The girl's grandmother would sprinkle white sage, juniper needles, and sweet grass over glowing embers, cedaring her and fanning her off. Sometimes the girl would stand naked, wrapped in a buffalo robe, straddling the smoking coals, sanctifying her womb in preparation for future motherhood.

Among the Navajo, a girl's coming-of-age ceremony was a very elaborate ritual, called kina'aldah. It lasted four nights, with an all-night singing at the end. A girl's first moon was something to be proud of, to be announced to all the people. The girl would have her hair washed ceremoniously with yucca suds. Each day at dawn she raced in a sacred manner toward the east. Friends and relatives would race along, but nobody was allowed to pass her. Each day there was a "molding" rite, during which an older woman would knead her body and straighten her hair. This would make her as shapely and beautiful as Changing Woman, which is to the Navajo what Ptesan Win is to us. Also, a huge corn cake was baked in a cornhusk-lined pit. The girl's possessions, blanket, jewelry, and clothes would be laid out to be blessed. Turquoise and silver bracelets, or maybe a squash blossom necklace, was sometimes given to her as a gift.

With the Apaches, a girl's puberty feast was a joyous, jubilant event, always attended by a large crowd of celebrants. The girl would, as in other tribes, stay for four days in a special tent. She would emerge dressed in a new, fringed, gorgeous buckskin outfit, the living embodiment of White Painted Woman, the All-mother and culture heroine of the Apaches. During this time she was enabled to bestow blessings, just like the goddess. A male singer supported her every day with sacred songs. At night the masked ghan dancers performed their mountain spirit dance, because the White Painted Woman said: "From now on we will have the girl's puberty ceremony. When the girls first menstruate, we will have a great feast. There shall be songs for those girls. The masked dancers shall dance in front." Because this was such a happy, joyous festival, the girl who just became a woman was called "she through whom we have a good time."

Among us Sioux and other Plains tribes, the ancient taboos connected with the puberty rite are not as strictly adhered to as before. But the belief of a woman having special great powers during her moontime is still widespread, and the fear of what that power might do to a medicine man's ritual is as strong as ever.

In my mother's family they ignored such customs because they were such staunch Christians. When I was growing up I didn't know anything about these matters. We just didn't talk about menstruation. Nobody ever mentioned it. As young girls growing up with Grandma we were not ever given a hint. And at the Catholic boarding school the priests and nuns discouraged any talk about subjects that had even the slightest connection with sex.

Early on I made a conscious choice. I made up my mind to believe in our old Lakota faith and follow the customs of our people. Therefore I keep the ancient rules pertaining to our moon-time. I won't let menstruating women into the sweat lodge or the sun dance circle. But when I went to church with my mother, or when I was in the Catholic boarding school at St. Francis, I sometimes wondered if the priests, or even the bishop, or the infallible pope, ever had a short moment of doubt about the immaculate conception, or the transubstantiation that changed the wine and the wafer into the blood and flesh of Christ. And may I not also indulge myself in a little twinge of doubt about whether that rattlesnake really dies if I spit on it while being on my moon?

CHAPTER SEVENTEEN

The Land Is Our Blood

Maka ke wakan—the land is sacred. These words are at the core of our being. The land is our mother, the rivers our blood. Take our land away and we die. That is, the Indian in us dies. We'd become just suntanned white men, the jetsam and flotsam of your great melting pot. The land is where even those Native Americans who live in the wasichu cities, far away from home, can come to renew themselves, where they can renew their Indianness. We have an umbilical cord binding us to the land and therefore to our ceremonies—the sun dance, the vision quest, the yuwipi. Here, the city Indians can relearn their language, talk to the elders, live for a short while on "Indian time," hear the howl of brother coyote greeting the moon, feel the prairie wind on their face, bringing with it the scent of sage and sweet grass. The white man can live disembodied within an artificial universe without ties to a particular tract of land. We cannot. We are bound to our Indian country.

It is no wonder that we love it so, because it is beautiful. There are majestic mountains, granite spires, rolling hills of buffalo grass studded with pines, and magic places where spirits dwell. It has badlands—moon landscapes of fantastic shapes looking like the towers of long-gone cities or strange, many-masted ships sailing across haunting deserts. It is strewn with the bones of long-extinct animals, of woolly elephants with gigantic tusks, huge dinosaurs, saber-toothed cats, and Unktehi—the great water monster. In the gullies and dry washes you can stumble upon large, seventy-million-year-old seashells, their mother-of-pearl skins glistening in rainbow colors. Here also are wondrous caves, their walls covered with crystals. Yet our country's greatest attraction, at least as far as I am concerned, is its vast, dreamlike emptiness, the prairie, the "Ocean of Grass," where there "is nothing between you and the North Pole but a barbed-wire fence." When Mom was a girl there were no fences. But that magic emptiness is now being filled and our land is forever shrinking.

Ten years ago we were fighting to keep the feds from driving our traditional Navajo brothers and sisters, the Diné elders, from their ancestral pastures on Big Mountain. From now on we will have to fight for our Lakota land, which means fighting for our survival.

There have been 341 treaties between Indian tribes and the American government that guaranteed us eternal ownership of our land "as long as the sun will shine and the rivers flow," and all of them have been broken. Our famous chief, Red Cloud, once said: "The white man has made us many promises, but he has kept only one. He said: 'We will take your land,' and he took it." In 1929 or 1930, in my grandmother's day, they were holding a sun dance. It was a secret dance in a hidden place, far from wasichu eyes, because at that time our religion was still outlawed and you could be arrested and jailed for putting on an Indian ceremony. On that occasion, the holy man, Hollow Horn Bear, of my own Ashké clan, spoke to the dancers, saying: "A day will come, and it is not far off, when Unchi, our Grandmother Earth, will weep bitter tears, asking you to save her for our unborn generations. If you fail to summon up your strength and power to defend her, then our people will die like dogs." That's heavy talk, and a heavy task that we must fulfill.

It was Sitting Bull who said: "You ask me to plow the ground. Shall I take a knife and tear my mother's breast? Then when I die she will not take me to her bosom to rest.

"You ask me to dig for stone. Shall I dig under her skin for bones? Then when I die I cannot enter her body to be born again.

"You ask me to cut grass and make hay and sell it, and be rich like the white man. But how dare I cut my mother's hair?"

Our land is now threatened as never before. After, as the wasichus put it, "the West was won, wresting virgin soil from bloodthirsty red savages," they at least left us the land they looked upon as worthless: land with little water, unsuited to farming, or deserts where nothing would grow. But then they discovered that this land had coal, copper, oil, natural gas, and uranium, and the wasichus suddenly discovered, or rather invented, "a patriotic need to develop these energy sources." Our res has become "a potential pay zone."

The history of the great wasichu land grab that robbed us of our ancient hunting grounds is a very sad one. In 1858, the government made a number of treaties with the tribes both east and west of the Missouri River. The chiefs were made to "touch the pen," to make their thumb marks on these treaties. They believed what the white man told them, that these strange pieces of paper would protect their land. They were lied to. At that time we still owned the western plains. In 1861, the Dakota Territory, also known as the Great Sioux Reservation, was established. It comprised a huge land area of what is now North and South Dakota, all of Nebraska north of the Platte River, and vast chunks of Montana and Wyoming east of the Great Divide. At the same time, our brothers, the Sioux tribes living east of the "Big Muddy," the Missouri, owned most of Minnesota. Their country was overrun by hordes of landhungry Europeans, mostly Swedes and Germans, and they were forced, at gunpoint, to surrender much of the land they owned. In return they were promised rations to make up for what was taken from them. But the rations were stolen by their white agent and his pals and the people faced starvation. The agent said: "Let them eat grass." In 1863, the Minnesota Dakotas rose in rebellion, killing the agent and stuffing his mouth with grass. This was called the Great Sioux Uprising. I have seen an old newspaper with the headline THE SIOUX MUST BE EXTERMINATED AND NOW IS A GOOD TIME TO DO IT. The article went on: "They have forfeited all rights to property and life. Extermination, swift, sure, and terrible, is the only thing that can satisfy us." The army acted accordingly. The Sioux were driven out of Minnesota, across the Missouri. At Mankato, there was a mass hanging of thirty-eight Sioux warriors, a better show, I'm sure, than a TV spectacular of today. The warriors met their fate singing their death songs.

In 1867, the whites began building the transcontinental railroad through Sioux land. At the same time they built a wagon road, the so-called Bozeman Trail, to reach the newly discovered gold fields in Montana. We called it the Thieves Road. We wanted no war with the whites. All we wanted was to be left alone. But they forced us to defend our land, and Red Cloud, Crazy Horse, and our Cheyenne allies fought the army along the Bozeman Trail. A certain Captain Fetterman swore that with eighty men he could ride over the whole Sioux Nation. He had exactly eighty men with him when we wiped them all out to the last man. The army was forced to give up the Thieves Road—for a while.

In 1868 we made the famous Treaty of Fort Laramie, with the government still promising us the vast plains known as the Great Sioux Reservation. It was broken before the ink was dry. It was just a little piece of paper for the white man to wipe his ass with. The Black Hills, our sacred Paha Sapa, are at the heart of what was the Great Sioux Reservation, given to us for all eternity. This was We Maka Ognaka Ichante, or Ichantognaka, the heart of the earth that is our blood, the heart of existence, the place from which, according to our legends, the Lakota people originated, the home of the wakinyan, the legendary thunderbirds. In 1874, in defiance of the treaty, General Custer led an army expedition into the Black Hills. He reported that "there was gold in the grass roots." Red Cloud said: "We knew that there was yellow metal in little chunks up there, but we didn't bother with it, because it was not good for anything." The whites did not think so and in no time gold-crazy prospectors overran our sacred hills. We never got those hills back, but at least we made Custer pay for what he had done. He had boasted that with his Seventh Cavalry he could ride over all the Indians on the Plains. At the Little Big Horn we proved him wrong. In the end we were defeated. We were outnumbered a hundred to one and we had no Gatling guns or cannon. The Montana and then Wyoming territories were established and each time we lost more land. The crooks in Washington handed over forty-seven million acres of Indian land to the railroads—the greatest land grab ever. In 1889, the government divided the Dakota Territory into the states of North and South Dakota, opening them up for settlement by homesteaders. The Lakota people were squeezed into five different reservations, but our Rosebud res still covered some six or seven million acres, bound by the Missouri River in the east, the Big White River in the north, and the Nebraska line in the south. Some of our people were forced to accept land allotments, usually about six hundred acres per family, often less. This was something new. We always thought the earth belonged to all the people and could not be "owned" by a single person, or even family. Also, suddenly you did not have to be a full-blood anymore to get an allotment. Having one-sixteenth Indian blood would do. Land could now be bought and sold.

One after another, Gregory, Tripp, and Mellette counties were opened to settlement. "Unallotted" land was given to white home-steaders. Indians were offered land to buy provided they had money. They didn't. Mom still has a little of the original Brave Bird land allotment left. The wasichus will probably find a way to steal it. By 1970, our once mighty reservation had shrunk to some

975,000 acres. Wow, you might think, those damn Indians still have too much land left. Think again. Most of the res is now a checkerboard of red- and white-owned parcels of land. Most of the Indian owned property is leased out to white ranchers. Lease money can be as little as twenty-five cents per acre or as high as a dollar and a half. The price is determined by the Bureau of Indian Affairs, "on behalf of the Indians," but mostly for the profit of the whites who run their cattle on our land. Often you wait for your lease money until your hair turns white.

More and more land is falling under state jurisdiction. Bit by bit the state has encroached upon our land. White residents and landowners have always fought for state jurisdiction over parts of our reservations. They are convinced, and rightly so, that state courts and law enforcement officers would better look after their interests in case of conflicts with our people than would either the federal government or tribal councils. Always in the back of their minds, but seldom publicly admitted, is the hope that state jurisdiction will eventually lead to state property taxes on Native Americans. As most Indian owners are too poor to pay taxes, they are bound to become delinquent in their payments and would be forced to sell their allotments for a pittance to eager white buyers. Over the years a number of jurisdiction bills have been passed by the South Dakota Legislature over the violent opposition of the tribes. Particularly during the term of the AIM-hating Governor Bill Janklow, more and more of the reservations fell under state jurisdiction. These bills were of course enacted "for the good of the Indians," who would be better off under the state than under our quaint tribal governments. We resisted. We won a few cases in federal courts but could not stop the steady nibbling at our rights and lands.

So now we are fighting the last Indian war to hold on to the little of what we have left. Some years ago, *Akwesasne Notes* published an article: "It is becoming clearer and clearer why AIM has been targeted by groups like the Law Enforcement Assistance Administration as one of the 'five most dangerous groups in the United States.' It is because of an intensive effort under way by powerful elements in U.S. society to obtain energy, water, and mineral resources that are now on Indian land." So, of course, they went after us with a vengeance. The movement was infiltrated by gangs of undercover agents, sowing dissension.

Most of our leaders were kept neutralized by new trials and indictments, with most of us being in jail at one time or other. Still AIM kept fighting for our land. But AIM is not what it used to be. Many of its leaders are dead, or burned out, or too old to fight. Still we must do what we can. All the confrontations I was involved in—the Trail of Broken Treaties, Wounded Knee, and Big Mountain—were fights for our land.

Our troubles are shared by the other Lakota reservations—Pine Ridge, Standing Rock, Cheyenne River, and Oak Creek. And they are shared by Native Americans all across the country.

After somehow surviving the first twenty or thirty years of reservation life, a time of starvation and utter misery, many families within our wider Ashké clan had gained their economic independence by becoming cattle owners and breeders of fine saddle horses. On Pine Ridge and Rosebud they had communal cattle herds and some Indians were becoming ranchers in a small way. But the government was quick to destroy our budding economy. World War I broke out and in 1917 the white superintendent sold off our cattle "because it was needed for the war effort." The land was then leased to white ranchers, who still run their livestock on our tribal land. It does not help much that the tribal governments on our Sioux reservations and elsewhere are mostly run by "apples"—red on the outside and white on the inside—that is, by the most assimilated, with the least Indian blood. They have little desire to defend our land. At a hearing on tribal sovereignty, my friend Agnes Lamont testified: "Nowadays, the tribal councils get a big board together and they don't let the people know what's going on. Well, it's just like when Chief Red Cloud got with the white people, they got him drunk . . . they say they got him drunk on firewater so he signed this land to them."

Old Henry had a whole trunkful of very impressive papers, yellow with age, covered with seals to which red and blue ribbons were attached. He always shuffled and reshuffled these documents, saying: "There it is, this proves all that land you see, from here to over there, belongs to us." Maybe, but way back in the 1880s, the government had unilaterally abrogated all the treaties they had made with us, taking our sovereignty, our nationhood, away. So all these thousands of pages, with their golden seals or their red wax impressions, aren't worth anything. When the old house burned up, Old Henry's camel-backed trunk with all these papers went up in flames, too.

But we fight not only for our own, much diminished, Rosebud Reservation. We also fight for what rightfully belongs, or did belong, to all Sioux and Cheyennes—the sacred Black Hills. There has been a legal battle going on over this for a lifetime, and the white lawyers who worked for us on our claims have become millionaires, and that is the only result so far. The government and the highest courts in the land have admitted that this huge area was stolen from us. But stolen or "bought," Uncle Sam never gives any Indian land back. Instead he has forked over some 122 million dollars to pay for the stolen land. But we have not accepted it. What we are saying is: "Give us the Black Hills back. Then, maybe we will accept the money you are holding in escrow for us as payment for all the gold and uranium you have taken, and are still taking, out of the hills." Fourteen billion dollars in gold alone have been taken out of our sacred land and they offer us 120 million in compensation! That's like someone stealing my brand-new car and coming back twenty years later saying: "I'm sorry I stole that car from you but I want to make it up to you. Here's twenty bucks." So we are at a dead end. As the *Crazy Horse Advocate* of December 1976 put it: "The Black Hills are sacred to the Lakota people. Both the sacred pipe and the Black Hills go hand in hand in our religion.

The Black Hills is our church, the place where we worship. The Black Hills is our burial grounds. The bones of our grandfathers lie buried in those hills. How can you expect us to sell our church and our cemeteries for a few token whiteman dollars? We will never sell." Of course, there are always some quarter-bloods who'd like to take the money and run. So far we who do not want to sell what is our Jerusalem, our Mecca, still outnumber them.

There should be billboards all over the Black Hills reading: CAUTION, RADIOACTIVE GROUND! About twenty-five years ago the Great Uranium Rush began. By 1980 there were 2,345 square miles of the Black Hills under uranium exploration, with almost six thousand uranium claims staked. Union Carbide had planned to stake out a full quarter of the Pine Ridge Reservation for uranium exploration. Luckily, the tribal council refused to let them come in. What did come in was a rumble of eastbound trucks transporting radioactive material through Pine Ridge and Rosebud. Most of the stuff came from the Edgemont area, at the southern edge of the Black Hills, which is the most contaminated part in South Dakota. Some people in that area had even used radioactive tailings for their foundations without being aware that this was "hot stuff." For them it was: "Get out or get cancer." Union Carbide dug some six thousand test holes prospecting for uranium throughout the area. Another center for this mining activity was Craven Canyon, which is the site of many rock paintings that are sacred to us. There is billions of dollars' worth of this dangerous stuff under Lakota treaty land and, as far as we are concerned, it should just stay there. The longer and deeper, the better. During a protest against the desecration of our sacred land, Russell Means, as I remember it, said: "They have to kill us first. They've shot me three times, and they've stabbed me, and they've clubbed me, but if they shoot me ten times more I'll keep fighting. I'll die fighting right here on this ground."

You can't even find out what these huge companies are up to. If we inquire about specifics they tell us: "This is classified, secret," or "This is competitive information." We get nowhere.

The way these companies were looking for uranium was to drill down, take water samples, and check them for radioactivity. If they got a high reading they knew that the uranium was there. When they were prospecting in Pine Ridge, they found that the water on the res was incredibly radioactive. The groundwater had already been contaminated by all the mining activity and shaft sinking in the areas around us. We started joking around: "Am I already glowing in the dark? Am I glow colored?" or "We want bread, they give us yellow cake." But the matter was serious as hell. At Pine Ridge, we had 101 miscarriages per 1,000 births, seven times the national average, and our cancer rate was four times higher. The closer you were to the mining and drilling, the more likely cancer occurred. We even had some mutations. It was Madonna Gilbert and WARN, Women of All the Red Nations, who, in the early eighties, led the fight and conducted the investigation. We demonstrated, carrying signs: GOLD KILLED CUSTER, URANIUM WILL KILL US ALL!" or HUG YOUR GEIGER COUNTER, HE'S GOT NEWS FOR YOU! I have been told that one pound of plutonium could give every man, woman, and child on this earth lung cancer. That is a good reason to worry.

I'll say something for Union Carbide, the TVA, Gulf, Chevron, Anaconda, Kerr-McGee, Peabody Coal, and all those other conglomerates. They are not racist. They'll drill and mine the land of white ranchers and farmers too if they think their area is "resource rich." So we told those white folks: "You'll be next, you'll be the next Indians." And they responded. One white guy in a bar told me: "This is cattle country, not uranium, coal, or oil country, and I have a gun over my mantelpiece that says so. We're all Indians now." As a result, the Black Hills Alliance was formed, uniting whites and Native Americans. They have done a lot of good work, but whenever we lose a battle, some people get discouraged and fall away. The big companies call the Lakota land a "Nuclear Energy Park," or "Black Hills Multinational Energy Domain," or even "National Sacrifice Area." I ask myself: "Who and what is to be sacrificed here?" It makes me shudder. Some people say: "The collapse of the Soviet Union will kill the uranium mining and that will be our Indian 'peace dividend.' " I don't believe it. They'll still find plenty of use for that evil stuff, and they'll always find Indian land as the ideal site to test their weapons on. In 1942, the government seized 133,000 acres of the Pine Ridge Reservation as a gunnery range to practice aerial bombing. This was near Sheep Mountain in one of the most scenic parts of South Dakota. We never got that land back. More recently, Honeywell tried to make Hell's Canyon, full of ancient rock paintings, into a testing range for something called the "antitank depleted-uranium-tip guided missile system." We barely managed to defeat that plan.

And then there is all that oil, gas, and coal under Indian land, in South Dakota as well as in Montana and Wyoming. On the Cheyenne Reservation, the strip miners in order to get at the coal actually uprooted old Indian graves, throwing skulls and bones all over the place. They even wanted to mine at Birney, where the Cheyennes' sacred tribal bundle, Issiwun, is kept. Coal companies are building so-called gasification plants near the res. They pump live steam through burning coal and "cook" it into gas. What this does to the environment is a horror story. All these various types of land exploitations are exposing us to toxic waste, radiation, and the pollution of our water supply. All these enterprises gulp up water at such a rate that some people predict that in thirty-five years our water will be gone. The little of it left will have turned into a toxic cesspool. To many of our people, who still make do with an old wood stove and a kerosene lamp, the white man's senseless waste of energy is mind-blowing. We have an old proverb: "Indian build little fire, keep close, keep warm. White man build big fire, keep warm chopping and hauling wood." Except that now poor minority people have to do the hauling for him.

We tried to reclaim the Black Hills on several occasions by taking over this or that site. In 1971 and 1972 some of us took over Mount Rushmore, which old John Fire always called the "Giant Tourist Curio Ashtray." It is the ultimate desecration, the faces of the conquerors squatting on top of the land of the conquered. Our guys formed a human chain, peeing on Teddy Roosevelt's nose, an action the women could not participate in, lacking the proper equipment. We also planted a feathered coup stick on top of the mountain. Most of the thousands of tourists below never noticed it. In 1981, AIM took over eight hundred acres inside the Black Hills to establish the Yellow Thunder Camp. It was named after Raymond Yellow Thunder, a gentle, sober Pine Ridge elder; he was attacked by some white racists who stripped him naked from the waist down, forced him to dance at gunpoint, and then beat him to death—just for the fun of it. I went to the camp with Crow Dog. He told the crowd: "Is this wonderful thing really taking place before my eyes? Do you see it, my Indian people? The spirit of Wounded Knee lives on. It lives right here in this camp. It never dies." Indians occupied the site for over a year, all the time under threat of arrest for "interfering with multiple use activity and environmental assessment." I can never get over the government's inventing word monstrosities when they want to get official. In the end, Yellow Thunder Camp died, like all such symbolic takeovers. You cannot get back land symbolically.

For me and for all the Lakota people, the Black Hills are not only sacred but also the most beautiful land in the whole USA. Here are majestic mountains, towers of granite soaring to the sky, sparkling lakes, pine-covered rolling hills, patches of grassland, and caves whose walls are covered with crystals. But this home of the thunderbirds is being transformed into a gigantic Disneyland and tourist trap. Wherever you go you run into such things as the Dakota Dragway ("Thrills and Chills"), the Horseless Carriage Museum, Doll Museum, Western Heritage Wax Musem, Wild West Wax Museum, Life of Christ Wax Museum, Reptile Gardens ("Ride the Giant Turtle"), Marine Life, Calamity Jane Cafe ("Buffalo Steaks, Buffalo Burgers"), Black Hills Gold Jewelry Store, Rockhound's Heaven, 1880 Train Ride, Taco Del Sol, Black Hills Passion Play, Boot Hill Fun Place, Black Hills Petrified

Forest, Buffalo Jeep Rides, Black Hills Greyhound Track, Genuine Indian Village, Flintstone City, and so on, and on, and on. The Grand Old Opry's put on "mellerdramas" like *The Hanging of Flyspeck Bill*, *The Shooting of Wild Bill*, *The Hanging of Cash McCall*, or *Sitting Bull's Last Fight*. Deadwood has become another Las Vegas or Atlantic City, a jungle of lit-up gambling saloons. Bear Butte, sacred to the Cheyennes and Lakotas, now has a parking area and a paved road leading to the top from where gawking tourists with binoculars can watch one of our holy men undergo his vision quest. But the land is still there, beautiful, waiting to be redeemed, and so long as there is still a shred of life left in us we will keep on fighting for it. HECHEL LENA OYATE KIN NIPI KTE, so that my people may live.

CHAPTER EIGHTEEN

Selling the Medicine

All across the country, among all the tribes, Native Americans are angry because the whites are selling our medicine. What Native Americans are saying is that our religion and ceremonies have become fads, and a fashionable pastime among many whites seeking for something that they hope will give meaning to their empty lives. And so our medicine is sold, and hawked about, by fake, non-Indian, so-called "plastic medicine men," giving themselves fancy Indian-sounding names like "Buffalo Grazing on the Mountainside," or "Golden Eagle Soaring to the Sky," or "Free Soul Wrapped in Morning Mist." Such names would not fool a ten-year-old Rosebud kid but are very impressive to the gullible wasichu. Their numbers are growing because there is money, real big bucks, to be made in the fake medicine man (or woman) business. It is an offshoot of the New Age movement and the result of Indians being "in," and of a flood of supposedly pro-Indian movies. After macrobiotics, Zen, and channeling, the "poor Vanishing Indian" is once more the subject of "deep and meaningful conversation" in the high-rises.

One white woman, who claims to have supernatural powers

taught to her by a Native American holy woman, and who also says that she belongs to a sisterhood of Indian spiritual women that doesn't actually exist, puts on mass sessions of Native teachings. She hires large auditoriums in which she teaches Native wisdom and spirituality to as many as six hundred white participants who pay over three hundred dollars apiece. Members of the audience also have to buy drums and drumsticks, crystals, smudge sticks, a special cushion to sit on, and, especially, the lady's books. Take pencil and paper and figure out the profits she makes. There are some self-styled medicine people who literally make a million dollars a year by selling our medicine.

Of course, exploiting of Indian religion and wisdom is nothing new. In the 1880s and 1890s the patent medicine entrepreneurs put on the big Indian medicine shows, selling fake Indian cure-alls. There was the Great Oregon Indian Medicine Company—"THEIR CUSTOMERS NUMBER MILLIONS WITH TESTIMONIALS BY THE THOUSANDS." There were the good folks who sold the Little Wonder Electric Cherokee Rheumatism Belt or the Great Mohee Indian Miracle Oil; there was the Jack Roach Indian Medicine Show and a dozen others.

The biggest of them all was the Kickapoo Indian Medicine Company, selling the "never-failing remedy" Kickapoo Snake Oil, Kickapoo Wonder Tapeworm Remedy, and something called Kickapoo Indian Sagwa, a concoction advertised as curing every sickness known to man. They also published the *Kickapoo Indian Magazine*. Some of their advertisements read:

"Is there some way you can delay, perhaps for many years, that final moment before your name is written down by a bony hand in the cold diary of death? Yes, ladies and gentlemen, there is, by means of that sovereign remedy—KICKAPOO INDIAN SAGWA!"

The company set up whole Indian villages with dozens of wigwams in which the public could see "Kickapoos brewing their Sagwa in steaming kettles." The company employed as agents some well-known former scouts and Indian fighters "who by their bravery in war have obtained such ascendancy over the Red Man that they willingly yield to their control." Most of the Indians in the medicine show were not Kickapoos at all; some were from Peru, and two were actually Irish immigrants. Among the supposed Kickapoo people on exhibit were such characters as Spirit Moon, Princess Red Fire, Dove Wing, Floating Poplar, and one Ma-Chu-Ta-Ga. The desolate, poverty-stricken Kickapoo reservation was described by the Sagwa manufacturers as a "veritable Garden of Eden, inhabited by a race of benevolent, primitive, but noble physicians who have plumbed the secrets of nature." For many years the company made millions of dollars from their Sagwa and Snake Oil. What is going on now is not too different from the Indian medicine shows of a hundred years ago.

Indian religion is at the center of my life. It is the spiritual side of myself. It is part of my heritage. It made me survive. And it angers me to see it profaned, exploited, misinterpreted, bought and sold. The white impersonators are giving people the wrong impressions about our beliefs, falsifying our traditions, and performing grotesque caricatures of our rituals. Whites should be forbidden to perform Native American ceremonies. Our religion should be protected from defilement. Our sacred things and medicine bundles stolen from us years ago, exhibited in museums and private collections to be gawked and laughed at, should be returned to us. Before 1930, we were forbidden to pray in our language. Our rituals were suppressed. For participating in a sweat lodge ceremony you could be jailed under the Indian Offenses Act. Our beliefs went underground and survived. In hidden places, far from the eyes of the missionaries, people kept on sun dancing, but what is happening now is worse than the old effort to stamp out our religion altogether. They tried to kill our faith and triumphantly proclaimed the "Death of the Great Spirit." They did not succeed. But they might succeed now by commercializing it and by giving the world the wrong idea of what the Indian way of life is about. They are selling our religion, selling the pipe, the sweat lodge, the fireplace, the peyote. Pretty soon whites will think of themselves as our teachers, telling us how to perform our rituals or how to use our sacred medicine. They might even say: "This divine plant is too good for those dumb primitives. Let's keep it for ourselves. Let's corner the peyote market."

And always it's money, money, MONEY! Not so long ago you could still go to Custer State Park, or to Wind Cave, and get a buffalo skull for free to use in a ceremony. Now you have to pay a lot for it, because every New Ager wants a buffalo skull for a wall decoration. There are phony medicine men, even Native Americans among them, who charge $750 for letting you go to a sweat lodge, $1,000 for taking you up on a mountain for a vision quest, and who will make a gullible white man, during one single weekend, into a genuine, gold-plated Lakota Medicine Man, complete with diploma, for $2,500. There are people who'll put you on a hill, give you a gaudy pipe from the curio shop, stick an eagle feather on your head, and take you for every cent you've got. But the real Native spiritual person never asks for money for a curing ceremony or some other rite. Our ceremonies are not for sale. So when money is asked for performing them, you know that something is very wrong. The quick-buck people are giving our tribes a bad name and should be stopped.

I was asked to run a sweat in Santa Fe. People asked me: "How much do you charge for it?" I backed out quick. They were polluting our way with their ignorance. To them a sweat is an experience. To us it's our sacred way, our connection to the Creator. There's one impersonator, in L.A. of course, who teaches "sacred Indian sex" in group sessions—for a few hundred dollars per person. A white groupie later wrote a long article about her experience. The headline read: I SOAKED UP INDIAN SPIRITUALITY THROUGH MY VAGINA! Actually, I put this more elegantly. She used a much shorter word for her private parts. She also claimed that sacred Indian sex had given her a "spiritual raging fire, atomic explosion orgasm."

I remember seeing a European movie once—the sun dance as conceived by a sick, fevered wasichu brain. It showed a single white dancer hanging from two meat hooks. He was totally nude except for a little fig leaf around his man thing. In real life there was a nude gay sun dance, also done exclusively by whites, with weird rituals invented for the occasion. I fight these desecrations of our most sacred ceremony, especially as they give outsiders a false and twisted image of the sun dance. It's just pure exploitation through nudity and sensationalism. It has to stop!

Then I was told of the White Coyote, a boy found of all places in the Pine Barrens of New Jersey by an ancient Apache sage. How the Apache got there must be looked upon as a miracle in itself. This aged Indian made the boy into a white shaman who now teaches survival skills to the unenlightened.

In California I saw a pamphlet that was being passed around, with a traditional-looking drawing on it, a pipe with eagle feathers, offering vision quests for $1,500. It said: "This includes your meals and four nights of camping." They even had children's rates. They were tacking these up all over the place. About a year later Rudi met the man in the Susanville penitentiary. The Indians were told: "We're going to bring in some spiritual advisers from the streets, to sweat with you, talk and teach you about the pipe," and so on. So who shows up but that fellow. I won't mention his name because he is dead now. Rudi confronted him on it: "Hey, bud, you're selling the medicine—I've seen your pamphlets around." The guy got mad, but he didn't deny it. And he left. Rudi apologized to the circle, but they said: "Right on. Fuck that dude." Later I heard that the guy was offering "sacred medicine bundles" for sale.

There is this elderly white woman in Texas who provides a perfect example of white people muscling in on the medicine. Again I won't mention her name. She is actually nice and sincere. She has witnessed a number of our ceremonies and it has gone to her head. She imagines that Crow Dog is her grandfather "who gave her the gift." She runs sweats, she puts people on the hill, and she "teaches the Lakota way." It's the same kind of bullshit—"Make your reservations now, parking included. And for $150 you are entitled to the following. . . ." This person actually believes in what she is doing, has her heart in the right place, sends us little gifts; but having witnessed our rituals makes her neither a medicine woman nor an Indian. Well-meaning people can do as much harm as the conniving bullshit artists. A few days spent on a reservation, and a few hours reading a book about our ceremonies, do not authorize a person to put on imitation Sioux rituals.

Mexicans do it, too. There's one fellow, who gave himself the name of a medieval Aztec chief, who says he is a Nahuatl medicine man. They ran him out of Mexico, and now he's floating around the good old USA, performing a mixture of so-called Aztec and Plains Indian rites.

Then there is a woman who has given herself a Sufi as well as a Sioux name, who performs in ashrams, a mishmash of Islamic and Lakota rites. She is white and from Brooklyn. Another man, actually a friend, witnessed a few sun dances, found spirituality overnight, and the next morning he was a great tribal leader with an Indian name. It's a disease and it's catching.

One character who claimed to be Indian and gave himself the usual Indian-sounding name was actually a ballet dancer of Greek and Near Eastern origin. For a while he was accepted by the white public as the great Native American guru and spokesman for the Indian tribes. He actually put himself in charge of the whole new Indian medicine show and became the darling of the media. After he was finally exposed he told an interviewer: "Shit, man, I am an Indian because I *say* I am an Indian!" All these people belong to the Wannabe Tribe. They get a pipe, and they misuse it. There's ways that go with the pipe, rituals that I've learned. But some people will take these sacred things and go the wrong way with them. When I was out in California this past winter, visiting friends for a couple of days, they said: "We're glad you're here; we need your help with a problem." There was this white lady who had bought a pipe at a powwow, and she wanted to use it. She'd been on this fasting trip, going up on the hill on her own. So they asked me: "Could you talk to her? We feel that she doesn't understand the power of these sacred objects." With us was an Assiniboin lady from Montana who knows and respects her tribe's ways. So they asked us both to talk to this white woman. Before we could say yes or no, they gave us tobacco, and asked us again if we'd talk to her. So we agreed. Well, this woman had been in sweats and she'd been fasting, and she wasn't quite all there. We told her to learn more about the ways and how to respect them before she used her pipe. She blew a fit, rolling around on the ground, throwing a temper tantrum, and got really mean and crazy. She said stuff like: "When I'm holding the pipe, it comes right through me." She was tripping on it like it was LSD. She didn't know the meaning of the pipe. She thought it was some kind of crystal, and that through it she could talk to the spirits. I told her how the pipe came to our people and what it represented. I told her that she should go to a ceremony, just be an observer—listen to the old people. You don't have to participate, just observe, and learn. Don't just try to jump into everything. We've shed blood, sweat, and tears over our religion for generations. I said to her: "If you want I can take your pipe back and give it to someone to keep, an elder, and if you ever come you can talk to someone who's knowledgeable." So she handed over the pipe, although she didn't want to. It's an example of how people get into these sacred things, and they're so powerful that if you mess it up, you can get hurt. And it's an example of a white person who wants to know about our religion but won't listen.

There are instances where people used the sacred medicine to snag a lover, or used it as an aphrodisiac. They want to have "genuine Indian orgies." All this makes our religion look cheap, like it can be bought. It is partly because some of these white people have lost their own gods and mislaid their souls. They have trouble dealing with reality, with death. They are vaguely bothered by the decay of their cities, the homeless lying in the streets, the collapse of their own ethics. They are looking to us for an answer that we cannot give them. They want us to fill the emptiness they have inside themselves. No thanks! There are white women, groupies, who are looking for "a medicine man who will put the power right into me." They are hungering for "a deep sexual experience." They'll sleep with anybody who wears braids or a choker.

I would like to warn those white "cosmic channelers" and "psychic interpreters" that it is very dangerous to play around with our sacred things. In the end it will hurt them, hurt them badly. What goes around comes around. Our faith cannot be bought. The grotesque things that these fake medicine men are doing are all aspects of a dying civilization. I only pray that its death will not drag us down with them and become our own undoing.

CHAPTER NINETEEN

A New Love

I was married to Rudi in Santa Fe on August 24, 1991, after being at the sun dance run by Crow Dog and Lame Deer. I had been married to Crow Dog in the Indian way. A medicine man had put a blanket around the two of us, put a pipe into our hands, feathered and cedared us. And that was that. It was not the kind of marriage recognized by white American officials, so we did not need a formal divorce. But my marriage to Rudi was a regular one, done by a justice of the peace in a proper setting, with an exchange of rings. Afterwards we got a marriage certificate, sealed, stamped, and signed. Also, I wore a dress and a white silk hat improvised by Marilyn Pailey, a white friend whom I had met during the 1970s in New York. And I got presents—from Richard and Jean a beautiful turquoise necklace, from Marilyn very fancy earrings, from Sid a southwestern blanket and, as he said, "A bunch of love," and from an Indian artist friend, Nelson Gipp, a sculptured eagle. I felt a little guilty. Here I was, a radical female Sioux activist doing such a bourgeois—or "bushway," as we used to pronounce it—thing: a legal wedding. But then it felt so good. After so many years of hardship, strife, and a nomad's life, wasn't I entitled to a little bit of normalcy? I wasn't getting out of the movement, which was barely breathing anyhow, but I was getting older. I was a thirty-six-year-old grandma. Still—a dress, hat, rings, and certificate—it felt a little strange.

Afterwards we celebrated at a campsite in the Santa Fe National Forest, halfway up to the ski basin, among the pines and aspen trees. The sun was shining, the air full of birdsong and the wonderful scent of cedar and wildflowers. We had a big table there and an outdoor fireplace with a big iron grill. And I was among old friends. I love Santa Fe because for some strange reason you always find there lots of skins, including many Lakotas, and friends who have been in the movement. So up there in the forest with us was Sid Eare St. Pierre. He had been, together with me, among the young AIM kids who had taken over the Bureau of Indian Affairs Building in Washington, D.C., in November of 1972, the culmination of the Trail of Broken Treaties march. And there was Jossie Ramos, with her beautiful full-blood face and the thickest, longest pigtail I ever saw, who, long ago, had painted red Teddy Roosevelt's statue in New York. And Richard and Jean Erdoes, at whose place in New York I had stayed, in 1975 and 1976, together with my baby boy while Crow Dog was doing time in Lewisburg Prison. There was Marilyn Pailey, another old friend from New York, and Al Lostetter, a very good artist, who had just pierced at the sun dance, together with his wife, Kathie, and their two sons, and Delbert Lee, a Sioux Mandan construction worker, and Nelson, the sculptor, a North Dakota Sioux. And my sister Sandra came with her baby daughter and Brad. We call Sandra "Poko," after Pogo, the comic-strip character.

We had steaks under the pines, along with hot dogs, hamburgers, corn, and spuds. Also quite a few twelvers of Bud and two bottles of vodka. I had been on the wagon for quite some time then, thanks to Rudi and the support he gave me, but, what the hell, you don't get married legally every day, so we made an exception and indulged. Anyhow, you could not have a Sioux wedding without booze. We didn't get totally itomni, just a little mellow, though one of the young skins later ran his car into a ditch. No harm done otherwise. I even forced Richard to play spinners and quarter pitch, but he has no talent that way. So, next morning I woke up legally married, still young, though a grandma. So, now we are respectable as well as civil rights minded.

My new husband, Rudi Olguin, is proud to call himself a Chicano. He is a Zapotec, from the same tribe to which Benito Juarez belonged. Rudi even has some Lakota relatives.

Rudi learned early about the Indian ways and the Chicano ways, which are mostly Indian anyhow. His dad was from Watrous, New Mexico. He used to go there when he was a kid. He remembers the old log cabin his grandfather used to live in, that his father was born in—in a frying pan—literally. Out of the womb into a frying pan. He remembers the herbs hanging from the ceiling, the pictures of saints and Montezuma, and his grandma mumbling strange incantations. They had their own medicine ways. His grandma always made different teas and yerbas. Osha was for the teeth and gums. There was one tea that was pretty much good for everything, good for your bones, good for your blood, but some of them really tasted wicked. Or they'd make medicine with potatoes. These were their medicine ways.

When he was in school he learned about George Washington, and baseball, and apple pie, but never about his own people. They never told him about Pancho Villa, or Emiliano Zapata, or for that matter, about Crazy Horse and Sitting Bull. Rudi knew his culture but not his people's history.

Rocky, Rudi's sister, is a curandera. She studied medicinal plants for years with many tribes in Mexico. She knows the secrets of healing herbs and should not be confused with one of the so-called New Age primitive healers. Whenever Rudi got sick he'd go and see Rocky, who would doctor him up. She has whole racks of plants, herbs, roots, and berries. She knows them all and is respected for this. She is chairperson of the National Chicano

Human Rights Council in Colorado and a teacher at the local college.

When Rudi was a kid, his grandma used to tell him about mountain spirits. He says he can still feel them in the Black Hills of South Dakota. He was told about witches who could change themselves into owls, and about the Jarona, an old Mexican witch who ripped the eyes out of her babies and then took them to the river and drowned them. The Jarona was blind, but would walk the streets at night and steal babies that were left alone in their cribs. She'd take them to the river and kill them. And she'd be on the rooftops crying for her babies. Another story was that she had red eyes that were like a cat's, and hooves like a goat's. There was a dance in an old barn, and a white dog appeared at the dance. They chased the dog down the street, and when they got close to it, it was the Jarona, dressed in a white veil. Earlier she had been at the dance, and she had eyes that were red. When she took off, she ran like a goat, and they couldn't catch her. The Jarona goes back thousands of years in the Mexican culture. Rudi said these stories scared the shit out of him and he would never tell them to our children.

His father kept fighting chickens and he had a real warrior of a rooster who was a prize bird, a killer. He murdered scores of opponents, particularly with steel spurs on. Cockfighting is outlawed now, but it still goes on. As for his dad's prize rooster, someone ran over it, I think on purpose. He had caused a lot of folks to lose a lot of money. Rudi's family always kept dogs and horses, too, and he learned to ride almost before he could walk.

Rudi was all right until he wound up in the Denver barrio. He was ten or eleven then, and on those mean streets he got into trouble with drugs and the law.

Rudi grew up in the days when the Chicano movement was going strong, with Corky Gonzales and César Chavez. Plenty was happening. In New Mexico, in the little town of Tierra Amarilla, there was a shoot-out as Reies Lopez Tijerina and his people faced tanks and armored cars when they tried to reclaim their ancient fields under the old Spanish land grant. In California, the Black Panthers made headlines. In South Dakota, AIM was on the rise. Kent State happened. All in the late sixties and early seventies. And then came Wounded Knee. Rudi got involved both with the struggle for Chicano rights and with AIM. He says that the fire still burns in his heart, that it will never die.

In Denver there was a lot of killing during the protest days. The Chicanos would have a demonstration and the police would show up in full riot gear, and a little confrontation would turn into a tear gassing and shooting. The police beat people to death and got away with it. An Indian brother, Sidney White Crane, was picked up on a drunk charge and they beat him to death in the elevator. When they put him in his cell he hemorrhaged and died. Nothing was ever done about it.

The protesters tried education and persuasion. They tried to be nonviolent. It was the cops who started the violence. Rudi told me that the police were always dying to stop a car full of Indians or Chicanos and beat the shit out of them for no reason. Detectives in Denver took Rudi to the mountains in Golden, Colorado, beat him severely, and left him up there—no arrest, no charges; they took him for a "Chicago ride," maybe because he was sporting a beret, or because he belonged to the movement, or because Rocky was one of the leaders. Then he got involved in the "Platte Valley Action" riot. This happened when a large group of Chicano and Indian people got together at the Platte Valley Action Center. The cops just pulled into the alley and started, as Rudi calls it, to "fuck the brothers over." The police opened up and started shooting into the crowd—at men, women, and children. They were firing tear gas, and shotguns with wooden plugs. If you get hit with one of those, it's going to bust you up, it's going to hurt. They bashed Rudi's head wide open and labeled him a no-good, violent criminal. But he was just a victim. He still has a bump on his head. So we had similar experiences at about the same time—he in Colorado and I in South Dakota. We were fighting for the same things.

Rudi got involved with AIM during the days when a lot of Chicano people from New Mexico, Colorado, and from below the border were coming to the sun dance, dancing at Big Mountain and Crow Dog's Paradise. It forged a bond between Native American and Mexican Indians. There were a bunch of sun dancers out of Colorado who called themselves the Red Vest Society and they all turned up at Crow Dog's place. That's when Rocky first started to dance with me. We became the closest of friends and called each other "sister" and adopted each other. And at that time my sister Barb adopted Rudi as a brother. Barb's husband, Jim, has the same background as Rudi.

Jim and Barb lived for a while in Colorado but eventually settled down on our Rosebud Reservation, at Mission. Rudi was always visiting them and that's how I met him. He fell in love with me right away. He often tells me that, but he did not dare to show it, because I was, at that time, still with Crow Dog. I have to admit that I was hardly aware of Rudi then, wrapped up in my own problems.

Rudi got into Lakota religion while in Denver. Whole caravans of AIM people and Native American Church members were always passing through Denver, on the way to Big Mountain, to the peyote gardens in South Texas, or to the Coast. Many pulled in at Rocky's place, whose house was always full of Indians. She knew all the AIM leaders and they were always welcome to stay with her.

A friend of Rudi's, Thomas Lopez, had a sweat lodge in Adams County. They called it the Eagle Lodge, and it was open to anybody who wanted to sweat. And Rudi went there a lot and through the lodge also met many of the movement people.

Rudi has done some crazy things for his Indian brothers. The Denver Museum of Natural History had in its possession a lot of medicine taken from a burial ground—a pipe bag, an old Indian war shirt, beaded and quilled artifacts—that belonged to the Red

Cloud family. Some people got mad and they "liberated" it. They said that stuff didn't belong there, that it belonged to Chief Red Cloud. The museum offered a reward for its return; they wanted these things back, bad. The FBI got involved. The people who had the artifacts came to Rudi, because at the time he knew Marlene and Marletta Red Cloud, descendants of the famous Red Cloud family. They wanted Rudi to take the stuff back to the Red Cloud family in South Dakota. This was before the Knee, and things were really bad in Pine Ridge. Everyone was carrying guns, and none of those sun dancers wanted to do it, so right away it was: "Put it on Rudi, he's not scared, he's got balls." He said no because he had just gotten out of the reformatory in Buena Vista and was on parole. If he got caught with these objects in his car, he'd go to federal prison. But they kept asking him, and they talked him into it. So he drove all the way up to South Dakota, where he met Marletta and Marlene's grandfather and all those Red Clouds. They really honored him up good and told him he was an adopted brother forever.

Now it's lawful to return these artifacts to the tribes or families from whom they were taken.

Rudi had a house in Denver and Jim and Barb moved in with him and shared the rent. That's when Rudi got really tight with Barb and found out that I was her sister. As I said, Rudi always had his eye on me, though I didn't know it. When he heard that I had left Crow Dog he at once came hotfooting up to South Dakota and snagged me. He was so obviously head over heels in love with me that it bowled me over. He said: "I'm glad I waited for you. I want you to be my wife. I think it was fated by the Great Spirit." So we got together.

Well, that's Rudi for you, where he is coming from. What is he like? He is a big teddy bear of a man. Right now he is putting in a flower bed for me. Last week he fixed Mom's roof. He is a talented artist, on paper and canvas. He can cut your hair or bake a pie. He can frame a house, or put in a swimming pool for some rich homeowner. He is good to me. So good that it makes me nervous, because I'm not used to it. Sometimes I am mean to him, snap at him, just because it makes me jittery to be pampered. He keeps me from drinking. I have not touched a Bud or Jack Daniel's in over a year.

I recently heard that Crow Dog also has a new wife, not merely in the Indian way, but legally, with a marriage license and all that. I am glad for them, and wish them all the best, but I am also much relieved. With Crow Dog having done this, it makes me feel less bourgeois and establishment for having done the same.

CHAPTER TWENTY

The Iron House

At least half of all the Indian men and women I know have spent some time in jail. I have. It seems that we can't help it. In South Dakota about 6 percent of the population are Indians, but we account for 43 percent of arrests and 50 percent of all convictions. You can walk into the infamous Pennington County jail at Rapid City and find that more than half of all inmates are skins. Many get jailed for political reasons, because of racial prejudice, because of cultural differences, or just because they are Indians. I think any white jury—and all the juries are white—would find even Jesus Christ himself guilty of murder or child molesting if he happened to be a skin and a member of AIM. Especially here in South Dakota people sometimes go to jail for having done the right, moral thing. I remember a case that was tried when I was still a young girl. A traditional family was having a wopila and give-away, an honoring feast for a dead relative. There are often up to a hundred or even more people at such a feast and all have to be fed. Well, the family sent one young man to get the food from the store. He took a friend along. At the store he said: "We are having a wopila. I need a side of beef from the freezer, and so many pounds of potatoes, coffee, sugar, and so on." The store owner and his clerk got those things and piled them up on the counter, or wherever. The owner was new. He said: "Well, that's so and so much. Just pay me and take your stuff." The young man said: "I can't pay you right now. We pay you when the lease money comes in. Write it down in your book and I'll sign my name to it." "Sorry," said the owner, "I don't sell on credit. It's cash on the barrelhead." "Don't you understand?" said the young man. "We're having an honoring feast. I just got to have that food. The old man who ran this store before you always let us have credit against the lease money." "That's probably why he sold the store. He was going broke. Sorry, no deal." The young man went back to his old pickup and took his double-barreled shotgun from the rack in back of his seat. It is common for people around here, both white and Indian, to have guns in their pickups. The young man pointed the gun at the owner and his helper, telling his friend to load the food on the pickup. "I've just got to do this," he told the storekeeper. "We're having a wopila and have to feed our guests. You get paid when the lease money comes in. You sure are a mean, tightfisted son of a bitch." Then he drove off with his friend, and his family had a nice giveaway. Of course, the store owner called the cops on him and the young man and his friend did time for armed robbery. But from our point of view they had done nothing wrong.

In my early teens, I and my friends stole things from the trading post—small stuff, like candy, or a can of food, or, in the case of the older teens, cigarettes. The trading post owner had started out as a little peddler and wound up as a millionaire by overcharging the "dumb Indians" and we felt perfectly justified taking a tiny little bit back. Again, the white folks did not see eye to eye with us on this.

Whites break the law too, but it is always the poor and the nonwhites who actually do the time in penitentiaries. Some of us just stay in there, forgotten by the outside world. A white judge will let a white defendant off with a gentle slap on the wrist but will put a Native American in the slammer for the same offense—particularly here, in South Dakota.

AIM, the American Indian Movement, was born in the "iron house." Four Ojibway brothers founded it while doing time in a Minnesota jail. And, of course, long after everybody was released at Attica for having taken part in the great prison riot there, one lonely young guy was kept behind bars, Decajawiah Hill, a Mohawk Indian. Native Americans, used to an outdoor life, going along unregulated, on "Indian time," have a really hard time being imprisoned. Many commit suicide in the pen. I know of a sixteen-year-old who hanged himself in his cell and I still grieve for my friend Pewee, who did the same thing.

I've been in jail quite a few times, in the white man's jail for political reasons, in tribal jails for drunk and disorderly or driving without a license. Tribal jails are not exactly pleasant, but not really bad. Tribes are allowed to handle only the petty stuff. Domestic arguments, speeding, driving while under the influence, penny-ante things. The feds handle the so-called major crimes, which are mostly not major at all but stuff just a cut above a misdemeanor.

Rudi has been in jail a few times. When he was fourteen years old his mother was in a car accident. She was the strength of the family, working as a private secretary. The accident left her crippled and brain damaged. It broke up the family and meant hard times for Rudi. It was the sixties and the barrio was drowning in drugs. His family had spread out in all directions so as a teenager Rudi was bouncing around more or less on his own. He hustled to keep from starving. He ran with a group of kids who were all in the same boat. They were not basically criminals, they just stole to survive. Then he started using heroin and stole in order to support his habit. Rudi grew up in the barrio on the east side of Denver where the poor had been crowded into the projects and the young did not have any alternatives but to shoplift or deal drugs. He told me: "Politicians, businessmen, and brokers steal money all the time, mostly in a legal way. The only difference is that they are much bigger thieves than a homeless kid from the barrios. I know I have to answer for what I did, but I don't have to answer to *them*."

Rudi is honest. If he likes you, he tells you, and if he doesn't like you he lets you know it. He lays his cards on the table. He doesn't bullshit you or play games with you. When I first met him, he leveled with me right away. He told me: "I've been in the joint. I've got a shady past and I don't lie about it. Thinking back, there's a lot of stuff I did that I'm not proud of, that makes me shake when I remember it, but when you're young and crazy, drinking wine and smoking weed, you do dumb things."

I told him that I didn't care, that I knew where he was coming from, that I had been there myself. He asked whether I cared that he wasn't a Sioux. I said: "You're a human being just like me."

He told me: "You're the first woman who didn't try to judge me. You're straight down. Some women I meet, when I tell them I've been in prison, it's like they smell shit. Yes, I did some things wrong, but that doesn't make me a bad person. I know one day I'll have to stand naked in front of Grandfather and he'll knock fire out of my ass—I'll have to answer for what I've done."

Rudi has a colorful way of expressing himself. Much of his language has been formed in the joint. But, he is an eloquent and fascinating speaker. He has been with AIM, taken part in ceremonies, and lived with us Lakotas. He told me that it was Indian tradition and religion that kept him going while he was in prison, that it was the pipe and the sweat lodge that made broken-down people whole, that made whitemanized men Indians again. He told me about the long struggle for Native Americans to be able to hold their ceremonies inside the joint, and to have medicine men come in, just as the others can have their priests, ministers, and rabbis. He told me about the battles he'd had with the wardens who call our rituals "heathen superstitions" and our holy men "bullshit artists."

He has seen a lot of people who came to the medicine in prison and it turned their lives around. He had one friend in prison, Pete, who came in hard-core, a killer off the streets, but he went back to the Indian beliefs and now is a sun dancer at Big Mountain and at Crow Dog's. Pete got out before Rudi and kept writing him letters of encouragement. Barb and Jim, who knew him long before he and I met, wrote to him also. He still treasures an old letter from his sister Rocky in which she wrote him words of strength:

"Brother, when you seem to get yourself down, teach yourself to think like the eagle always, and let your spirit soar high. Feel the strength of his wings, and feel the beat of his heart so that your spirit soars high and you can look down and see just how small things really are." That kind of support helped Rudi overcome days of despair, when he was just ready to go off and hang himself, or try to escape. That's when he'd have to smoke his pipe, pray, and think like that eagle.

When Rudi was in prison, he worked a lot for the Indian and Chicano cause, and for the Freedom of Religion Act, so that we could worship and have the pipe, sweat lodge, feathers, and medicine in the institution. He helped mostly with the legal work and typing. He had a friend named Owl, an old man who was a Mono from the Tule River Reservation, who was very instrumental in bringing the sweats into Folsom and San Quentin. They were broke, and it cost a lot of money to file the motions and the writs. Oddly enough, Charlie Manson lent the Indian people a lot of money to get the sweat lodge into Vacaville. He gets royalties on his book, and he came through.

The first prison sweat lodge erected in the country was in San Quentin. The second one was in Vacaville, then Susanville, then Folsom, and so on, until now there's been a lodge in just about every institution. The first time Rudi sweated in a prison was in California, in San Quentin. A fenced-in area called "Indian land" is where they erect the lodge, and Indians from the outside come and help to build it. This area also serves as a meeting place, which is good because in California there's a lot of gangs, and Indian

people are not into that. There are many tribes in California—
Pomo, Karok, Mono, Hupa, a lot of different nations, while in the
Los Angeles area you can find Native Americans from every part
of the country. So the lodge was always intertribal. The spiritual
advisers who run the sweats come from the outside, and to get in
they have to have what's called a brown card, just as if they were
a priest in the Catholic or Protestant church. Rudi sweated a few
times with an adviser named Cedro, who got fired over an incident
involving a death row inmate whose grandmother had died. The
inmate cut off his braids and wrapped them in sage. Then he asked
Cedro to take them to be buried with his grandmother. When
Cedro was leaving the prison, they found them on him and fired
him for violating the strict rule that forbids anything going in or
out of the prison. That's when Richard Williams took over as
spiritual adviser to the lodge. He was in charge of the northern part
of California—Folsom, San Quentin, Tracy. He'd go to a different
institution each week, and sweat with the brothers, and teach them.

For years Rocky sun danced with me. She'd visit Rudi and show
him the scars, saying: "These are for you. We suffer so that you'll
straighten up." She would always pray that Rudi would stay with
the medicine, with the red road. And he'd tell her: "Your prayers
are felt, and they help a lot."

When Rudi was fourteen he met Archie Fire Lame Deer in
Lompoc. Back then Archie's father was still alive, and Archie was
the spiritual adviser to the lodge. It was good, because Rudi came
in young, and he was able to learn about these traditional teachings
before he got caught up in the bullshit that goes on in penitentiaries—gangs, stabbings, and drugs. I'm grateful to Archie for that.
Rudi sweated with spiritual men from different tribes—Shoshones,
Navajos, Huroks, Karoks, Lakotas—and was able to learn their
different ways. He learned songs from many different tribes. And
he learned respect—for everything—the whole universe—man-
kind, animals, the earth, the air, the water. Without spiritual
strength I don't think you can make it in this world.

If you're in prison you're stereotyped as a tough guy, a criminal.

It's not like that. Most Indians in prison are there because they've made mistakes in their life, because their culture is different, that's all it is. Less than one in ten are hard-core criminals. Most are young guys who got into trouble either drinking or doing drugs, or hurt someone in a bar fight. Rudi first went in when he was fourteen years old under what they called the Youth Act. They don't have it anymore because it was declared unconstitutional. At that time if you were arrested for a federal crime you were tried as an adult. There were a lot of young kids, fourteen or fifteen years old, in the federal institutions then.

A lot of Indian inmates would sometimes have a problem with the northern Mexicans in the yard, or the blacks, and they always had Rudi represent the Indians and talk it out. Usually they were fighting about stupid stuff—a pack of cigarettes, a dirty look in the hall, a TV program, or some other crap—but it would lead to a war, so Rudi became a mediator in the institution.

One time there was almost a full-scale riot involving the Crips, a black gang out of East L.A. The Indians had gone into a dorm and were watching some TV when the black guys came in and turned it off. The Indians turned it back on, and it turned into a fight. This time it involved the southern Mexicans, because two of them were Mexican and two of them were Indians, so they had all the Indian and Chicano people backing them up and the Crips backing up the black guys. That's a lot of people. You're talking about five or six hundred people ready to get down. They were ready for war. The cops were already on the tower with guns. So Rudi, representing the Native Americans, the shot caller of the Crips, and the shot caller of the Mexicans were brought to the lieutenant's office and told: "You dudes better talk and get this thing over with, or we're going to lock down the whole institution." Rudi talked to the others and got it all settled. When you talk man to man from the heart they listen to you, and Rudi is a good talker. They all prayed together and everybody shook hands. So that's how Rudi kept peace in the institution.

Native Americans doing time had a lot of outside support,

especially from people praying for them at the sun dance. At San Quentin every year the prisoners used to make a staff, tie their medicine bags and feathers to it, and make offerings. Then Richard Williams would take it to Big Mountain for them. A lot of people prayed for Rudi at Big Mountain and at Crow Dog's Paradise. In the eighties, after the Longest Walk and the Longest Run, people started having runs to support the prisoners, the Indian people who were doing time. They would have runs to the prison, and in there they'd have a powwow, a lecture, or a ceremony. That was going pretty well until Ted Means's daughter, Kimberly, died. They had been running relays along the highway, between Rose-bud and the prison at Sioux Falls. She ran across the road, was run over by a car, and died. She must have been around ten years old. I don't think they've had many runs after that. But they have annual powwows. Such medicine men as Archie Fire Lame Deer and Crow Dog have done a lot to bring Indian religion into the penitentiaries. Two years ago, they even managed to get Indians out on a short leave from prisons at Sioux Falls and elsewhere to sun dance at Crow Dog's Paradise—even a man like White Hawk, who's doing life for murder.

All the institutions in California have Indian groups. Since Rudi could type, every time he'd go to a joint, they'd say: "Hey, Rudi, why don't you be the secretary of the Indian group? Why don't you help us with the paperwork?" Sometimes he'd get into trouble because of his involvement with Indian groups. They'd bother him because he was a talker, a spokesman for the Indians, and he was right up front about this. And he'd be the first person called to the captain's office whenever something happened. They'd threaten him, or move him—like from San Quentin to Soledad. He'd stay there four or five months, and after he filed papers, they'd send him back to San Quentin. By then he'd have lost his cell, his job, and all his property. They were good at that. Whenever you were sent to another institution, somehow your TV, your property and stuff, would take six months to get there, and when it did, you'd find that your books and paperwork somehow were destroyed or misplaced. They set Rudi up with minor shit like: "We found a razor blade in your locker; that's a concealed weapon." Stupid shit like that. They were always screwing the Indian brothers around. They'd get ready to have a sweat and there'd be no wood. They had to get paperwork done in triplicate just to get the wood brought in. One thing about California was that each Indian group kept in touch with the others. Every month Rudi would write a letter to the Indian circle in every institution and let them know what was happening. And he'd get letters from brothers in Folsom, or Chino, or wherever. It was their way of reaching out to each other. People had to fight for everything—to have a powwow, or to take the drum out into the yard and play it and learn some songs. And every time they would have to go through security and they'd search everything. They knew they were just taking the drum to sing some songs in the yard, but they make a big issue out of everything.

Rudi met a lot of Chicano gang members from L.A. who said to him: "Hey brother, I'm part Indian, but I don't know nothing about it, I grew up in the barrio, right in East L.A., but I'd like to learn something about Indian ways." And Rudi would take them aside and teach them. There were even full-blood Indians in the joint but they grew up in East Oakland, or San Francisco, and they'd never been on the res, and they'd want to know more about their culture. The drum used to really bring them together. When you start drumming, people gather. They want to see what it's about. And that's when they start to learn. That's when you feel that you really accomplished something. To sit by the fire and sing, and hear the drumming, sitting with Indian and mestizo people, talking about the res; it's like you aren't a part of the joint anymore when you're on Indian ground. Rudi would be on Indian ground drumming, and the gangs were inside fighting each other. They had their knives. The Indians had the pipe. The Indians were better off.

Rudi learned barbering in prison. He still cuts hair very well. He also got certificates in bricklaying, welding, and in carpentry, and he did electrical work and plumbing. He learned drafting and design too. He can read and write music and he plays a number of instruments: the guitar, bass, congas, and a little bit of drums, piano, and flute. And he can cook and bake for a thousand people.

Rudi escaped a couple of times from prison. They took him to the hospital one time and he escaped from there but was immediately busted. He escaped again from the institution and got caught. The last time he ran, he got into a high-speed chase with the Denver police. They had a hard time catching him because he's a good driver, but they eventually ran him off the road with a roadblock. He went off a bridge and got hurt pretty bad, breaking his ribs and shoulder. He woke up days later in the hospital. He lucked out, though, because he ended up beating all the escape charges, and just got returned to the penitentiary.

After Rudi had served his sentence, he got into a fight in Denver in which he ended up in the hospital with a broken leg. After Rudi got out of the hospital he was walking down Forty-fourth Street early one morning, really bummed out, sick of the city, and the bars, and the drugs, and everything that goes on there. Then a blue van pulled up beside him, the door swung open, and there was my sister Barb and Jim, who had just pulled into Denver. They asked him: "Do you want to split?" Rudi said: "Yeah," and left with them for South Dakota without even bringing clothes or anything. He just had on a pair of shorts, a tank top, and a hat. He was so sick of Denver, and the kind of life he was leading, that he just wanted to leave. He made a promise to himself that drugs would not be a part of his life anymore. He made a promise to Tunkashila to follow his ways, to give the medicine a try, to go back to the good red road. And he prayed that he'd meet a woman who would take him for what he is. He had known about me for a long time through his sister Rocky, and had talked to my family over the phone, from inside prison. And when we finally met, we gave each other strength. He was at Jim's house, and was really nervous—he didn't know what to talk to me about. He had looked forward to meeting me for years, but he never had the opportunity to because he was in and out of prison. I never thought I would fall in love again, but I dug Rudi. Then, as we got to know each other more, and we were talking about our lives, it turned out that he was at the same point that I was—he was disgusted with the drugs; I was getting that way about alcohol. So along he came for me, and along I came for him. We've got a lot of struggles ahead of us, but we'll hang with each other. We'll deal with whatever lies ahead.

CHAPTER TWENTY-ONE

Skin Art

Traditional Lakota people, and even the not quite traditional, have tattoos, mostly on their wrists. These are not the elaborate designs you see in tattoo parlors, but lines, little stars, unconnected letters—small blue marks pricked into the skin for no apparent reason, certainly not for their beauty. But there is a reason. Our people hold the widespread belief that, after death, the ghosts start out on Tachanku, the Spirit Road, which is the Milky Way, to go to Wanagi Tamakoche, the Spirit Land. On the way they have to pass Hinhan Kaga, the Owl Woman, who acts as a sort of gatekeeper to the Land of Many Lodges. She examines every passing soul, looking for tattoos on their wrists, which are a sort of passport to the spirit world, and if Owl Woman does not find such marks, she throws the soul down from the Milky Way into bottomless space. I was told that in the old days there was always one man or woman to do the tattooing. Such persons marked out the design on the skin with clay and, with an awl, pierced the skin. Blue clay was put over this, even when there was still bleeding. When the clay dried, it was rubbed off and the dark blue marks remained. A long time ago, people were tattooed with a blue spot on their foreheads or with two lines down their chins so that the Owl Woman would let them pass. Nowadays, it seems any kind of simple design will do, but faces are no longer marked that way, just the wrists.

Tattooing was performed in almost all Indian tribes, usually having religious or ceremonial significance. Often rituals and special songs were performed while somebody was tattooed. Awls, needles, sharpened bones, cactus spines, porcupine quills, or fish bones and teeth were used for skin pricking, depending on the tribe. The Wichita used the most elaborate forms of tattooing, covering large parts of their bodies, which is why early French travelers called them the Peaux Piquées, the Pricked Skins. Among the Osages, pipe keepers and members of the medicine society were tattooed, the men on their eyelids. The Caddos marked themselves with the designs of plants and animals, tattooing also the corners of their eyes. Among the Assiniboins, women had three vertical stripes tattooed on their chins, below the lower lip. Omaha women were marked with a circle on their foreheads, representing the sun and daylight, and with a star on their breast, symbolizing night. The Kiowas tattooed round dots on their women's foreheads. The Ojibways got themselves tattooed as a cure for toothache. The Hidatsas also used simple designs to denote war honors. Early depictions of southeastern Indians show their entire bodies covered with elaborate tattoos. Most men I have met from among Plains tribes bear some tattoo marks, even if they no longer know their significance and just follow an old tradition out of habit. I know a man in Rosebud, the son of a former tribal chairman, who has WINE tattooed under one nipple and BEER under the other.

For all these reasons I was intrigued to find that Rudi was into tattooing. He calls it "skin art." He learned it in prison—naturally. He is a good artist, anyhow, and that shows in his tattooing. Tattooing was developed years ago in the Orient, and they used to tattoo with bamboo. For a long time in the U.S. it was identified with prisoners and bikers, but now it has become fashionable among the public. Now every year they have tattoo conventions. The best tattooists will get together and compare their work. They have contests just like an art show. Rudi entered his stuff, and a lot of it has come out in *Outlaw Biker* magazine and *Easy Rider*. He did a tattoo on an Indian brother, of a medicine wheel with some pipes, and out of the smoke an Indian was holding a pipe to the sun, and it came out really good. He sent it to *Easy Rider* magazine, and they displayed it on a color page. Rudi has been tattooing for fifteen years. He uses a cassette motor and a guitar string. He makes an electric pencil with the motor and bends the guitar string like a little drive shaft, so that it runs through the ink pen, and the needle comes up and down. You just dip it in ink and draw with it. It's really easy. There was a biker in prison with Rudi, a Hell's Angel named Shotgun, who was a fantastic tattooist. And his wife, Star, owned one of the biggest tattoo parlors in San Francisco. When Rudi got out, he got a job working there for Star. Right now tribal designs are really hot. That's what people want. Down their chin, or on their shoulder, African or Indian tribal designs. There's good money to be made, and there's a big market for it. Nowadays if you open a parlor, you have to have the Department of Health in there, to make sure you sterilize your needles and wear rubber gloves. One time Rudi made about thirty-four hundred dollars in three days at Sturgis, tattooing the bikers at their yearly get-together. He's done that a few times. He has tattooed on the boardwalk in Santa Cruz. He says that he's easily done five thousand tattoos in California. When he first started, Rudi was really good at tattooing skulls, demons, lizards—that's what people go for. They don't want a deer drinking water on their back. They'd rather have a skull with a snake, and crossbones.

There's a lot of gang stuff that one has to be careful with. Sometimes guys would bring Rudi a pattern, and it would be a Hell's Angel's logo, their colors, and you're not allowed to wear that if you're not one of them. He'd have to tell a lot of them: "I can't put that on you, bud." If you ever see someone with stars, they got that tattoo in a federal prison, and each star means five years. The teardrops coming out of dudes' eyes, representing killings in the joint, those are gang symbols. A lot of people don't know that—they'll want a teardrop on their eye because they think it looks good. And you have to tell them that this identifies you as a gang member.

Rudi likes to do Indian art and biker art. Usually women will want something small and dainty like a flower. One time he did barbed wire on a woman's breast. She asked him to do it, and it came out really nice. After that he must have had a hundred women come in: "Are you the one who did the barbed wire?" It became a hot item. He put it on their ankles, on their wrists, on their breasts; some wanted it around their necks. On one woman he put a holster with bullets around her waist, with a .45 on the side of her leg. Janis Joplin had a little red heart on her tit; they used to call it the Janis Joplin heart. A lot of girls wanted that. It used to take him five minutes to do it, and he'd charge them sixty dollars.

Then you've got the nuts. Bikers who want a picture of a woman naked, with her legs spread open. One man wanted a picture of a dog with a big old weenie pissing on a fire hydrant. Rudi said: "Man, do you really want this on you?" They'd bring him nasty pornography. In *Hustler* magazine, they had a little penis in tennis shoes chasing a little pussy in tennis shoes. He tattooed that design on some guys. He asked them: "Does your mom know you're putting this on you? What'll your wife think?" Bikers don't care. You can tell by a man's tattoo whether he's a sailor, thief, pimp, mafioso, or biker. Some people won't rest until every inch of their body is covered with designs—flowers, butterflies, snakes, skulls, and daggers. Rudi met a guy who had Christ's head put on his bald pate. Another had two eyes tattooed, one on each of his buttocks, making his ass look like a face. People who want to be tattooed don't always have good taste.

An old Apache man told me a story, that years ago the elders had gone into the mountains to make medicine and Grandfather came down, and he opened up the earth and showed them hell, and a lot of the people down there were tattooed. In the Bible, God tells you that your body is a temple and not to abuse it. But among bikers it's the fashion, and among Native Americans, it's a tradition.

I was toying with the idea of Rudi putting the design of a waterbird on me—the symbol of the peyote church—but I quickly dropped the idea. He has been working for over a year on my brother-in-law's stomach. It is very big—the stomach as well as the design. It's a very ambitious project—eagles, and tipis, and Sitting Bull, and whatnot. I wonder whether he'll ever finish it, call it part of an Indian-Chicano-biker-prison tradition. Well, this was just a little wandering off the track of my story.

CHAPTER TWENTY-TWO

Here and Now

After my marriage to Rudi, we both moved for a few months to Phoenix, Arizona. I made and sold beaded and feathered earrings. Rudi did some construction work. But then I got homesick for the res and all my relatives and friends there. So here I am again, back at Rosebud. Rudi and I, together with all the kids, now have a home on the res. It's a tiny, so-called transitional house way out in the boondocks but we like it. While it's small inside, it is big outside. We have a large garden, a ceremonial ground for rituals, and a corral for horses, though we don't have any at the moment. The place is situated in a little valley between two hills, with a big old creek running through the grounds. There are lots of trees all around and you can see eagles and hawks sitting on the branches. You can't see any other house, just endless prairie wherever you look. In the evening, at twilight, mule deer come down to the creek. At night there is a tremendous sky with millions of stars—pure magic—and you can hear the coyotes howling at the moon when they are not busy going after rabbits. Silhouetted against the moonlight, the cottonwoods along the brook look like mighty ghosts waving their arms around. So the nature around us is inspiring, but living so far out on the prairie has its drawbacks. The road is terrible. When it rains we are surrounded by a sea of mud so that we can't even get the car out. Last winter, after a blizzard, we were snowed in for three days and just had to stay put, cut off from the rest of the world. But the beauty around us makes up for everything. The house once belonged to my uncle, Clifford Broken Leg. It was in terrible shape when we first moved in. I called it a bunkhouse. It must have been a place for cowboys once, because the designs of cattle brands were scrawled all over the walls. It consists of two very small bedrooms and a tiny front room. So, with three kids and the new baby, we are kind of cramped, but we are used to that. We have an old cast-iron stove and, in winter, Rudi is constantly hauling wood to keep us warm. We use propane for cooking.

Rudi has done wonders to make the place livable. He repaired the plumbing and the electrical system, laid tiles, put in a new floor, and painted the walls. Outside, he put in flower beds for me in the front yard. He pulls up weeds, rakes the grounds, and makes the kids help him. Financially, the setup is not so good. The house belongs to my cousin Clifford, who is a tribal councilman. He charges us only seventy-five dollars per month, which is very reasonable, though I tried to get him down to fifty bucks. But that's the good part. The house is about three-quarters of a mile from the nearest drivable road. It is six miles from Parmelee and twenty-eight miles from Mission, where we have to go for our groceries and all other supplies, and where we go with our food stamps. So a round trip to the local supermarket is about sixty miles. It takes a full tank for our old crate. The businesses on the res have no competition, so they mark up all prices 15 percent. A full tank, which would cost us twenty dollars anywhere else, is thirty dollars on the res. Often we are marooned for the simple reason of having no gas money. That's also one reason why rents are cheap out here.

Rudi tries everything he can think of to support his "instant" family. He discovered that he has many relatives on and around the res—on Grass Mountain, in Yankton, in Rosebud—people like Uncle Robert Moorehouse, who just died, Edna Whipple, and several DeCoras. But the few jobs around here—and you can practically count them on the fingers of your two hands—are reserved for tribally enrolled Rosebud Sioux, and that disqualifies him. He jokes: "You can't even support a family anymore as a criminal. You'd need a regular job during daytime and do your robbing moonlighting at night." So he hustles every way he can. He hauls wood for three dollars an hour and hot-tars roofs for four or five bucks. He always works with his hands. He makes beautiful peyote fans and falls back on his old standby—tattooing. Some people want just a little symbol, a star or sun circle, to please the Owl Woman, but others want more elaborate designs. He did a nice picture on a man's shoulder blade, and then covered another guy's whole back with a beautiful, intricate design. It shows an Indian dressed for the sun dance in a fringed shirt, holding a sacred pipe up to the sun. The whole is framed by a medicine wheel surrounded by zigzag lightning bolts. Rudi got paid sixty bucks for this. The man is so proud of it he shows off his back everywhere—a living advertisement for Rudi. June Bug, who has a talent for art, is fascinated by Rudi doing tattoos. He can sit next to Rudi for hours, watching every move, asking questions like: "How do you do this shading? Does it hurt? How do you get ideas for your designs?" Rudi said that this drawing on the man's back "has motion," that it is "severe."

Rudi is a good father. He cusses a lot, using every four-letter word there is, but he is kind and patient, spending a lot of time with the kids, and they love him for it. One thing that a lot of people would consider a drawback turned into a blessing for us. Situated in a hollow overshadowed by the hills of a rolling prairie, we have very bad TV reception. So, instead of sitting before the idiot box, with my and Rudi's encouragement the kids read a lot. June Bug and Jennifer got good grades and became honor students.

I have a harder time with Pedro and Anwah. Pedro is twenty

years old and now the father of two. He dropped out of school a few years ago. He looked up to Crow Dog, who saw no value in education. That's understandable. But things are different now. Archie Fire Lame Deer is a medicine man and sun dance leader, but his daughter Josephine is a mathematical and scientific genius and Archie has encouraged her to apply for a top college. We have enough medicine men and enough high school dropouts. What we need are Indian lawyers, doctors, teachers, and scientists. Illiteracy will get us nowhere. There is no reason why you can't perform a ceremony even if you *can* read and write or maybe know enough to balance your bankbook, if that's the road you want to travel. Pedro doesn't like school. He thinks education is a lot of crap because it doesn't seem to get a young man a job. He thinks it is ridiculous for a father of two to go back to school for his GED. But he has no income and his family is on welfare. Now and then he'll try turning over a new leaf, try to get interested in school again, but Pedro never gets along with his instructors. He's always had trouble because he grew up in the movement, learning to be antigovernment, anti–the system. He had such a hard time that he just dropped out. I told him that he should go back to school because now that he has a wife and two children, he can't support them with just doing powwows. I always told him to keep away from the violent element, then he'll be okay. If he could channel his energy somewhere else, it would be good. I even told him to try boxing—there's a boxing team for boys—but he was against it. Pedro's seen a lot of spiritual ways, but he's seen a lot of the dark side, too—the drinking and the violence.

If my kid does something wrong with another kid, I'll go to the parent and talk to them about it, and straighten it out. And I'll tell my kid what's right and wrong. And the other parents have to correct their children too. If the other parents can't correct their children, that's where the law will come in. That's about the only time I'll call the police, when my kids are involved, because it puts me in jeopardy too. Then I'll tell the cops straight out: "I tried to

make peace, I tried to do the right thing, but please talk to them."
Sometimes it's better to have someone in the middle to talk to
them, because it gets bigger, it gets into gangs, and it gets into
family feuds, and it might be over a little thing that's not even
worth it. It's really sad. My friend Debbie, who I had the talk with
after I wrecked, had a son about thirteen years old who died in a
wreck. There's a lot of tragedies like that. This year a lot of young
people died in wrecks. There's usually alcohol or drugs involved.

But Pedro is a grown man now. You can't tell a father: "Behave
yourself," tell him what to do. Pedro is becoming very mature. He
and Anwah run yuwipi ceremonies. You have to be respected in
order to do this. He still has some eggshells from the old he-
warrior mentality sticking to him, but they are falling off. He's
growing up. He and Percetta live in a small apartment in Antelope
together with their little daughters. Like everybody else on the res,
they struggle to survive.

As for me and Rudi, life is in some ways idyllic, down to basics,
to the simplest kind of life—still, you have to pay for rent, gas,
electricity, groceries, everything. It's hard. The politicians, the
part-time Indians up there, have nice homes and ranches with
horses, but everybody else is barely surviving. Some wasichus
grow rich on the liquor they sell—the bar owners and those who
have the package stores. You can sometimes see a guy on a horse,
with a big Uncle Joe hat, riding up to the liquor store's window for
his bottle of Jack, then galloping off with it after paying twice as
much for it as somebody in a big city.

Rudi's trying hard to make a good life for me. He's gifted. He'd
like to do something with art or sculpture, maybe do book illustra-
tions. He is a good musician and plays the Spanish guitar well. But
what can you do with that on the res? If it doesn't work out at
Rosebud, we'll pretty well have to move to a city. Jim and Barb are
struggling too. They have a little burrito business going. Jim gets
up at four in the morning to cook up his burritos—some with and
some without meat. At seven-thirty in the morning, Barb starts

driving around selling them. By ten or eleven they're through and they have the rest of the day for themselves. But they have their problems. Their car barely makes it from day to day and needs constant repairs. The business depends on Barb's being able to drive around. So when the old crate is in the shop she has to borrow one from a friend. She once borrowed my ancient lemon and that promptly broke down too. So on that day there was no business. They now have a "new" car, an ancient Lincoln Continental they bought for fifty bucks. Then they got a motor for it for another fifty.

Life is not without excitement even now. When Rudi and I moved in together on the res, in 1991, bounty hunters came after us. It was like a Grade B movie. Some time back, Rudi had gotten into an argument with some racists in Denver who called him some names. It resulted in a fight in which Rudi came off second best because it was two against one. As a matter of fact he had his ankle broken and was still limping and bleeding when I met him. He was up for a misdemeanor charge—kid stuff. But a thousand-dollar bond was posted for him pending trial. Since he was leaving Denver for South Dakota with Jim and Barb, he ignored it. Well, there is a guy in Denver who has had it in for Rudi ever since they were young kids. This guy is a bounty hunter and he saw his chance to get after Rudi. They came to the trailer I lived in then, in Antelope, the one with the sign I had put up: INSURED BY SMITH AND WESSON. Rudi and I were out and Pedro threw them out of the house. We had pulled up to Jim and Barb's place just as those guys had left. It was perfect timing.

The bounty hunters came back. I don't know who gave them the address. They really played me cheap. The guy who hated Rudi said: "My dad's a chief here on the reservation." I said: "Oh yeah?" He went on: "That Rudi's a convict—he's extremely dangerous." I made a face: "No shit? I'd better be careful." They didn't connect me. I went back to Jim's, picked up Rudi in the car, and lit out for my mom's place at He Dog. They got my mom's phone number

but had no idea where we were. They called us up: "Better surrender. We are at the Mission Police Department, right across the
street, with the detectives, and we're going to arrest you." Right
across the street was twenty-eight miles away. I started laughing:
"Just try to find us. The res is a big, wild place." They went on:
"We're going to bring the tribal police and the U.S. marshals." I
told them: "Fine, bring them, but you'd better have search warrants."

I was a bit concerned because I didn't need the Man coming
around. I didn't need the heat after the recent run-in I'd had in
Pine Ridge, when tribal cops stopped me for having booze in my
car. Rudi told my mother: "I've got warrants, and the bounty
hunters showed up at Mary's place." Mom was cool about it. She
said: "Well, you stay here, down in the basement. They ain't
coming on my land." Right away she was in our corner. Mom's real
straitlaced, but I think she liked the action, the excitement. The
way the bounty hunters work, if they arrest you and bring you in,
they get 10 percent of the bond. Rudi's bond was only a thousand
dollars—so the bounty hunters would have gotten only a hundred
dollars, not even enough to pay for their gas from Denver to
Rosebud. It was all bullshit, a teenage vendetta. Before hanging up
on him, I said: "Mister bounty hunter, get your ass out of here or
I'll call the tribal police on you. You are in Indian country, on my
turf. But thanks for the entertainment." We never heard from them
again.

As far as the res is concerned, things are getting worse and
worse. We are getting poorer and poorer. Under the Carter administration, .04 percent of the federal budget was earmarked for us
noble savages, that is, for all the Native Americans, from the East
Coast to the Pacific and from Alaska to the Rio Grande. In 1981,
Reagan cut this by five hundred million dollars, and Bush cut it
again—"got to cut that deficit." There's nothing left to cut now.
Whatever little money comes in is skimmed off at the top. The
bureaucrats have taken the cream off the milk. Otherwise things go

on as usual. The tribal chairman had a heart attack. There is the fight about the renewal of grazing rights. The people who want to dump the nation's garbage on our res still seem to have the upper hand and still have a chance to turn the place into a toilet. We had a bunch of rape cases, one involving a tribal policeman, and some of our councilmen—or should I say council persons—are pushing for a scheme to put up a big gambling casino on the res in order to raise money. Gambling on Indian land is now all the rage. State and federal gambling laws don't apply to reservations. That's about the only instance where our "sovereignty" is respected, and so the tribes are under siege from a whole mob of promoters smelling big bucks. I don't think it's a good idea. I can't see the high rollers traveling great distances to get rid of their money at Rosebud, of all places. There are no towns of any size near us. In the north there's Kadoka, Murdo, Interior, Scenic—jerkwater towns, all of them. To the south is Valentine, Nebraska, not exactly a metropolis either. It's 170 miles to Rapid City to the west. There's nothing to attract the high roller to the res, no amenities, no glitter, no gourmet restaurants. And we have too many problems of our own to handle an influx of tinhorn gamblers.

A cop in Gordon, Nebraska, shot and killed a doddering, intoxicated Indian. AIM has sent a team to investigate. When I heard this I thought: "Here we go again! That's where I came in." Gordon, Nebraska, that's where it all started, over twenty years ago, with the senseless and brutal murder of Raymond Yellow Thunder by a bunch of drunken rednecks and American Legionnaires. That's when AIM came out from Minnesota to join the Lakota traditionalists, and that was the beginning of the movement.

AIM did a lot of good because it brought back awareness of the treaty, and of the danger of losing the Black Hills, awareness of the land's sacredness. It made us conscious of being Indians and what that means. It made medicine men radical activists, and it made radical activists into sun dancers and vision seekers. It gave a new purpose in life to young drifters who knew nothing of their proud past. It gave a voice to our women and brought them into the tribal councils. It changed my life. AIM will always live in our hearts. It still exists, but it has grown middle-aged.

Nowadays, the status of AIM on the res is pretty much a matter of individual efforts. The old AIM people still relate to each other and reminisce about the glorious past, but it's not a real strong organization anymore. It's more of a personal thing. There are other things to occupy our thoughts now—treaty rights, studying at the Sinte Gleska College, fighting legal battles, handling our local problems. Last year AIM started coming in again. Clyde Bellecourt came down, with Joe Nogeeshik, from the Twin Cities. They travel from one res to another, speaking to groups, dealing with drug problems, counseling young people. That's the main preoccupation now. And I think AIM is more strong in Minnesota, where it started, than anywhere else. It is weak in South Dakota because people have gone back to the old traditions, to the sweats and the ceremonies, and to them that's the movement right there—a spiritual movement. And, of course, for that revival they have to thank AIM, but they no longer remember that. AIM and its old leaders are hardly mentioned anymore. There's a thin line between the spiritual part and the radical part. There are other organizations now and most of them, even though they recognize what AIM has done for all Native Americans, don't want to go about doing things the way we once did, through confrontations. They'd rather go through legal channels now. AIM was never meant to be violent, but, as at Custer, the other side always started swinging first. Thinking back on it all, comparing what has been and what is now, I feel like an old, old woman, though I'm only thirty-seven. Being involved wears you out. AIM is now sensitizing the world to our plight by organizing running groups—running all the way from Alaska to the tip of South America, or running through whole continents. I'm a little too old for that. My legs are not what they were in those good red days. But there's something to be said for slowing down, for being slower but more effective, more sure of yourself, for thinking with your brain instead of some other parts of your body. Power does not always come from the barrel of a gun—in the end the spirit wins out. Anyhow, I had a lump in my throat when, at the last sun dance, some of us veterans were honored by being given a new rainbow-colored patch with the words WOUNDED KNEE. Everyone who was at the Knee in 1973 wore it with pride.

There is an old Lakota song that begins: "To be a man it is difficult, they say." Well, to be a Native American woman is even harder. I do the dishes and I am again changing diapers. But I'm still fighting. I try to be sincere, try to hold on to the medicine, try to make my kids understand what it means to be Indian. I have become an environmentalist, because it is over the environment that the last of the Indian Wars will be fought. I try to help other women to cope with life. It does not necessarily have to be ceremonial, but just through understanding, and friendship, and support. And I think that unless our men can be free, we won't make it either. I rejoice because there are now medicine women, who have their own medicine bundles and their pipes and feathers, taking good care of these sacred things, passing on what they know to future generations. I try to raise my own kids in a traditional way while also trying to get them a modern education. I know that this is a hopeless contradiction, but then I've never lost hope yet. I will endure. I will fight to the end of my days—for everything that lives. MITAKUYE OYASIN—ALL MY RELATIONS.